*Oracle Press*™

Introducing JavaFX™ 8 Programming

About the Author

Best-selling author **Herbert Schildt** has written extensively about programming for three decades and is a leading authority on the Java language. His books have sold millions of copies worldwide and have been translated into all major foreign languages. He is the author of numerous books on Java, including *Java: The Complete Reference, Java: A Beginner's Guide, Herb Schildt's Java Programming Cookbook,* and *Swing: A Beginner's Guide*. He has also written extensively about C, C++, and C#. Although interested in all facets of computing, his primary focus is computer languages. Schildt holds both graduate and undergraduate degrees from the University of Illinois. He can be reached at his consulting office at (217) 586–4683. His website is **www.HerbSchildt.com**.

About the Technical Editor

Gerrit Grunwald is a software engineer with more than ten years of experience in software development. He has been involved in Java desktop application and controls development. Gerrit is interested in Java-driven embedded technologies based on JavaSE and JavaME. He is a true believer in open source and has participated in popular projects like JFXtras.org as well as his own projects (Enzo, SteelSeries Swing, and SteelSeries Canvas). Gerrit is an active member of the Java community, where he founded and leads the Java User Group Münster (Germany), co-leads the JavaFX and IoT community, and is a JavaOne Rock Star and Java Champion. He is a speaker at conferences and user groups internationally and writes for several magazines.

Oracle Press™

Introducing
JavaFX™ 8 Programming

Herbert Schildt

New York   Chicago   San Francisco
Athens   London   Madrid   Mexico City
Milan   New Delhi   Singapore   Sydney   Toronto

Cataloging-in-Publication Data is on file with the Library of Congress

McGraw-Hill Education books are available at special quantity discounts to use as premiums and sales promotions, or for use in corporate training programs. To contact a representative, please visit the Contact Us pages at www.mhprofessional.com.

Introducing JavaFX™ 8 Programming

1 2 3 4 5 6 7 8 9 0 DOC DOC 1 0 9 8 7 6 5

ISBN   978-0-07-184255-6
MHID   0-07-184255-1

Sponsoring Editor	**Copy Editor**	**Composition**
Brandi Shailer	LeeAnn Pickrell	Cenveo® Publisher Services
Editorial Supervisor	**Proofreader**	**Illustration**
Patty Mon	Lisa McCoy	Cenveo Publisher Services
Project Editor	**Indexer**	**Art Director, Cover**
LeeAnn Pickrell	Sherry Schildt	Jeff Weeks
Technical Editor	**Production Supervisor**	
Gerrit Grunwald	Jean Bodeaux	

Contents

Preface

S ince its original 1.0 release, Java has been an innovative force that has driven both the art and science of programming forward. Although it has now been several years since that initial release, Java remains vibrant and alive, constituting what is arguably the world's most important computer language. One reason for Java's long-term success has been its ability to adapt to the many and varied changes that have occurred in the realm of computing. As you will see in the course of this book, JavaFX 8 carries forward this rich legacy of innovation.

JavaFX is Java's next-generation graphical user interface (GUI) framework. Not only does JavaFX provide a rich, powerful, flexible framework, it is also easy to use. Thus, if you have programmed in one of Java's previous GUI frameworks, such as Swing, you will be pleasantly surprised by how easy it is to create a GUI with JavaFX. Perhaps more importantly, JavaFX gives you features that let you add the "visual sparkle" that is so crucial to the success of modern applications. In short, JavaFX represents the future of GUI programming in Java. It is truly that important. The goal of this book is to present in a fast-paced manner, the fundamentals of JavaFX programming.

At the time of this writing, the latest version of JavaFX is JavaFX 8. JavaFX 8 was released with JDK 8, and this is the version of JavaFX described in this book. Therefore, as a general rule, when the term JavaFX is used in this book, it refers to JavaFX 8.

A Book for All Java Programmers

This book is for all Java programmers, whether you are a novice or an experienced pro. Of course, you must have a basic, working knowledge of the Java language. This is because all of the examples are in Java. Therefore, no understanding of Cascading Style Sheets (CSS) or FXML is needed. Furthermore, prior experience with other Java GUIs is *not* required. If you already know another Java GUI, such as Swing, you may be able to advance more quickly, but a careful reading is still suggested because there are several important differences between JavaFX and the other Java GUI frameworks.

What's Inside

This book is an introduction to JavaFX 8, Java's newest GUI framework. It describes several of its key features and includes numerous examples that illustrate their use. The discussions are fast paced, but designed for ease of understanding. Although the topic of JavaFX is quite large, the goal of this book is to present core topics—those that will be important to nearly any type of GUI design.

The book starts with the basics, such as the general form of a JavaFX program, event handling, and the basic controls. It then moves on to layouts, images, and fonts. The book continues with some of JavaFX's most exciting features: effects, transforms, and animation (including 3-D animation). The book concludes with a look at menus, charts, the **WebView** class, and drawing directly on a canvas. Once you finish this book, you will have a foundation on which you can build your further study of JavaFX.

Don't Forget: Code on the Web

Remember, the source code for all of the examples in this book is available free of charge on the Web at **www.oraclepressbooks.com**.

Special Thanks

Special thanks to Gerrit Grunwald, the technical editor for this book. His advice, insights, and suggestions are much appreciated.

HERBERT SCHILDT

For Further Study

Introducing JavaFX 8 Programming is just one in the Herb Schildt series of Java programming books. Here are others that you will find of interest:

Java: The Complete Reference

Herb Schildt's Java Programming Cookbook

Java: A Beginner's Guide

Swing: A Beginner's Guide

The Art of Java

CHAPTER
1

JavaFX Fundamentals

In today's computing environment the user interface is a key factor in determining a program's success or failure. The reasons for this are easy to understand. First, the look and feel of a program defines the initial user experience. Thus, it forms the user's first impression—and first impressions matter because they often become lasting impressions. Second, the user interface is the way in which a user interacts with a program each time it is used. Therefore, the overall quality of a program is judged, in part, by the usability and appeal of its interface. To be successful, a user interface must be convenient, well organized, and consistent. It must also have one thing more: that "visual sparkle" that users have come to expect. For today's Java programmer, JavaFX is the best way to provide such interfaces.

JavaFX is a collection of classes and interfaces that defines Java's modern graphical user interface (GUI). It can be used to create the types of GUIs demanded by rich client applications in the contemporary marketplace. JavaFX supplies a diverse set of controls, such as buttons, scroll panes, text fields, check boxes, trees, and tables, that can be tailored to fit nearly any application. Furthermore, effects, transforms, and animation can be employed to enhance the visual appeal of the controls. JavaFX also streamlines the creation of an application by simplifying the management of its GUI elements and the application's deployment. Thus, JavaFX not only enables you to build more exciting, visually appealing user interfaces, it also makes your job easier in the process. Simply put: JavaFX is a powerful, state-of-the-art GUI framework that is defining the future of GUI programming in Java.

This book provides a compact, fast-paced introduction to JavaFX programming. As you will soon see, JavaFX is a large, feature-rich system, and in many cases, one feature interacts with or supports another. As a result, it can be difficult to discuss one aspect of JavaFX without involving others. The purpose of this chapter is to introduce the fundamentals of JavaFX, including its history, basic concepts, core features, and the general form of a JavaFX program. Subsequent chapters will expand on the foundation presented here, so a careful reading is advised.

One more point: This book assumes that you have a working knowledge of Java. You need not be a Java expert, but you should be comfortable with the fundamentals of the language. However, prior experience with other GUI frameworks is *not* required, although such prior experience may help you advance more quickly.

We will begin by putting JavaFX into its historical context.

A Brief History of Java's GUI Frameworks

Like most things in programming, the GUI frameworks defined by Java have evolved over time, and JavaFX is Java's third such framework. Before you begin programming with JavaFX, it is helpful to understand in a general way why JavaFX was created and how it relates to and improves on Java's previous GUIs.

The AWT: Java's First GUI Framework

Java's original GUI framework was the Abstract Window Toolkit (AWT). The AWT offered only rudimentary support for GUI programming. For example, its set of controls is quite limited by today's standard. One reason for the limited nature of the AWT is that it translates its various visual components into their corresponding platform-specific equivalents, or *peers*. Because the AWT components rely on native code resources, they are referred to as *heavyweight*.

The AWT's use of native peers led to several problems. For example, because of variations between operating systems, a component might act differently on different platforms. This potential variability threatened the overarching philosophy of Java: write once, run anywhere. Also, the look and feel of each component was fixed (because it is defined by the platform) and could not be (easily) changed. Furthermore, the use of heavyweight components caused some frustrating restrictions. For example, a heavyweight component was always opaque.

Swing

Not long after Java's original release, it became apparent that the limitations and restrictions present in the AWT were sufficiently serious that a better approach was needed. The solution was Swing. Introduced in 1997, Swing was included as part of the Java Foundation Classes (JFC). Swing was initially available for use with Java 1.1 as a separate library. However, beginning with Java 1.2, Swing (and the rest of the JFC) was fully integrated into Java.

Swing addressed the limitations associated with the AWT's components through the use of two key features: *lightweight components* and a *pluggable look and feel*. Let's look briefly at each. With very few exceptions, Swing components are *lightweight*. This means the components are written entirely in Java. They do not rely on platform-specific peers. Lightweight components have some important advantages, including efficiency and flexibility. Furthermore, because lightweight components do not translate into platform-specific peers, the look and feel of each component is determined by Swing, not by the underlying operating system. This means that each component can work in a consistent manner across all platforms. It is also possible to separate the look and feel of a component from the logic of the component, and this is what Swing does. Separating out the look and feel provides a significant advantage: you can "plug in" a new look and feel. In other words, it becomes possible to change the way that a component is rendered without affecting any of its other aspects or creating side effects in the code that uses the component. In short, Swing solved the problems of the AWT in an effective, elegant manner.

There is one other important aspect of Swing: it uses an architecture based on a modified Model-View-Controller (MVC) concept. In MVC terminology, the *model* corresponds to the state information associated with a component. The *view* determines how the control is displayed on the screen. The *controller* determines how the component reacts to the user. The MVC approach enables any of its pieces to be changed without affecting the other two. For example, you can change the view without affecting the model. In Swing, the high level of separation between the view and the controller was not beneficial. Instead, Swing uses a modified version of MVC that combines the view and the controller into a single logical entity. This is called *separable model architecture*. However, the benefits of the MVC concept are still attained, providing support for Swing's pluggable look-and-feel capabilities.

JavaFX

Swing was so successful that it remained the primary Java GUI framework for over a decade, which is a very long time in the fast-paced world of computing. Of course, computing continued to move forward. Today the trend is toward more dramatic, visually engaging effects—that "visual sparkle" mentioned earlier. Such effects were troublesome to create with Swing. Furthermore, the conceptual basis that underpins the design of GUI frameworks has advanced beyond that used by Swing. To better handle the demands of the modern GUI and utilize advances in GUI design, a new approach was needed. The result is JavaFX: Java's next-generation GUI framework.

JavaFX offers all of the advantages of Swing but provides a substantially updated and improved approach. For example, it defines a set of modern GUI controls and enables you to easily incorporate special effects into those controls. Its improved architecture, based on the *scene graph* feature described later in this chapter, streamlines the management of a program's windows. For example, it automates the once-tedious repaint process. Like Swing, JavaFX uses an MVC-based architecture. Deployment is simplified because JavaFX applications can be run in a variety of environments without recoding. Although not the focus of this book, JavaFX also supports the use of CSS and FXML to style and build a GUI. In short, JavaFX sets a new standard for the contemporary GUI framework.

It is important to mention that the development of JavaFX occurred in two main phases. The original JavaFX was based on a scripting language called *JavaFX Script*. However, JavaFX Script has been discontinued. Beginning with the release of JavaFX 2.0, JavaFX has been programmed in Java itself and provides a comprehensive API. JavaFX has been bundled with Java since JDK 7, update 4. At the time of this writing, the latest version of JavaFX is JavaFX 8, which is included with JDK 8. (The version number is 8 to align with the JDK version. Thus, the numbers 3 through 7 were skipped.) JavaFX 8 is the version of JavaFX described in this book. When the term *JavaFX* is used, it refers to JavaFX 8.

Before we continue, it is useful to answer one question that naturally arises relating to JavaFX: Is JavaFX designed as a replacement for Swing? The answer is, essentially, Yes. However, Swing will continue to be part of Java programming for some time to come. The reason is that there is a large amount of Swing legacy code. Furthermore, there are legions of programmers who know how to program for

Swing, Nevertheless, JavaFX has clearly been positioned as the GUI framework of the future. It is expected that over the next few years, JavaFX will supplant Swing for new projects, and many Swing-based applications will migrate to JavaFX. One other point: it is also possible to use both JavaFX and Swing in an application, thus enabling a smooth transition from Swing to JavaFX.

JavaFX Basic Concepts

Before you can create a JavaFX application, there are several key concepts and features you must understand. Although JavaFX has similarities with Java's other GUIs, it has substantial differences. For example, the overall organization of JavaFX and the relationship of its main components differ significantly from either Swing or the AWT. Therefore, even if you have experience in coding for one of Java's other GUI frameworks, a careful reading of the following sections is advised.

The JavaFX Packages

The JavaFX framework is contained in packages that begin with the **javafx** prefix. At the time of this writing, there are more than 30 JavaFX packages in its API library. Here are four examples: **javafx.application**, **javafx.stage**, **javafx.scene**, and **javafx.scene.layout**. Although we will use only a few JavaFX packages in this chapter, you might want to spend some time browsing the JavaFX packages. Doing so will give you an idea of the wide array of functionality that JavaFX offers.

Setting the Stage with the Stage and Scene Classes

The central metaphor implemented by JavaFX is the *stage*. As in the case of an actual stage play, a stage contains a *scene*. Thus, loosely speaking, a stage defines a space and a scene defines what goes in that space. Or, put another way, a stage is a container for scenes and a scene is a container for the items that comprise the scene. As a result, all JavaFX applications have at least one stage and one scene. These elements are encapsulated in the JavaFX API by the **Stage** and **Scene** classes. To create a JavaFX application, you will, at a minimum, add at least one **Scene** object to a **Stage**. Let's look a bit more closely at these two classes.

Stage is a top-level container. All JavaFX applications automatically have access to one **Stage**, called the *primary stage*. The primary stage is supplied by the run-time system when a JavaFX application is started. Although you can create other stages, for many applications, the primary stage will be the only one required.

As mentioned, **Scene** is a container for the items that comprise the scene. These can consist of various types of GUI elements, such as controls, text, and graphics. To create a scene, you will add elements to an instance of **Scene**. Then, set that **Scene** on a **Stage**.

Nodes and Scene Graphs

The elements of a scene are called *nodes*. For example, a push button control is a node. However, nodes can also consist of groups of nodes. Furthermore, a node can have a child node. In this case, a node with a child is called a *parent node* or *branch node*. Nodes without children are terminal nodes and are called *leaves*. The collection of all nodes in a scene creates what is referred to as a *scene graph,* which comprises a *tree*.

There is one special type of node in the scene graph, called the *root node*. This is the top-level node and is the only node in the scene graph tree that does not have a parent. Thus, with the exception of the root node, all other nodes have parents, and all nodes either directly or indirectly descend from the root node.

The base class for all nodes is **Node**. There are several other classes that are, either directly or indirectly, subclasses of **Node**. These include **Parent**, **Group**, **Region,** and **Control**, to name a few.

Layouts

JavaFX provides several layout panes that manage the process of placing elements in a scene. For example, the **FlowPane** class provides a flow layout and the **GridPane** class supports a row/column grid-based layout. Several other layouts, such as **BorderPane**, which organizes output within four border areas and a center, are available. Each inherits **Node**. The layouts are packaged in **javafx.scene.layout.**

The Application Class and the Life-Cycle Methods

A JavaFX application must be a subclass of the **Application** class, which is packaged in **javafx.application**. Thus, your application class will extend **Application**. The **Application** class defines three life-cycle methods that your application can override. These are called **init( )**, **start( )**, and **stop( )**, and are shown here, in the order in which they are called:

    void init( )

    abstract void start(Stage *primaryStage*)

    void stop( )

The **init( )** method is called when the application begins execution. It is used to perform various initializations. As will be explained, it *cannot,* however, be used to create a stage or build a scene. If no initializations are required, this method need not be overridden because an empty, default version is provided.

The **start( )** method is called after **init( )**. This is where your application begins, and it *can* be used to construct and set the scene. Notice that it is passed a reference to a **Stage** object. This is the stage provided by the run-time system and is the primary stage. Also notice that this method is abstract. Thus, it must be overridden by your application.

When your application is terminated, the **stop( )** method is called. It is here that you can handle any cleanup or shutdown chores. In cases in which no such actions are needed, an empty, default version is provided.

Launching a JavaFX Application

In general, when a JavaFX application begins execution, an instance of the subclass of **Application** defined by the application is created. Then **init( )**, followed by **start( )**, is executed. However, sometimes, such as in the case of a free-standing, self-contained JavaFX application, a call to the **launch( )** method defined by **Application** may be needed. So that the examples in this book can be run in all of the ways supported by JavaFX, **launch( )** is included in all of the programs.

The **launch( )** method has two forms. Here is the one used in this book:

public static void launch(String ... *args*)

Here, *args* is a possibly empty list of strings that typically specifies command-line arguments. When called, **launch( )** causes the application to be constructed, followed by calls to **init( )** and **start( )**. The **launch( )** method will not return until after the application has terminated. This version of **launch( )** starts the subclass of **Application** from which **launch( )** is called. The second form of **launch( )** lets you specify a class other than the enclosing class to start. As a general rule, **launch( )** is called from **main( )**.

It is important to emphasize that neither a **main( )** method nor a call to **launch( )** is necessary in all cases for a JavaFX program. So don't be surprised when you see other JavaFX code that does not include them. However, including **main( )** and **launch( )** ensures that the code can be used in the widest range of circumstances. Also, an explicit call to **launch( )** is needed if your application requires a **main( )** method for a purpose other than starting the JavaFX application. Thus, the programs in this book include both **main( )** and **launch( )** methods.

A JavaFX Application Skeleton

All JavaFX applications share the same basic skeleton. Therefore, before looking at any more JavaFX features, it will be useful to see what that skeleton looks like. In addition to showing the general form of a JavaFX application, the skeleton illustrates how to launch the application and demonstrates when the life-cycle methods are called. A message noting when each life-cycle method executes is displayed on the console via **System.out**. The complete skeleton is shown here:

```
// A JavaFX application skeleton.

import javafx.application.*;
import javafx.scene.*;
```

```java
import javafx.stage.*;
import javafx.scene.layout.*;

public class JavaFXSkel extends Application {

  public static void main(String[] args) {

    System.out.println("Launching JavaFX application.");

    // Start the JavaFX application by calling launch().
    launch(args);
  }

  // Override the init() method.
  public void init() {
    System.out.println("Inside the init() method.");
  }

  // Override the start() method.
  public void start(Stage myStage) {

    System.out.println("Inside the start() method.");

    // Give the stage a title.
    myStage.setTitle("JavaFX Skeleton");

    // Create a root node. In this case, a flow layout
    // is used, but several alternatives exist.
    FlowPane rootNode = new FlowPane();

    // Create a scene.
    Scene myScene = new Scene(rootNode, 300, 200);

    // Set the scene on the stage.
    myStage.setScene(myScene);

    // Show the stage and its scene.
    myStage.show();
  }

  // Override the stop() method.
  public void stop() {
    System.out.println("Inside the stop() method.");
  }
}
```

Although the skeleton is quite short, it can be compiled and run. It produces the empty window, shown here:

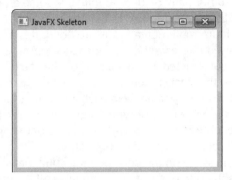

The skeleton also produces the following output on the console:

```
Launching JavaFX application.
Inside the init() method.
Inside the start() method.
```

When you close the window, this message is displayed:

```
Inside the stop() method.
```

Of course, in a real program, the life-cycle methods would not normally output anything to **System.out**. They do so here simply to illustrate when each method is called. Furthermore, as explained earlier, you will need to override the **init( )** and **stop( )** methods only if your application must perform special startup or shutdown actions. Otherwise, you can use the default implementations of these methods provided by the **Application** class.

Let's examine this program in detail. It begins by importing four packages. The first is **javafx.application**, which contains the **Application** class. The **Scene** class is packaged in **javafx.scene**, and **Stage** is packaged in **javafx.stage**. The **javafx.scene.layout** package provides several layout panes. The one used by the program is **FlowPane**.

Next, the application class **JavaFXSkel** is created. Notice that it extends **Application**. As explained, **Application** is the class from which all JavaFX applications are derived. **JavaFXSkel** contains four methods. The first is **main( )**. It is used to launch the application via a call to **launch( )**. Notice that the **args** parameter to **main( )** is passed to the **launch( )** method. Although this is a common approach, you can pass a different set of parameters to **launch( )**, or none at all. One other point: as mentioned earlier, **launch( )** and **main( )** are not required in all cases. However, for reasons already explained, both **main( )** and **launch( )** are included in the programs in this book.

When the application begins, the **init( )** method is called first by the JavaFX run-time system. For the sake of illustration, it simply displays a message on **System.out**, but it would normally be used to initialize some aspect of the application. Of course, if no initialization is required, it is not necessary to override **init( )** because an empty, default implementation is provided. It is important to emphasize that **init( )** cannot be used to create the stage or scene portions of a GUI. Rather, these items should be constructed and displayed by the **start( )** method.

After **init( )** finishes, the **start( )** method executes. It is here that the initial scene is created and set to the primary stage. Let's look at this method line by line. First, notice that **start( )** has a parameter of type **Stage**. When **start( )** is called, this parameter will receive a reference to the primary stage of the application. It is on this stage that you will set a scene for the application.

After displaying a message on the console indicating that **start( )** has begun execution, **start( )** sets the title of the stage using this call to **setTitle( )**:

```
myStage.setTitle("JavaFX Skeleton");
```

Although this step is not necessarily required, it is customary for stand-alone applications. This title becomes the name of the main application window.

Next, a root node for a scene is created. The root node is the only node in a scene graph tree that does not have a parent. In this case, a **FlowPane** is used for the root node, but there are several other classes that can be used for the root.

```
FlowPane rootNode = new FlowPane();
```

As mentioned, a **FlowPane** uses a flow layout. This is a layout in which elements are positioned line by line, with lines wrapping as needed. (Thus, it works much like the **FlowLayout** class used by the AWT and Swing.) By default, a horizontal flow is used, but it is possible to specify a vertical flow. Although not needed by this skeletal application, it is also possible to specify other layout properties, such as a vertical and horizontal gap between elements and an alignment.

The following line uses the root node to construct a **Scene**:

```
Scene myScene = new Scene(rootNode, 300, 200);
```

Scene provides several versions of its constructor. The one used here creates a scene that has the specified root with the specified width and height. It is shown here:

Scene(Parent *rootnode*, double *width*, double *height*)

Notice that the type of *rootnode* is **Parent**. It is a subclass of **Node** and encapsulates nodes that can have children. Also notice that the width and the height are **double** values. This lets you pass fractional values, if needed. In the skeleton, the root is **rootNode**, the width is 300, and the height is 200.

The next line in the program sets **myScene** as the scene for **myStage**:

```
myStage.setScene(myScene);
```

Here, **setScene( )** is a method defined by **Stage** that sets the scene to that specified by its argument.

The last line in **start( )** displays the stage and its scene:

```
myStage.show();
```

In essence, **show( )** shows the window that was created by the stage and scene.

When you close the application, its window is removed from the screen and the **stop( )** method is called by the JavaFX run-time system. In this case, **stop( )** simply displays a message on the console, illustrating when it is called. However, **stop( )** would not normally display anything. Furthermore, if your application does not need to handle any shutdown actions, there is no reason to override **stop( )** because an empty, default implementation is provided.

Compiling and Running a JavaFX Program

One important advantage of JavaFX is that the same program can be run in a variety of different execution environments. For example, you can run a JavaFX program as a stand-alone desktop application, inside a web browser, or as a Web Start application. However, different ancillary files may be needed in some cases, such as a JAR file, an HTML file, or a Java Network Launch Protocol (JNLP) file.

In general, a JavaFX program is compiled like any other Java program. However, depending on the target execution environment, some additional steps may be required. For this reason, often the easiest way to compile a JavaFX application is to use an Integrated Development Environment (IDE) that fully supports JavaFX programming, such as NetBeans. Although the specific instructions for using an IDE differ among IDEs, as a general rule, to compile and run a JavaFX program, first create a JavaFX project and then enter the JavaFX program as the project's source file.

Alternatively, if you are accustomed to using the command line and just want to compile and run the JavaFX applications shown in this book, you can easily do so using Java's command-line tools. First, compile the application in the way you do any other Java program, using **javac**. This creates a **.class** file that can then be run by **java**. For example, to compile and run **JavaFXSkel.java**, you can use this command-line sequence:

```
javac JavaFXSkel.java
java JavaFXSkel
```

If you are comfortable using the command-line tools, they offer the easiest way to try the examples in this book.

NOTE
*If you use the command-line tools, you can still convert a JavaFX application contained in .class files into a fully deployable form by use of the **javapackager** command-line tool. (This tool was previously called **javafxpackager**, but has been renamed.) Consult Oracle's online documentation for details.*

The JavaFX Application Thread

In the preceding discussion, it was mentioned that you cannot use the **init( )** method to construct a stage or scene. You also cannot create these items inside the application's constructor. The reason is that a stage or scene must be constructed on the JavaFX *application thread*. However, the application's constructor and the **init( )** method are called on the main thread, also called the *launcher thread*. Thus, they can't be used to construct a stage or scene. Instead, you must use the **start( )** method, as the skeleton demonstrates, to create the initial GUI because **start( )** is called on the application thread.

Furthermore, any changes to the GUI currently displayed must be made from the application thread. Fortunately, this is a fairly easy rule to follow because, as a general rule, interactions with your program, such as user input, take place on the application thread. The **stop( )** method is also called on the application thread.

Build a Simple Scene Graph

Although the preceding skeleton is fully functional, its scene graph is empty. Thus, it does not contain any elements and its window is blank. Of course, the point of JavaFX is to build user interfaces. To do this, you must build a scene graph. To introduce the process, we will build a very simple one that contains only one element: a label.

The label is one of the controls provided by JavaFX. As mentioned earlier, JavaFX contains a rich assortment of controls. Controls are the means by which the user interacts with an application. The simplest control is the label because it just displays a message or an image. Because it is quite easy to use, the label is a good way to introduce the techniques needed to begin building a scene graph.

In JavaFX, a label is an instance of the **Label** class, which is packaged in **javafx.scene.control**. **Label** inherits **Labeled** and **Control**, among other classes. The **Labeled** class defines several features that are common to all labeled elements (that is, those that can contain text), and **Control** defines features related to all controls.

The **Label** constructor that we will use is shown here:

Label(String *str*)

The string that is displayed is specified by *str*.

Once you have created a label (or any other control), it must be added to the scene's content, which means adding it to the scene graph. Here is the technique we will use: First call **getChildren( )** on the root node of the scene graph. It returns a list of the child nodes in the form of an **ObservableList<Node>**. **ObservableList** is packaged in **javafx.collections**, and it inherits **java.util.List**, which is part of Java's Collections Framework. **List** defines a collection that represents a list of objects. Although a discussion of **List** and the Collections Framework is outside the scope of this book, it is easy to use **ObservableList** to add child nodes. Simply call **add( )** on the list of child nodes returned by **getChildren( )**, passing in a reference to the node to add, which in this case is a label.

The following program puts the preceding discussion into action by creating a simple JavaFX application that displays a label:

```java
// Demonstrate a simple scene graph that contains a label.

import javafx.application.*;
import javafx.scene.*;
import javafx.stage.*;
import javafx.scene.layout.*;
import javafx.scene.control.*;

public class SimpleSceneGraphDemo extends Application {

  public static void main(String[] args) {

    // Start the JavaFX application by calling launch().
    launch(args);
  }

  // Override the start() method.
  public void start(Stage myStage) {

    // Give the stage a title.
    myStage.setTitle("Demonstrate A Simple Scene Graph");

    // Use a FlowPane for the root node.
    FlowPane rootNode = new FlowPane();

    // Create a scene.
    Scene myScene = new Scene(rootNode, 300, 200);

    // Set the scene on the stage.
    myStage.setScene(myScene);

    // Create a label.
```

```
    Label myLabel = new Label("A simple JavaFX label.");

    // Add the label to the scene graph.
    rootNode.getChildren().add(myLabel);

    // Show the stage and its scene.
    myStage.show();
  }
}
```

This program produces the following window:

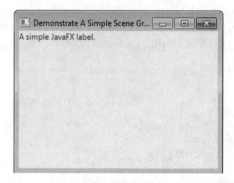

In the program, pay special attention to this line:

```
rootNode.getChildren().add(myLabel);
```

It adds the label to the list of children for which **rootNode** is the parent. Although this line could be separated into its individual pieces if necessary, you will often see it as shown here.

Of course, a scene graph can contain more than one control. Simply add each control to the scene graph, as just shown. For example, this version of **start( )** adds three labels:

```
// Override the start() method. This time, add three labels
// to the scene graph.
public void start(Stage myStage) {

  // Give the stage a title.
  myStage.setTitle("Demonstrate A Simple Scene Graph");

  // Use a FlowPane for the root node.
  FlowPane rootNode = new FlowPane();

  // Create a scene.
  Scene myScene = new Scene(rootNode, 300, 200);
```

```
  // Set the scene on the stage.
  myStage.setScene(myScene);

  // Create a label.
  Label myLabel = new Label("Label One   ");

  // Create a second label.
  Label myLabel2 = new Label("Label Two   ");

  // Create a third label.
  Label myLabel3 = new Label("Label Three");

  // Add three labels to the scene graph.
  rootNode.getChildren().add(myLabel);
  rootNode.getChildren().add(myLabel2);
  rootNode.getChildren().add(myLabel3);

  // Show the stage and its scene.
  myStage.show();
}
```

Here, the sequence

```
rootNode.getChildren().add(myLabel);
rootNode.getChildren().add(myLabel2);
rootNode.getChildren().add(myLabel3);
```

adds **myLabel**, **myLabel2**, and **myLabel3** to the root node of the graph. Thus, after this sequence executes, **rootNode** will have three child nodes.

If you substitute this version of **start( )** into the preceding program, it will produce the following window:

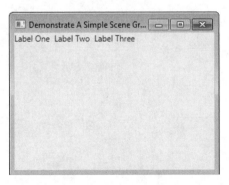

Notice that the three labels are positioned left to right in the order in which they were added to the scene graph. This is because a flow layout is used. With a flow layout, elements in the scene graph are displayed line by line. When the end of a line is reached, the next line is begun. You can see this if you narrow the window produced by the program. At some point, one of the labels will automatically wrap down to the next line. If you want a different layout strategy, simply use a different layout pane. The rest of the program remains the same. Various layout panes are described later in this book, but for now, the flow layout is sufficient for our purposes.

Before moving on, it is useful to point out that **ObservableList** provides a method called **addAll( )** that can be used to add two or more children to the scene graph in a single call. For example, this line adds three labels to the scene graph in a single call:

```
// Add all three labels to the scene graph in one call
// rootNode.getChildren().addAll(myLabel, myLabel2, myLabel3);
```

Thus, it produces the same scene graph as the one created by the three separate calls to **add( )** shown earlier. The only difference is that it is accomplished by a single call to **addAll( )**.

In addition to adding a control to a scene graph, you can remove one. This is done by calling **remove( )** on the **ObservableList** returned by **getChildren( )**. For example,

```
rootNode.getChildren().remove(myLabel);
```

removes **myLabel** from the scene.

In general, **ObservableList** supports a wide range of list-management methods. Here are two examples: You can determine if the list is empty by calling **isEmpty( )**. You can obtain the number of nodes in the list by calling **size( )**. You will want to explore **ObservableList** in greater depth as you advance in your study of JavaFX.

CHAPTER
2

Introducing Events
and Controls

The program shown at the end of the previous chapter presented a simple example that constructed a scene graph and introduced the **Label** control. However, it did not show one important feature found in most JavaFX programs: event handling. In JavaFX, an *event* is an object that describes some action that has affected the program, such as when the user interacts with the program by clicking a button. Because **Label** does not take input from the user, it does not generate events, so no event handling was needed to use it. However, other JavaFX controls *do* generate events in response to user input. For example, buttons, check boxes, and lists all generate events when they are used, and those events are handled by your program. Therefore, all but the most simple JavaFX programs contain one or more controls and will need to handle the events generated by those controls. For this reason, controls and event handling are introduced together in this chapter.

Event Basics

JavaFX uses what is, in essence, the *delegation event model* approach to event handling. The concept behind this model is quite simple: a source, such as a control, generates an event and sends it to one or more listeners, which handle the event. To receive an event, the handler for the event must first be registered with the event source. When the event occurs, the handler is called. It must then respond to the event and return. Thus, a user-interface element *delegates* the processing of an event to a separate event handler. The following sections provide an overview of how the process works.

The Event Class

The base class for JavaFX events is the **Event** class, which is packaged in **javafx.event**. **Event** inherits **java.util.EventObject**, which means that JavaFX events share the same basic functionality as other Java events. When a JavaFX event is generated, it is encapsulated within an **Event** instance. **Event** supports several methods that help you manage events. For example, you can obtain the source of the event and the event type. Several subclasses of **Event** are defined, which represent various types of events. The one that we will use to introduce event handling is **ActionEvent**. It encapsulates action events generated by several JavaFX controls, including the push button.

The EventHandler Interface

Events are handled by implementing the **EventHandler** interface, which is also in **javafx.event**. It is a generic interface with the following form:

Interface EventHandler<T extends Event>

Here, **T** specifies the type of event that the handler will handle. It defines one method, called **handle( )**, which receives the event object as an argument. It is shown here:

    void handle(T *eventObj*)

Here, *eventObj* is the event that was generated. Typically, event handlers are implemented through anonymous inner classes or lambda expressions. However, you can use stand-alone classes for this purpose if it is more appropriate to your application, such as when one event handler will handle events from more than one source.

There are two basic ways to specify a handler for an event. First, you can call **addEventHandler( )**, which is defined by the **Node** class, among others. Second, in many cases, you can use what is referred to as a *convenience method*. Convenience methods use the prefix **setOn** and set an event handler property. In general, if a convenience method exists for the event that you want to handle, it is the recommended approach, and is the approach used here. With either approach, when an event is generated, its handler is called on the program's application thread. One other point: if you want to unregister an event handler, call **removeEventHandler( )**.

The Event Dispatch Chain

In JavaFX, events are processed via an *event dispatch chain*. As it relates to a GUI, the event dispatch chain is a path from the top element in the scene graph (typically the stage) to the target of the event, which is the control that generated the event. When an event is processed, two main phases occur. First, the event is passed from the top element down the chain to the target of the event. This is called *event capturing*. After the target node processes the event, the event is passed back up the chain, thus allowing parent nodes a chance to process the event, if required. This is called *event bubbling*. Event handlers are called during the event bubbling phase.

It is also possible for an application to implement an *event filter*. An event filter is, in essence, a special type of event handler. Event filters are called during the event capturing phase. Thus, an event filter for an event will execute before an event handler for the same event. It is also possible for a node in the chain to *consume* an event, which prevents it from being processed further. Therefore, if a filter consumes an event, an event handler for that event will not execute. In general, event filters constitute a special case and are not often needed, but when they *are* needed, they can be very useful.

Introducing the Button Control

Before we can develop an example that demonstrates the basics of event handling, a source of events is needed. As mentioned, nearly all JavaFX controls generate events. Perhaps the most commonly used control is the button, and button events are some of the most frequently handled in a JavaFX program. Therefore, handling button events is a good way to get started.

In JavaFX, the push button control is provided by the **Button** class, which is in **javafx.scene.control**. **Button** inherits a fairly long list of base classes that includes **ButtonBase**, **Labeled**, **Region**, **Control**, **Parent**, and **Node**. If you examine the API documentation for **Button**, you will see that much of its functionality comes from its base classes. **Button**s can contain text, graphics, or both. Here, text-based buttons are used. Furthermore, **Button** supports a wide array of options, but we will use the default form.

Button has three constructors. The first is the default constructor. The second **Button** constructor lets you specify a string to be displayed. It is shown here:

Button(String *str*)

In this case, *str* is the message that is shown in the button. The third constructor lets you include an image and is described in Chapter 5.

When a button is pressed, an **ActionEvent** is generated. **ActionEvent** is packaged in **javafx.event**. **ActionEvent** defines two event types, called **ACTION** and **ALL**, which are objects of **EventType**. **ALL** refers to all action event types, which at the time of this writing is only one: **ACTION**. You can use **ACTION** to register a handler for an action event via the **addEventHandler( )** method. However, it is easier to register an action event handler by calling the convenience method **setOnAction( )** on the button. It has this general form:

final void setOnAction(EventHandler<ActionEvent> *handler*)

Here, *handler* is the handler being registered.

As mentioned, often you will use an anonymous inner class or lambda expression for the handler. As with all other Java event handling, your handler must respond to the event as quickly as possible and then return. If your handler consumes too much time, it will noticeably slow your application. For lengthy operations, you must use a separate thread of execution.

Demonstrating Event Handling and the Button

The following program puts the preceding discussion into action, demonstrating both event handling and the **Button** control. It uses two buttons and a label. The buttons are called First and Second. Each time a button is pressed, the content of the label is set to display which button was pressed.

```
// Introduce JavaFX events and buttons.

import javafx.application.*;
import javafx.scene.*;
import javafx.stage.*;
```

```
import javafx.scene.layout.*;
import javafx.scene.control.*;
import javafx.event.*;
import javafx.geometry.*;

public class JavaFXEventDemo extends Application {

  Label response;

  public static void main(String[] args) {

    // Start the JavaFX application by calling launch().
    launch(args);
  }

  // Override the start() method.
  public void start(Stage myStage) {

    // Give the stage a title.
    myStage.setTitle("Introducing Buttons and Events");

    // Use a FlowPane for the root node. In this case,
    // vertical and horizontal gaps of 10.
    FlowPane rootNode = new FlowPane(10, 10);

    // Center the controls in the scene.
    rootNode.setAlignment(Pos.CENTER);

    // Create a scene.
    Scene myScene = new Scene(rootNode, 300, 100);

    // Set the scene on the stage.
    myStage.setScene(myScene);

    // Create a label.
    response = new Label("Push a Button");

    // Create two push buttons.
    Button btnFirst = new Button("First");
    Button btnSecond = new Button("Second");

    // Handle the action events for the First button.
    btnFirst.setOnAction(new EventHandler<ActionEvent>() {
      public void handle(ActionEvent ae) {
        response.setText("First button was pressed.");
      }
    });
```

```
   // Handle the action events for the Second button.
   btnSecond.setOnAction(new EventHandler<ActionEvent>() {
     public void handle(ActionEvent ae) {
       response.setText("Second button was pressed.");
     }
   });

   // Add the label and buttons to the scene graph.
   rootNode.getChildren().addAll(btnFirst, btnSecond, response);

   // Show the stage and its scene.
   myStage.show();
  }
}
```

Sample output from this program is shown here:

Let's examine a few key portions of this program. First, notice how buttons are created by these two lines:

```
Button btnFirst = new Button("First");
Button btnSecond = new Button("Second");
```

This creates two text-based buttons. The first displays the string "First"; the second displays "Second".

Next, an action event handler is set for each of these buttons. The sequence for the First button is shown here:

```
// Handle the action events for the First button.
btnFirst.setOnAction(new EventHandler<ActionEvent>() {
  public void handle(ActionEvent ae) {
    response.setText("First button was pressed.");
  }
});
```

As explained, buttons respond to events of type **ActionEvent**. To register a handler for these events, the **setOnAction( )** method is called on the button. It uses an anonymous inner class to implement the **EventHandler** interface. (Recall that **EventHandler** defines only the **handle( )** method.) Inside **handle( )**, the text in the

response label is set to reflect the fact that the First button was pressed. Notice that this is done by calling the **setText( )** method on the label. The **setText( )** method is defined by the **Labeled** class. As mentioned in the previous chapter, **Labeled** is a superclass of any control that can contain text. It is used here to set the text in a label. Events are handled by the Second button in the same way.

After the event handlers have been set, the **response** label and the buttons **btnFirst** and **btnSecond** are added to the scene graph by using a call to **addAll( )**:

```
rootNode.getChildren().addAll(btnFirst, btnSecond, response);
```

The **addAll( )** method adds a list of nodes to the invoking parent node. Of course, these nodes could have been added by three separate calls to **add( )**, but the **addAll( )** method is more convenient to use in this situation.

There are two other things of interest in this program that relate to the way the controls are displayed in the window. First, when the root node is created, this statement is used:

```
FlowPane rootNode = new FlowPane(10, 10);
```

Here, the **FlowPane** constructor is passed two values. These specify the horizontal and vertical gap that will surround elements in the scene. If these gaps are not specified, then two elements (such as two buttons) would be positioned in such a way that no space is between them. Thus, the controls would run together, creating a very unappealing user interface. Specifying gaps prevents this.

The second point of interest is the following line, which sets the alignment of the elements in the **FlowPane**:

```
rootNode.setAlignment(Pos.CENTER);
```

Here, the alignment of the elements is centered. This is done by calling **setAlignment( )** on the **FlowPane**. The value **Pos.CENTER** specifies that both a vertical and horizontal center will be used. Other alignments are possible. **Pos** is an enumeration that specifies alignment constants. It is packaged in **javafx.geometry**.

Before moving on, one more point needs to be made. The preceding program uses anonymous inner classes to handle button events. However, because the **EventHandler** interface defines only one abstract method, **handle( )**, it is a functional interface. This means that a lambda expression could have been passed to **setOnAction( )**. For example, here is the handler for the First button, rewritten to use a lambda expression:

```
btnFirst.setOnAction( (ae) ->
                response.setText("First button was pressed.")
              );
```

Notice that the lambda expression is more compact than the anonymous inner class. Because the lambda expression is a relatively new Java feature, but the anonymous inner class is a widely used construct readily understood by most Java programmers, the majority of the examples in this book will use anonymous inner classes. However, lambda expressions are an important part of Java programming going forward. You should consider using them wherever applicable.

Another JavaFX Control: CheckBox

JavaFX defines a rich set of controls that are packaged in **javafx.scene.control**. You have already seen two, **Label** and **Button**. Although we will explore the controls at greater length in Chapter 3, it is helpful to look at one more here. The control we will use is **CheckBox**. **CheckBox** encapsulates the functionality of a check box. Beyond offering another example of handling events, **CheckBox** also shows an example of a JavaFX control that provides enhanced functionality.

The immediate superclass of **CheckBox** is **ButtonBase**. Thus, **CheckBox** represents a special type of button. Although you are no doubt familiar with check boxes because they are widely used controls, the JavaFX check box is a bit more sophisticated than you may at first think. This is because **CheckBox** supports three states. The first two are checked or unchecked, as you would expect, and this is the default behavior. The third state is *indeterminate* (also called *undefined*). The inclusion of the indeterminate state enables the check box to better fit certain uses. For example, it can indicate that the state of some option has not been set or that the option is not relevant to a specific situation. If you need the indeterminate state, you will need to explicitly enable it.

CheckBox defines two constructors. The first is the default constructor. The second lets you specify a string that identifies the box. It is shown here:

CheckBox(String *str*)

It creates a check box that has the text specified by *str* as a label.

CheckBox generates an action event when it is clicked. You can set the action event handler on a **CheckBox** by calling **setOnAction( )**, described earlier.

You can obtain the state of a check box by calling **isSelected( )**. It is shown here:

final boolean isSelected( )

It returns **true** if the check box is selected and **false** otherwise. Depending on the specific situation, it may also be possible to ignore events when using a check box and simply obtain the state of the box when your program needs it.

Here is a program that demonstrates check boxes. The check boxes let the user select various input device options, which are keyboard, mouse, and touch screen. Each time a check box is clicked, an action event is generated. The event handlers display the new state (selected or cleared) of the affected check box. Then, a list of all selected boxes is displayed. The program also makes use of two new layout features: vertical alignment and padding.

```java
// Demonstrate check boxes.

import javafx.application.*;
import javafx.scene.*;
import javafx.stage.*;
import javafx.scene.layout.*;
import javafx.scene.control.*;
import javafx.event.*;
import javafx.geometry.*;

public class CheckBoxDemo extends Application {

  CheckBox cbKeyboard;
  CheckBox cbMouse;
  CheckBox cbTouchScreen;

  Label response;
  Label selected;

  String inputDevices = "";

  public static void main(String[] args) {

    // Start the JavaFX application by calling launch().
    launch(args);
  }

  // Override the start() method.
  public void start(Stage myStage) {

    // Give the stage a title.
    myStage.setTitle("Demonstrate Check Boxes");

    // Use a FlowPane for the root node. In this case,
    // vertical gap of 10.
    FlowPane rootNode = new FlowPane(Orientation.VERTICAL, 0, 10);

    // Center the controls vertically; left-align them horizontally.
    rootNode.setAlignment(Pos.CENTER_LEFT);

    // Set a padding value of 10 on the left for the flow pane.
    rootNode.setPadding(new Insets(0, 0, 0, 10));

    // Create a scene.
```

```java
Scene myScene = new Scene(rootNode, 300, 180);

// Set the scene on the stage.
myStage.setScene(myScene);

Label heading = new Label("Select Input Devices");

// Create a label that will report the state of the
// selected check box.
response = new Label("No Devices Selected");

// Create a label that will report all input devices selected.
selected = new Label("Supported devices: <none>");

// Create the check boxes.
cbKeyboard = new CheckBox("Keyboard");
cbMouse = new CheckBox("Mouse");
cbTouchScreen = new CheckBox("Touch Screen");

// Handle action events for the check boxes.
cbKeyboard.setOnAction(new EventHandler<ActionEvent>() {
  public void handle(ActionEvent ae) {
    if(cbKeyboard.isSelected())
      response.setText("Keyboard selected.");
    else
      response.setText("Keyboard cleared.");

    showAll();
  }
});

cbMouse.setOnAction(new EventHandler<ActionEvent>() {
  public void handle(ActionEvent ae) {
    if(cbMouse.isSelected())
      response.setText("Mouse selected.");
    else
      response.setText("Mouse cleared.");

    showAll();
  }
});

cbTouchScreen.setOnAction(new EventHandler<ActionEvent>() {
  public void handle(ActionEvent ae) {
    if(cbTouchScreen.isSelected())
      response.setText("Touch Screen selected.");
    else
      response.setText("Touch Screen cleared.");
```

```
        showAll();
    }
});

// Add controls to the scene graph.
rootNode.getChildren().addAll(heading, cbKeyboard, cbMouse,
                             cbTouchScreen, response, selected);

// Show the stage and its scene.
myStage.show();
}

// Update and show the input devices list.
void showAll() {
    inputDevices = "";

    // Use isSelected() to determine the state of the check boxes.
    if(cbKeyboard.isSelected()) inputDevices = "Keyboard ";
    if(cbMouse.isSelected()) inputDevices += "Mouse ";
    if(cbTouchScreen.isSelected()) inputDevices += "Touch Screen";

    if(inputDevices.equals("")) inputDevices = "<none>";

    selected.setText("Supported devices: " + inputDevices);
}
}
```

Sample output is shown here:

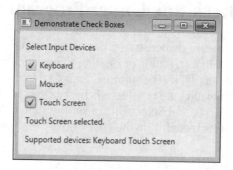

The operation of this program is straightforward. Each time the check box is clicked, an action event is generated. These events are handled by the event handler registered to the affected box. Each handler determines what has occurred by calling **isSelected( )** to obtain the new state of the control. It then sets the text in the **response** label to indicate the new state. For example, when the user selects Mouse, the message "Mouse selected." is displayed. Each handler then calls **showAll( )**, which reports all selected options in the **selected** label. Notice that the method **showAll( )** also uses the **isSelected( )** method to test the state of each box, in turn.

There are three other points of interest in the program. First, notice that it uses a vertical flow pane for the layout, as shown here:

```
FlowPane rootNode = new FlowPane(Orientation.VERTICAL, 0, 10);
```

By default, **FlowPane** flows horizontally. A vertical flow is created by passing the value **Orientation.VERTICAL** as the first argument to the **FlowPane** constructor. Also notice that no horizontal gap is needed, but a vertical gap of 10 is specified.

Second, notice that the alignment in the **FlowPane** is set to **CENTER_LEFT**:

```
rootNode.setAlignment(Pos.CENTER_LEFT);
```

CENTER_LEFT is another alignment option specified in the **Pos** class. It causes the content of the pane to be centered vertically and aligned left.

Finally, notice this line:

```
rootNode.setPadding(new Insets(0, 0, 0, 10));
```

This sets a padding value for the **FlowPane**. It does so by specifying a set of insets, which are encapsulated by the **Insets** class in **javafx.geometry**. The values specify the amount of space that the content will be inset from the edges, in the order of top, right, bottom, left. By default, a **FlowPane** has insets of zero. In this case, an inset of 10 is specified on the left. The other insets remain 0. Taken together, the use of vertical orientation, left alignment, and the left inset value improves the GUI's visual appearance

Selecting a Check Box Under Program Control

A check box can be selected or cleared in two ways. First, the user can set or clear a box, as the previous program demonstrated. Second, the state of a check box can be changed by the program. In fact, setting or clearing a check box under program control is quite common. For example, it is not unusual for a GUI to include buttons that reset all check boxes to their default state or select all check boxes. Such buttons are typically called something like Reset and Select All. To set the state of a check box under program control, call **setSelected( )** on the check box. It is shown here:

```
void setSelected(boolean set)
```

Here, if *set* is true, the check box is selected (checked). If *set* is false, the check box is cleared (unchecked).

To see the effect of **setSelected( )**, try adding the following code to the previous program. It adds two buttons. The first is called Reset, which clears all check boxes when pressed. The second button is called Select All. It selects all check boxes when pressed.

```
// Create the Reset button.
Button btnReset = new Button("Reset");

// Add action event handler for the Reset button.
btnReset.setOnAction(new EventHandler<ActionEvent>() {
  public void handle(ActionEvent ae) {
    // Clear all the check boxes.
    cbKeyboard.setSelected(false);
    cbMouse.setSelected(false);
    cbTouchScreen.setSelected(false);

    response.setText("All options cleared.");

    showAll();
  }
});

// Create the Select All button.
Button btnSelectAll = new Button("Select All");

// Add action event handler for the Select All button.
btnSelectAll.setOnAction(new EventHandler<ActionEvent>() {
  public void handle(ActionEvent ae) {
    // Select all the check boxes.
    cbKeyboard.setSelected(true);
    cbMouse.setSelected(true);
    cbTouchScreen.setSelected(true);

    response.setText("All options selected.");

    showAll();
  }
});
```

Next, add the two buttons to the scene graph, as shown here:

```
// Add controls to the scene graph.
rootNode.getChildren().addAll(heading, cbKeyboard, cbMouse,
                              cbTouchScreen, response, selected,
                              btnReset, btnSelectAll);
```

Finally, change the dimensions of the **myScene** to **300** by **240**.

Here is sample output from the program:

As the output shows, the Select All button has just been used to select all check boxes. This is accomplished by the following lines in the **btnSelectAll** button event handler:

```
cbKeyboard.setSelected(true);
cbMouse.setSelected(true);
cbTouchScreen.setSelected(true);
```

A similar approach is used to clear all the check boxes, except that **false** is passed to **setSelected( )**.

This example also illustrates another important aspect of event handling: the ability of an event handler for one control to alter the state of another control. This is possible because, as mentioned earlier, event handlers are called on the application thread. Thus, they can be used to affect elements of the GUI other than themselves.

Another way you can change the state of a check box is by use of the **fire( )** method. When called, it acts as if a user had clicked on the box. Thus, if the box was cleared, it will be selected. If the box was already selected, it will be cleared. You can see this effect by substituting the following code for the calls to **setSelected( )** in the **btnReset** button event handler:

```
// Reverse the state of all the check boxes.
cbKeyboard.fire();
cbMouse.fire();
cbTouchScreen.fire();
```

Now, each time the Reset button is pressed, the state of the check boxes will be reversed.

One last point: The **fire( )** method is inherited from **ButtonBase**. Thus, it can be used to fire an event for several other controls that are subclasses of **ButtonBase**. For example, it can be used to press a button under program control. That is, when you call **fire( )** on a **Button** instance, its action event handler is called. You might want to experiment with it by having the Select All button call **fire( )** on the Reset button. If you do this, then both buttons will result in the check boxes being cleared.

Create a Three-State Check Box

As explained, by default, **CheckBox** implements two states: checked and unchecked. This is the traditional way in which a check box works. For example, it is how check boxes work in both the AWT and Swing. However, **CheckBox** provides an expanded capability because it adds support for a third, indeterminate state. Among other uses, this indeterminate state can indicate that the status of the box has not yet been set, that an option is not applicable to a situation, or that the state of the box is unknown. The indeterminate state for a check box must be explicitly enabled. It is not provided by default. Also, the event handler for the check box must handle the indeterminate state.

To enable the indeterminate state, call **setAllowIndeterminate( )**, shown here:

final void setAllowIndeterminate(boolean *enable*)

Here, if *enable* is **true**, the indeterminate state is enabled. Otherwise, it is disabled. When the indeterminate state is enabled, the user can select between checked, unchecked, and indeterminate.

You can determine if a check box is in the indeterminate state by calling **isIndeterminate( )**, shown here:

final boolean isIndeterminate( )

It returns **true** if the state is indeterminate and **false** otherwise.

You can see the effect of a three-state check box by modifying the preceding program. First, enable the indeterminate state on the check boxes by calling **setAllowIndeterminate( )** on each check box, as shown here:

```
cbKeyboard.setAllowIndeterminate(true);
cbMouse.setAllowIndeterminate(true);
cbTouchScreen.setAllowIndeterminate(true);
```

Next, handle the indeterminate state inside the action event handlers. For example, here is the modified handler for **cbKeyboard**:

```
cbKeyboard.setOnAction(new EventHandler<ActionEvent>() {
  public void handle(ActionEvent ae) {

    if(cbKeyboard.isIndeterminate())
      response.setText("Keyboard support is indeterminate.");
    else if(cbKeyboard.isSelected())
      response.setText("Keyboard selected.");
    else
      response.setText("Keyboard cleared.");

    showAll();
  }
});
```

Now, all three states are tested. Update the other two handlers in the same way. After making these changes, the indeterminate state can be used, as this sample output shows:

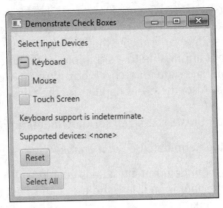

Here, the Keyboard check box is indeterminate.

Handle Key and Mouse Events

As a general rule, the events you will most often handle are generated by controls. However, other types of events are possible. Perhaps the two most important of those are events generated from the keyboard and from the mouse. Although input from these devices is automatically handled for you by a control, you can also respond to these events on their own. Before continuing, it is important to point out that many (if not most) applications will *not* require you to explicitly handle mouse or key events. However, for those situations in which you want to handle these events, the following introduction will be helpful.

Key Events

When a key is typed on the keyboard, a **KeyEvent** is generated. **KeyEvent**s can be handled by instances of various classes, and both the **Node** and **Scene** classes define convenience methods that support **KeyEvent**s. When a key event is handled by a **Node**, events are received only when that node has input focus. When a key event is handled by a **Scene**, events are received when the scene has input focus. **KeyEvent** is packaged in **javafx.scene.input**.

There are three types of key events: a key is pressed; a key is released; and a key is typed. These events are represented by the fields **KEY_PRESSED**, **KEY_RELEASED**, and **KEY_TYPED**, which are defined by **KeyEvent** as objects of **EventType**. (The **ALL** type is also defined.) A key-pressed event is generated when a key is pressed on the keyboard. A key-released event is generated when the key is released. Although handling these events is sometimes useful, often you will simply handle key-typed events. A key-typed event is generated when a normal character on the keyboard, such as A, K, 9, or + is typed. Thus, for normal keyboard input, you can usually just handle key-typed events. A key-pressed event is mostly used when you need to watch for special keys, such as the function, SHIFT, ALT, or ARROW keys.

As mentioned, both **Node** and **Scene** define convenience methods that make it easy to register an event handler for the various types of key events. They are shown here:

final void setOnKeyPressed(EventHandler<? super KeyEvent> *handler*)

final void setOnKeyReleased(EventHandler<? super KeyEvent> *handler*)

final void setOnKeyTyped(EventHandler<? super KeyEvent> *handler*)

For all, *handler* specifies the event handler.

When a key-typed event is received, you can obtain the character by calling **getCharacter( )** on the event. It is shown here:

final String getCharacter( )

It returns a string that contains the character. A string is returned because in some cases more than one character may be required, which is true with certain Unicode characters. However, most often, only one character is returned, encapsulated in a string. It is important to point out that **getCharacter( )** should be used only for key-typed events. For both key-pressed and key-released events, **getCharacter( )** does *not* return a valid character. Instead, it returns **CHAR_UNDEFINED**, which is a string defined by **KeyEvent**.

For key-pressed and key-released events, you can obtain the key code associated with the event. Key codes are enumeration constants defined by **KeyCode**, which is packaged in **javafx.scene.input**. A large number of codes are defined because they represent the various keys on a keyboard. Here are a few examples:

Key Code	Meaning
RIGHT	The stand-alone RIGHT ARROW key
LEFT	The stand-alone LEFT ARROW key
KP_RIGHT	The RIGHT ARROW key on the number pad
KP_LEFT	The LEFT ARROW key on the number pad
F1	The F1 key
F10	The F10 key
ALT	The ALT key
CONTROL	The CTRL key
SHIFT	The SHIFT key

You can obtain the key code by calling **getCode( )** on the key event. It is shown here:

```
final KeyCode getCode( )
```

It is important to understand that this method should be called only when handling a key-pressed or key-released event. For key-typed events, the return value does not represent a key. Instead, the value **KeyCode.UNDEFINED** is returned.

The following program puts the preceding discussion into action. It registers key-typed and key-pressed event handlers on the program's scene. The key-typed handler simply displays the character in a label. The key-pressed handler recognizes the RIGHT and LEFT ARROW keys, F10, and ALT. If the key pressed is one of these keys, it is reported. Otherwise, no other action takes place. It is important to emphasize that all key presses generate a key-pressed event. However, only those that result in a character generate a key-typed event.

```java
// Handle events generated by the keyboard.

import javafx.application.*;
import javafx.scene.*;
import javafx.stage.*;
import javafx.scene.layout.*;
import javafx.scene.control.*;
import javafx.event.*;
import javafx.geometry.*;
import javafx.scene.input.*;

public class KeyEventDemo extends Application {

  Label prompt;
  Label showKey;

  public static void main(String[] args) {

    // Start the JavaFX application by calling launch().
    launch(args);
  }

  // Override the start() method.
  public void start(Stage myStage) {

    // Give the stage a title.
    myStage.setTitle("Handle Keyboard Events");

    // Use a FlowPane for the root node. In this case,
    // the horizontal gap is 10.
    FlowPane rootNode = new FlowPane(Orientation.VERTICAL, 0, 10);
```

```java
    // Center the controls in the scene.
    rootNode.setAlignment(Pos.CENTER);

    // Create a scene.
    Scene myScene = new Scene(rootNode, 300, 100);

    // Set the scene on the stage.
    myStage.setScene(myScene);

    // Create labels.
    prompt = new Label("Press a key.");
    showKey = new Label("");

    // Handle a key-typed event on the scene.
    myScene.setOnKeyTyped(new EventHandler<KeyEvent>() {
      public void handle(KeyEvent ke) {
        showKey.setText("You typed " + ke.getCharacter());
      }
    });

    // Handle a key-pressed event on the scene.
    myScene.setOnKeyPressed(new EventHandler<KeyEvent>() {
      public void handle(KeyEvent ke) {
        switch(ke.getCode()) {
          case RIGHT:
            showKey.setText("You pressed Right Arrow.");
            break;
          case LEFT:
            showKey.setText("You pressed Left Arrow.");
            break;
          case F10:
            showKey.setText("You pressed F10.");
            break;
          case ALT:
            showKey.setText("You pressed Alt.");
            break;
        }
      }
    });

    // Add the labels to the scene graph.
    rootNode.getChildren().addAll(prompt, showKey);

    // Show the stage and its scene.
    myStage.show();
  }
}
```

Sample output is shown here:

Mouse Events

Mouse events are represented by the **MouseEvent** class, which is packaged in **javafx.scene.input**. Like **KeyEvent**, a **MouseEvent** can be handled by instances of various classes, and the **Node** and **Scene** classes define convenience methods for mouse events. When a mouse event is handled by a **Node**, mouse events are received only when that node has input focus. When a mouse event is handled by a **Scene**, mouse events are received when the scene has input focus.

There are a number of different types of events that can be generated by the mouse. For example, an event is generated when the mouse is moved, when a button is clicked or released, when the mouse enters or exits an element that handles mouse events, or when the mouse is dragged. As a result, a number of **EventType** objects are defined by **MouseEvent** that represent the events, such as **MOUSE_CLICKED** and **MOUSE_MOVED**.

As mentioned, both **Node** and **Scene** define convenience methods that can be used to register event handlers for mouse events. The two used in the example that follows are shown here:

final void setOnMouseClicked(EventHandler<? super MouseEvent> *handler*)

final void setOnMouseMoved(EventHandler<? super MouseEvent> *handler*)

For both, *handler* specifies the event handler.

MouseEvent defines a number of methods that help you determine precisely what has occurred. The ones used in the following example are described here. When the mouse is clicked, you can find out which button was used by calling **getButton( )**, shown next:

final MouseButton getButton( )

The button that was clicked is returned as one of the values defined by the **MouseButton** enumeration. In general, if the left button was clicked, **MouseButton.PRIMARY** is returned. If the right button was clicked, the return value is **MouseButton.SECONDARY**. For a mouse with a middle button, clicking it causes **MouseButton.MIDDLE** to be returned. If no button was clicked, such as in the case of **MouseEvent** resulting from a move, then **getButton( )** returns **MouseButton.NONE**.

You can obtain the number of times a mouse button has been clicked by calling **getClickCount( )**, shown here:

final int getClickCount( )

It returns the number of times the button has been pressed. For example, a single-click has the value 1. Clicks in quick succession in the same location result in values greater than 1. For example, a double-click has the value 2. If this method is called when a non-click event has occurred, then the return value is 0.

You can obtain the location of the mouse at the time an event occurred in three different ways. You can get its X,Y coordinates relative to the element on which the mouse event handler is registered, relative to the scene that contains the element or relative to the screen. In all cases, the origin is the upper-left corner. Here, we will obtain the mouse location relative to the scene. To do this, we will use the **getSceneX( )** and **getSceneY( )** methods, shown here:

final double getSceneX( )

final double getSceneY( )

For example, if the mouse is 10 units right and 5 units down from the upper-left corner, then **getSceneX( )** will return 10 and **getSceneY( )** will return 5.

The following program puts the preceding discussion into action. It reports when the mouse is clicked, what button was clicked, and how many times it was clicked in rapid succession. It also displays the location of the mouse relative to the scene.

```
// Handle mouse events.

import javafx.application.*;
import javafx.scene.*;
import javafx.stage.*;
import javafx.scene.layout.*;
import javafx.scene.control.*;
import javafx.event.*;
import javafx.geometry.*;
import javafx.scene.input.*;

public class MouseEventDemo extends Application {

  Label showEvent;
  Label showLocation;

  public static void main(String[] args) {

    // Start the JavaFX application by calling launch().
    launch(args);
  }
```

```java
    // Override the start() method.
    public void start(Stage myStage) {

      // Give the stage a title.
      myStage.setTitle("Handle Mouse Events");

      // Use a FlowPane for the root node. In this case,
      // the horizontal gap is 10.
      FlowPane rootNode = new FlowPane(Orientation.VERTICAL, 0, 10);

      // Center the controls in the scene.
      rootNode.setAlignment(Pos.CENTER);

      // Create a scene.
      Scene myScene = new Scene(rootNode, 300, 100);

      // Set the scene on the stage.
      myStage.setScene(myScene);

      // Create labels.
      showEvent = new Label("Use the mouse.");
      showLocation = new Label("");

      // Handle a mouse click event on the scene.
      myScene.setOnMouseClicked(new EventHandler<MouseEvent>() {
        public void handle(MouseEvent me) {
          int clickcount = me.getClickCount( );
          String times = "time";
          if(clickcount > 1) times += "s";

          switch(me.getButton()) {
            case PRIMARY:
              showEvent.setText("Primary button clicked " + clickcount +
                          " " + times);
              break;
            case MIDDLE:
              showEvent.setText("Middle button clicked " + clickcount +
                          " " + times);
              break;
            case SECONDARY:
              showEvent.setText("Secondary button clicked " + clickcount

                          " " + times);
              break;
          }
        }
      });
```
+

```
  // Handle a mouse move event on the scene.
  myScene.setOnMouseMoved(new EventHandler<MouseEvent>() {
    public void handle(MouseEvent me) {
      showLocation.setText("Mouse at " + me.getSceneX() +", " +
                            me.getSceneY());
    }
  });

  // Add the labels to the scene graph.
  rootNode.getChildren().addAll(showEvent, showLocation);

  // Show the stage and its scene.
  myStage.show();
  }
}
```

Sample output is shown here:

NOTE
*JavaFX also supports touch-screen events. You might
find it interesting to explore them on your own,
especially if you will be writing specifically for touch-
screen devices. In general, touch-screen events are
handled in much the same fashion as mouse and
key events. For example, both the **Node** and **Scene**
classes provide convenience methods that can be
used to register touch-screen event handlers.*

Filtering and Consuming Events

As mentioned earlier in this chapter, the event handling mechanism in JavaFX occurs
in two phases: event capturing and event bubbling. Event handlers, such as those
shown in the previous examples, execute during the event bubbling phase. Event
filters execute during the event capturing phase. Thus, event filters execute *before*
event handlers. This means an event filter can act on an event before it is received
by the event handler registered to the event target.

To register an event filter, use the **addEventFilter( )** method. It is defined for **Node**, **Scene**, and **Stage**, among others. It is shown here:

```
final <T extends Event> void addEventFilter(EventType<T> eType,
                                  EventHandler<? super T> handler)
```

Here, *eType* specifies the type of event to be captured, such as **ActionEvent.ACTION** or **MouseEvent.MOUSE_MOVED**. The event handler is passed to *handler*. You can remove an event filter by calling **removeEventFilter( )**.

One way that a filter can be used is to prevent an event from reaching its target. Recall that the event dispatch chain starts at the top and works its way down. Therefore, an event filter inserted into the chain prior to the element that generated the event can prevent that element from receiving the event. A filter does this by *consuming* the event. This is done by calling **consume( )** on the event. The **consume( )** method is defined by **Event**, as shown here:

```
void consume( )
```

After **consume( )** has been called on an event, the processing of the event is terminated. Thus, a consumed event will never reach an event handler.

To see a filter in action, try adding this one to the first program in this chapter, which is **JavaFXEventDemo**. It consumes all action events that occur inside **myScene**, which includes those generated by the First and Second buttons.

```
// A filter that consumes action events on myScene.
myScene.addEventFilter(ActionEvent.ACTION,
        new EventHandler<ActionEvent>() {
          public void handle(ActionEvent ae) {
            ae.consume();
          }
        });
```

Because this filter is called before the button event handlers, the **consume( )** method will prevent either button handler from being called. Thus, neither button will appear to work because neither button will ever receive an action event.

You can also use a filter to handle events for a group of controls. Here is a very simple example. This version of the previous filter simply reports that a button was pressed, but does not identify which one:

```
// A filter that responds to all action events in myScene the same way
// and then consumes them.
myScene.addEventFilter(ActionEvent.ACTION,
        new EventHandler<ActionEvent>() {
          public void handle(ActionEvent ae) {
            response.setText("A button was pressed.");
```

```
        ae.consume();
      }
   });
```

Thus, in this case, one filter handles events for both buttons.

Of course, it is not necessary for a filter to consume an event. It may allow further processing in some cases, but not in others. Here is a simple example that uses the **MouseEventDemo** program shown earlier. It consumes a mouse moved event only if the mouse's horizontal location is greater than 150.

```
// Add a filter that consumes mouse move events if the mouse's
// horizontal location is greater than 150.
myScene.addEventFilter(MouseEvent.MOUSE_MOVED,
         new EventHandler<MouseEvent>() {
           public void handle(MouseEvent me) {
             if(me.getSceneX() > 150) me.consume();
           }
        });
```

If you add this to the **MouseEventDemo** program, when you move the mouse, you will see its location reported, as before, until its horizontal position exceeds 150. At that point, mouse move events are consumed, and the location of the mouse is no longer reported. However, other mouse events, such as mouse clicked, will continue to be active. Also, when the mouse is moved such that its horizontal location is less than 150, the mouse move events are no longer consumed and the mouse move event handler becomes active again.

CHAPTER
3

Exploring JavaFX
Controls, Part One

The previous chapters described several of the core concepts relating to JavaFX. In the process, they introduced three controls: **Label**, **Button**, and **CheckBox**. Controls are at the foundation of JavaFX because they define the way a user interacts with an application. Furthermore, the techniques needed to utilize and manage controls have a substantial impact on the design of an application. Therefore, a general understanding of controls is necessary before you advance to other aspects of JavaFX. For this reason, this and the following chapter explore several more JavaFX controls.

Before we begin, it is important to emphasize that JavaFX is an extraordinarily rich and powerful framework that provides a wide range of controls. We won't explore them all in this book. The primary purpose of this and the following chapter is to introduce a representative sampling and to illustrate a number of techniques. Once you understand the basics, learning the other JavaFX controls is straightforward.

The control classes introduced in this chapter are shown here:

- ToggleButton
- RadioButton
- ListView
- ComboBox
- ChoiceBox

These and the other JavaFX controls are packaged in **javafx.scene.control**. Also discussed are **Tooltip**, which is used to add tooltips to a control, and **Separator**, which provides visual separation between screen elements.

ToggleButton

JavaFX provides a useful variation on the push button called a *toggle button*. It can be used to streamline the coding in cases in which an on/off type button is desired. A toggle button looks just like a push button, but it acts differently because it has two states: pressed and released. That is, when you press a toggle button, it stays pressed rather than popping back up as a regular push button does. When you click the toggle button a second time, it releases (pops up). Therefore, each time a toggle button is pushed, it toggles between these two states. In JavaFX, a toggle button is encapsulated in the **ToggleButton** class. Like **Button**, **ToggleButton** is also derived from **ButtonBase**. It implements the **Toggle** interface, which defines functionality common to all types of two-state buttons.

ToggleButton defines three constructors. The one we will use is shown here:

ToggleButton(String *str*)

Here, *str* is the text displayed in the button. Like a push button, a **ToggleButton** generates an action event when it is clicked.

Because **ToggleButton** defines a two-state control, it is commonly used to let the user select an option. When the button is pressed, the option is selected. When the button is released, the option is deselected. For this reason, a program will usually need to determine the toggle button's state. To do this, use the **isSelected( )** method, shown here:

    final boolean isSelected( )

It returns **true** if the button is pressed and **false** otherwise.

Here is a short program that demonstrates **ToggleButton**:

```
// Demonstrate a toggle button.

import javafx.application.*;
import javafx.scene.*;
import javafx.stage.*;
import javafx.scene.layout.*;
import javafx.scene.control.*;
import javafx.event.*;
import javafx.geometry.*;

public class ToggleButtonDemo extends Application {

  ToggleButton tbToggle;
  Label response;

  public static void main(String[] args) {

    // Start the JavaFX application by calling launch().
    launch(args);
  }

  // Override the start() method.
  public void start(Stage myStage) {

    // Give the stage a title.
    myStage.setTitle("Demonstrate a Toggle Button");

    // Use a FlowPane for the root node. In this case,
    // vertical and horizontal gaps of 10.
    FlowPane rootNode = new FlowPane(10, 10);

    // Center the controls in the scene.
    rootNode.setAlignment(Pos.CENTER);
```

```
    // Create a scene.
    Scene myScene = new Scene(rootNode, 200, 100);

    // Set the scene on the stage.
    myStage.setScene(myScene);

    // Create a label.
    response = new Label("Push the Button.");

    // Create the toggle button.
    tbToggle = new ToggleButton("Toggle");

    // Handle action events for the toggle button.
    tbToggle.setOnAction(new EventHandler<ActionEvent>() {
      public void handle(ActionEvent ae) {
        if(tbToggle.isSelected()) response.setText("Button is down.");
        else response.setText("Button is up.");
      }
    });

    // Add the label and buttons to the scene graph.
    rootNode.getChildren().addAll(tbToggle, response);

    // Show the stage and its scene.
    myStage.show();
  }
}
```

Sample output produced by the program is shown here, with the button pressed:

In the program, notice how the pressed/released state of the toggle button is determined by the following lines of code inside the button's action event handler.

```
if(tbToggle.isSelected()) response.setText("Button is down.");
else response.setText("Button is up.");
```

When the button is pressed, **isSelected( )** returns **true**. When the button is released, **isSelected( )** returns **false**.

One other point: It is possible to use two or more toggle buttons in a group. In this case, only one button can be in its pressed state at any one time. The process of creating and using a group of toggle buttons is similar to that required to use radio buttons, which are described in the next section.

Radio Buttons

Another commonly used control supported by JavaFX is the *radio button*. Radio buttons are typically used to manage a group of mutually exclusive buttons. In such a group, only one button can be selected at any one time. They are supported by the **RadioButton** class, which extends both **ButtonBase** and **ToggleButton**. **RadioButton** also implements the **Toggle** interface. In essence, **RadioButton** is a unique style of **ToggleButton**. Radio buttons are the primary control employed when the user must select only one option among several alternatives.

　　RadioButton defines two constructors. The first is the default constructor. The second is shown here:

　　RadioButton(String *str*)

Here, *str* is the label for the button.

　　In order for their mutually exclusive nature to be activated, radio buttons must be configured into a group. Only one of the buttons in the group can be selected at any time. For example, if a user presses a radio button that is in a group, any previously selected button in that group is automatically cleared. A button group is created by the **ToggleGroup** class, which is packaged in **javafx.scene.control**. **ToggleGroup** provides only a default constructor.

　　Radio buttons are added to the toggle group by calling the **setToggleGroup( )** method on the button. It is shown here:

　　final void setToggleGroup(ToggleGroup *tg*)

Here, *tg* is a reference to the toggle group to which the button is added. After all radio buttons have been added to the same group, their mutually exclusive behavior will be enabled.

　　When a **RadioButton** is part of a **ToggleGroup**, an action event is generated when the button is clicked only if the button was previously cleared. Thus, an action event is generated only when a new button is selected. If an already selected radio button is clicked, no event is generated.

　　It is important to point out that, although not the common usage, a **RadioButton** can be used in a stand-alone manner. In this case, it will behave like a check box or toggle button, changing state each time it is pressed. Here, we are concerned only with the typical radio button use, which is to support a group of mutually exclusive options.

　　In general, when radio buttons are used in a group, one of the buttons is selected when the group is first displayed in the GUI. One way to do this is by calling **setSelected( )** on the button that you want to select. It is shown here:

　　final void setSelected(boolean *state*)

If *state* is **true**, the button is selected. Otherwise, it is deselected. Although the button is selected, no action event is generated.

In some cases, you might find it easier to initially select a radio button by calling **fire( )** on the button that you want to set. If the button was previously not selected, then calling **fire( )** will generate an action event for the button, and the button will be selected. The button will also receive input focus. This approach is demonstrated by the example that follows.

There are a number of different ways to handle radio buttons. Perhaps the most intuitive is to simply respond to the action event that is generated when one is selected. The following program shows an example of this approach. It uses radio buttons to allow the user to select a primary input device. Thus, it is a variation of the check box example from the previous chapter. In this version, only one device can be selected at a time.

```
// A simple demonstration of Radio Buttons.
//
// This program responds to the action events generated
// by a radio button selection. It also uses fire() to set
// the initial selection.

import javafx.application.*;
import javafx.scene.*;
import javafx.stage.*;
import javafx.scene.layout.*;
import javafx.scene.control.*;
import javafx.event.*;
import javafx.geometry.*;

public class RadioButtonDemo extends Application {

    Label response;
    Label prompt;

    RadioButton rbKeyboard;
    RadioButton rbMouse;
    RadioButton rbTouchScreen;

    ToggleGroup tg;

    public static void main(String[] args) {

        // Start the JavaFX application by calling launch().
        launch(args);
    }

    // Override the start() method.
```

```java
public void start(Stage myStage) {

  // Give the stage a title.
  myStage.setTitle("Demonstrate Radio Buttons");

  // Use a FlowPane for the root node. In this case,
  // vertical gap of 10.
  FlowPane rootNode = new FlowPane(Orientation.VERTICAL, 0, 10);

  // Center the controls vertically, left-align them horizontally.
  rootNode.setAlignment(Pos.CENTER_LEFT);

  // Set a padding value of 10 on the left for the flow pane.
  rootNode.setPadding(new Insets(0, 0, 0, 10));

  // Create a scene.
  Scene myScene = new Scene(rootNode, 220, 140);

  // Set the scene on the stage.
  myStage.setScene(myScene);

  // Create the prompting label.
  prompt = new Label("Select Primary Input Device");

  // Create a label that will report the selection.
  response = new Label("");

  // Create the radio buttons.
  rbKeyboard = new RadioButton("Keyboard");
  rbMouse = new RadioButton("Mouse");
  rbTouchScreen = new RadioButton("Touch Screen");

  // Create a toggle group.
  tg = new ToggleGroup();

  // Add each button to a toggle group.
  rbKeyboard.setToggleGroup(tg);
  rbMouse.setToggleGroup(tg);
  rbTouchScreen.setToggleGroup(tg);

  // Handle action events for the radio buttons.
  rbKeyboard.setOnAction(new EventHandler<ActionEvent>() {
    public void handle(ActionEvent ae) {
      response.setText("Primary input device is keyboard.");
    }
  });

  rbMouse.setOnAction(new EventHandler<ActionEvent>() {
```

```
      public void handle(ActionEvent ae) {
        response.setText("Primary input device is mouse.");
      }
    });

    rbTouchScreen.setOnAction(new EventHandler<ActionEvent>() {
      public void handle(ActionEvent ae) {
        response.setText("Primary input device is touch screen.");
      }
    });

    // Fire the event for the first selection. This causes
    // that radio button to be selected and an action event
    // for that button to occur.
    rbKeyboard.fire();

    // Add the label and buttons to the scene graph.
    rootNode.getChildren().addAll(prompt, rbKeyboard, rbMouse,
                                  rbTouchScreen, response);

    // Show the stage and its scene.
    myStage.show();
  }
}
```

Sample output is shown here:

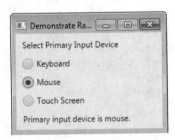

In the program, pay special attention to how the radio buttons and the toggle group are created. First, the buttons are created using this sequence:

```
rbKeyboard = new RadioButton("Keyboard");
rbMouse = new RadioButton("Mouse");
rbTouchScreen = new RadioButton("Touch Screen");
```

Next, a **ToggleGroup** is constructed:

```
tg = new ToggleGroup();
```

Finally, each radio button is added to the **ToggleGroup**:

```
rbKeyboard.setToggleGroup(tg);
rbMouse.setToggleGroup(tg);
rbTouchScreen.setToggleGroup(tg);
```

As explained, radio buttons must be part of a toggle group for their mutually exclusive behavior to be activated.

After the event handlers for each radio button have been defined, **fire( )** is called on **rbKeyboard**. This causes that button to be selected, input focus to be on that button, and an action event to be generated for that button. Thus, the toggle group is initialized with a default selection.

Watch for Changes in a Toggle Group

Although there is nothing wrong, per se, with managing radio buttons by handling action events, as just shown, sometimes it is more appropriate (and easier) to listen to the entire toggle group for changes. When a change takes place, the event handler can easily determine which radio button has been selected and take action accordingly. To use this approach, you must register a **ChangeListener** on the toggle group. When a change occurs to the toggle group, the listener is executed. Inside the listener, you can determine which button was selected. Thus, one piece of code can watch for a change to a group of radio buttons.

To try this approach, remove the action event handlers and the call to **fire( )** from the preceding program and substitute the following:

```
// Use a change listener to respond to a change of selection within
// a ToggleGroup of radio buttons.
tg.selectedToggleProperty().addListener(new ChangeListener<Toggle>() {
  public void changed(ObservableValue<? extends Toggle> changed,
                      Toggle oldVal, Toggle newVal) {

    // Cast newVal to RadioButton.
    RadioButton rb = (RadioButton) newVal;

    // Display the selection.
    response.setText("Device selected is " + rb.getText());
  }
});

// Select the first button. This will cause a change event
// on the toggle group.
rbKeyboard.setSelected(true);
```

You will also need to add this **import** statement:

```
import javafx.beans.value.*;
```

It supports the **ChangeListener** interface.

The output from this program is the same as before; each time a selection is made, the **response** label is updated. However, in this case, only one event handler is needed for the entire group, rather than three (one for each button). Let's now look at how this code works.

To listen for change events, an implementation of the **ChangeListener** interface is required. **ChangeListener** defines only one method, called **changed( )**. It is shown here:

void changed(ObservableValue<? extends T> *changed*, T *oldVal*, T *newVal*)

Here, *changed* is the instance of **ObservableValue<T>** that encapsulates an object that can be watched for changes. The *oldVal* and *newVal* parameters receive the previous value and the new value, respectively. Thus, in this case, *newVal* holds a reference to the radio button that has just been selected.

Next, the change listener must be registered for the toggle group. This is done by calling **addListener( )** on the object returned by **selectedToggleProperty( )**, which is called on the toggle group. This object represents the selection and is of type **ReadOnlyObjectProperty<T>**. It is packaged in **javafx.beans.property**. In this case, **T** is **Toggle**. As its name suggests, **ReadOnlyObjectProperty** provides support for read-only properties. Once the change listener has been registered, any change to the toggle group will result in a call to the change listener and the new selection will be reported.

One other point: In this example, the **setSelected( )** method, rather than **fire( )**, is called to set the initial selection. Because setting the initial selection causes a change to the toggle group, it results in a change event being generated when the program first begins. You can also use **fire( )**, but here **setSelected( )** is used to demonstrate that any change to the toggle group generates a change event.

Obtain the Selected Radio Button in a Toggle Group

Although handling events generated by radio buttons is quite common, in some cases it may be better to ignore those events and simply obtain the currently selected button in the toggle group when that setting is needed. For example, you may want to wait until a user has confirmed a choice before your program acts on it. This approach is demonstrated by the following program. It adds a button called Confirm Device. When this button is pressed, the currently selected radio button in the toggle group is obtained and then the selection is displayed in a label. When you try the program, notice that changing the selected radio button does not cause the confirmed device to change until you press the Confirm Device button.

```
// In this example, no radio button events are handled.
// Instead, the current selection is obtained when the
// Confirm Device push button is pressed.
```

```
import javafx.application.*;
import javafx.scene.*;
import javafx.stage.*;
import javafx.scene.layout.*;
import javafx.scene.control.*;
import javafx.event.*;
import javafx.geometry.*;

public class RadioButtonDemoAlt extends Application {

  Label response;
  Label prompt;

  Button btnConfirm;

  RadioButton rbKeyboard;
  RadioButton rbMouse;
  RadioButton rbTouchScreen;

  ToggleGroup tg;

  public static void main(String[] args) {

    // Start the JavaFX application by calling launch().
    launch(args);
  }

  // Override the start() method.
  public void start(Stage myStage) {

    // Give the stage a title.
    myStage.setTitle("Another Way to Use Radio Buttons");

    // Use a FlowPane for the root node. In this case,
    // vertical gap of 10.
    FlowPane rootNode = new FlowPane(Orientation.VERTICAL, 0, 10);

    // Center the controls vertically, left-align them horizontally.
    rootNode.setAlignment(Pos.CENTER_LEFT);

    // Set a padding value of 10 on the left for the flow pane.
    rootNode.setPadding(new Insets(0, 0, 0, 10));

    // Create a scene.
    Scene myScene = new Scene(rootNode, 220, 200);

    // Set the scene on the stage.
```

```
myStage.setScene(myScene);

// Create the prompting label.
prompt = new Label("Choose Primary Input Device");

// Create a label that will report the selection.
response = new Label("No device confirmed.");

// Create the confirm device button.
btnConfirm = new Button("Confirm Device");

// Create the radio buttons.
rbKeyboard = new RadioButton("Keyboard");
rbMouse = new RadioButton("Mouse");
rbTouchScreen = new RadioButton("Touch Screen");

// Create a toggle group.
tg = new ToggleGroup();

// Add each button to a toggle group.
rbKeyboard.setToggleGroup(tg);
rbMouse.setToggleGroup(tg);
rbTouchScreen.setToggleGroup(tg);

// Initially select one of the radio buttons.
rbKeyboard.setSelected(true);

// Handle action events for the confirm device button.
btnConfirm.setOnAction(new EventHandler<ActionEvent>() {
  public void handle(ActionEvent ae) {
    // Get the radio button that is currently selected.
    RadioButton rb = (RadioButton) tg.getSelectedToggle();

    // Display the selection.
    response.setText(rb.getText() + " is confirmed.");
  }
});

// Add the label and buttons to the scene graph.
rootNode.getChildren().addAll(prompt, rbKeyboard, rbMouse,
                     rbTouchScreen, btnConfirm, response);

// Show the stage and its scene.
myStage.show();
  }
}
```

The output from the program is shown here:

There is one point of special interest in the program. Inside the action event handler for the **btnConfirm** button, notice that the selected radio button is obtained by the following line:

```
RadioButton rb = (RadioButton) tg.getSelectedToggle();
```

Here, the **getSelectedToggle( )** method (defined by **ToggleGroup**) obtains the current selection for the toggle group (which in this case is a group of radio buttons). It is shown here:

final Toggle getSelectedToggle( )

It returns a reference to the **Toggle** that is selected. In this case, the return value is cast to **RadioButton** because this is the type of button in the group.

ListView

Controls such as check boxes and radio buttons are certainly very useful, but they are best for representing a small, fixed number of options. In cases in which you want to present a list of items to the user, another of JavaFX's controls, the **ListView**, offers a solution. The **ListView** class encapsulates a list view. *List views* are controls that display a list of entries from which you can select one or more. Furthermore, the number of entries in the list can increase or decrease during the execution of the program. They also make efficient use of limited screen space. As a result, they are popular alternatives to other types of selection controls.

ListView is a generic class that is declared like this:

class ListView<T>

Here, **T** specifies the type of entries stored in the list view. Often, these are entries of type **String**, but other types are also allowed.

ListView defines two constructors. The first is the default constructor, which creates an empty **ListView**. The second lets you specify the list of entries in the list. It is shown here:

ListView(ObservableList<T> *list*)

Here, *list* specifies a list of the items that will be displayed. It is an object of type **ObservableList**, which defines a list of observable objects. As explained in Chapter 1, **ObservableList** inherits **java.util.List**. Thus, it supports the standard list collection methods. **ObservableList** is packaged in **javafx.collections**.

An easy way to create an **ObservableList** for use in a **ListView** is to use the factory method **observableArrayList( )**, which is a static method defined by the **FXCollections** class (which is also packaged in **javafx.collections**). The version we will use is shown here:

static <E> ObservableList<E> observableArrayList(E ... *elements*)

Here, **E** specifies the type of elements, which are passed via *elements*.

Although **ListView** will provide a default size, sometimes you will want to set the preferred height and/or width to best match your needs. One way to do this is to call the **setPrefHeight( )** and **setPrefWidth( )** methods, shown here:

final void setPrefHeight(double *height*)
final void setPrefWidth(double *width*)

Alternatively, you can use a single call to set both dimensions at the same time by use of **setPrefSize( )**, shown here:

void setPrefSize(double *width*, double *height*)

In general, you don't need to worry about the size of the list exceeding the size of the **ListView** control. **ListView** will automatically provide scroll bars when the items in the list exceed the size of the control. Specifically, when the number of items in the list exceeds the number that can be displayed within its height, vertical scroll bars are added. When the length of an entry exceeds the control's length, horizontal scroll bars are added. This means you can set the size of a **ListView** so it best fits your screen space without having to be overly worried about size limitations.

By default, a **ListView** allows only one item in the list to be selected at any one time. However, you can allow multiple selections by changing the selection mode. For now, we will use the default single-selection model.

There are two basic ways in which you can use a **ListView**. First, you can ignore events generated by the list and simply obtain the selection in the list when your program needs it. Second, you can monitor the list for changes by registering a change listener. This lets you respond each time the user changes a selection in the list. This is the approach used in the next example.

To listen for change events, you must first obtain the selection model used by the **ListView**. This is done by calling **getSelectionModel( )** on the list. It is shown here:

final MultipleSelectionModel<T> getSelectionModel( )

It returns a reference to the model. **MultipleSelectionModel** is a class that defines the model used for multiple selections, and it inherits **SelectionModel**. It is important to emphasize that, although **MultipleSelectionModel** is used by **ListView**, multiple selections are allowed only if multiple-selection mode is turned on. You will see an example of this shortly.

Using the model returned by **getSelectionModel( )**, there are two basic ways to identify the list item selected. You can obtain a reference to the item, or you can obtain its index. Let's begin with the first method. To start, obtain a reference to the selected item property. This property defines what takes place when an element in the list is selected. This is done by calling **selectedItemProperty( )**, shown here:

final ReadOnlyObjectProperty<T> selectedItemProperty( )

You will add the change listener to this property by calling **addListener( )** on the property, passing in the change listener. This process is similar to that used for radio buttons, described previously.

The following example puts the preceding discussion into action. It creates a list view that displays various types of apples, allowing the user to select one. When one is chosen, the selection is displayed.

```
// Demonstrate ListView.

import javafx.application.*;
import javafx.scene.*;
import javafx.stage.*;
import javafx.scene.layout.*;
import javafx.scene.control.*;
import javafx.geometry.*;
import javafx.beans.value.*;
import javafx.collections.*;

public class ListViewDemo extends Application {

  Label response;

  ListView<String> lvApple;

  public static void main(String[] args) {

    // Start the JavaFX application by calling launch().
    launch(args);
  }
```

```
// Override the start() method.
public void start(Stage myStage) {

  // Give the stage a title.
  myStage.setTitle("ListView Demo");

  // Use a FlowPane for the root node. In this case,
  // vertical and horizontal gaps of 10.
  FlowPane rootNode = new FlowPane(10, 10);

  // Center the controls in the scene.
  rootNode.setAlignment(Pos.CENTER);

  // Create a scene.
  Scene myScene = new Scene(rootNode, 220, 140);

  // Set the scene on the stage.
  myStage.setScene(myScene);

  // Create a label.
  response = new Label("Select Your Apple");

  // Create an ObservableList of entries for the list view.
  ObservableList<String> appleTypes =
    FXCollections.observableArrayList("Winesap", "Cortland", "Gala",
                                      "Golden Delicious", "Fuji",
                                      "Jonathan");

  // Create the list view.
  lvApple = new ListView<String>(appleTypes);

  // Set the preferred height and width.
  lvApple.setPrefSize(80, 80);

  // Get the list view selection model.
  MultipleSelectionModel<String> lvSelModel =
                                lvApple.getSelectionModel();

  // Use a change listener to respond to a change of selection within
  // a list view.
  lvSelModel.selectedItemProperty().addListener(
                                new ChangeListener<String>() {
    public void changed(ObservableValue<? extends String> changed,
                     String oldVal, String newVal) {

      // Display the selection.
      response.setText("Apple selected is " + newVal);
```

```
    }
  });

  // Add the label and list view to the scene graph.
  rootNode.getChildren().addAll(lvApple, response);

  // Show the stage and its scene.
  myStage.show();
  }
}
```

Sample output is shown here:

In the program, pay special attention to how the **ListView** is constructed. First, an **ObservableList** is created by this line:

```
ObservableList<String> appleTypes =
  FXCollections.observableArrayList("Winesap", "Cortland", "Gala",
                                    "Golden Delicious", "Fuji",
                                    "Jonathan");
```

It uses the **observableArrayList( )** method to create a list of strings. Next, the observable list is passed to **ListView**, as shown here:

```
lvApple = new ListView<String>(appleTypes);
```

After this statement executes, **lvApple** will have been initialized with the list of apples. The program then sets the preferred width and height of the control. In this case, the size of the list view is purposely set too small to display all of the entries. As a result, scroll bars are automatically included, as the sample output shows.

Now, notice how the selection model is obtained for **lvApple**:

```
MultipleSelectionModel<String> lvSelModel =
                             lvApple.getSelectionModel();
```

As explained, **ListView**s use **MultipleSelectionModel**, even when only a single selection is allowed. The **selectedItemProperty( )** method is then called on the model and a change listener is registered to the returned item.

As stated, scroll bars are automatically added when the size of the list exceeds what the **ListView** instance can hold. Of course, if the entries will fit within the dimensions of the control, no scroll bars will be shown. You can confirm this by reducing the number of items in the declaration of **appleTypes**, as shown here:

```
ObservableList<String> appleTypes =
   FXCollections.observableArrayList("Winesap", "Cortland", "Gala");
```

After making this change, the **lvApple** control will now look like the one shown here:

One other point before moving on: it is possible to create a **ListView** in which the values can be edited. However, this technique is beyond the scope of this book. You might, however, want to explore it on your own. In general, if you simply want to edit a list that contains strings, then the **ComboBox** described later in this chapter offers an easy solution.

Enabling Multiple Selections

If you want to allow more than one item to be selected, you must explicitly request it. To do so, set the selection mode to **SelectionMode.MULTIPLE** by calling **setSelectionMode( )** on the **ListView** model. It is shown here:

    final void setSelectionMode(SelectionMode *mode*)

Here, *mode* must be either **SelectionMode.MULTIPLE** or **SelectionMode.SINGLE**. **SelectionMode** is an enumeration packaged in **javafx.scene.control**.

When multiple-selection mode is enabled, you can obtain the list of the selections in two ways: as a list of selected indices or as a list of selected items. We will use a list of the selected items, but the procedure is similar when using a list of the indices.

To retrieve a list of the selected items, call **getSelectedItems( )** on the selection model. It is shown here:

    ObservableList<T> getSelectedItems( )

It returns an **ObservableList** of the items. Because **ObservableList** extends **java.util.List**, you can access the items in the list just as you would any other **List** collection.

To try multiple selections, modify the preceding program as follows. First, add this line:

```
lvSelModel.setSelectionMode(SelectionMode.MULTIPLE);
```

It enables multiple-selection mode for **lvApple**. Next, replace the change event handler with the one shown here:

```
lvSelModel.selectedItemProperty().addListener(
                                new ChangeListener<String>() {
  public void changed(ObservableValue<? extends String> changed,
               String oldVal, String newVal) {

    String selItems = "";
    ObservableList<String> selected =
           lvSelModel.getSelectedItems();

    // Display the selections.
    for(String item : selected)
      selItems += "\n       " + item;

    response.setText("All selected apples: " + selItems);
  }
});
```

After making these changes, the program will display all selected apples, as the following output shows:

As a point of interest, you can use the selection model to set a selection in a list view by calling **select( )**, specifying either the index or the object to be selected. Other selection methods are also supported.

Changing the ListView Dynamically

Once a list has been created, you can add to or remove items from it by adding or removing them from the **ObservableList** that backs it. To add an item, use **add( )**. To add a list of items, use **addAll( )**. To remove an item, use **remove( )**. Various forms of these methods are supported. Making a change to an **ObservableList** results in the same change in the **ListView** that uses the list. For example, the following lines add Red Delicious to the list and remove Fuji from the **ListViewDemo** program.

```
appleTypes.add("Red Delicious");
appleTypes.remove("Fuji");
```

In this example, the name of the backing list **appleTypes** is known, so it is used explicitly. However, it is possible to obtain a reference to the backing list from the **ListView** control, itself. This is done by calling **getItems( )** on the **ListView** instance. It is shown here:

final ObservableList<T> getItems( )

It returns a reference to the backing list. Using **getItems( )**, the previous statements can be rewritten like this:

```
lvApple.getItems().add("Red Delicious");
lvApple.getItems().remove("Fuji");
```

One other point: you can set the backing list after the **ListView** instance has been created by using **setItems( )**:

final void setItems(ObservableList<T> *itemList*)

Here, *itemList* is a reference to the new backing list.

Obtaining ListView Item Indices

As mentioned earlier, when listening for change events on a **ListView**, you can identify what item was selected by obtaining a reference to it or by obtaining its index in the list. The first approach was shown by the preceding examples. Here, we will look at using indices. Although the two processes are similar, different methods are needed.

To obtain the index of a selected item when a change event occurs, first obtain the selection model by calling **getSelectionModel( )** on the list, as before. Then, using this model, obtain a reference to the selected index property by calling **selectedIndexProperty( )**, shown next:

final ReadOnlyIntegerProperty selectedIndexProperty( )

Notice that this method returns a **ReadOnlyIntegerProperty**. This is because the index of a selection is represented by an integer value. Next, add a change listener to the object returned by **selectedIndexProperty( )**. For example, here is one way to recode the change listener for the **ListViewDemo** program:

```
lvSelModel.selectedIndexProperty().addListener(
                        new ChangeListener<Number>() {
    public void changed(ObservableValue<? extends Number> changed,
```

```
                    Number oldVal, Number newVal) {

     // Display the selection.
     response.setText("The index of the apple selected is " + newVal);
   }
 });
```

After making this change, the program will report the index of the newly selected apple. Sample output is shown here:

One other point: When multiple selections have been enabled, you can obtain a list of the selected indices by calling **getSelectedIndices( )** on the selection model. You might want to try this on your own.

ComboBox

JavaFX provides a variation of a list control called the *combo box,* which is implemented by the **ComboBox** class. A combo box displays one selection, but it will also display a drop-down list that allows the user to select a different item. Additionally, you can allow the user to edit a selection. **ComboBox** inherits **ComboBoxBase**, which provides much of its functionality. Unlike **ListView**, which can allow multiple selections, **ComboBox** is designed for single selection.

ComboBox is a generic class that is declared like this:

class ComboBox<T>

Here, **T** specifies the type of entries. Often, these are entries of type **String**, but other types are also allowed.

ComboBox defines two constructors. The first is the default constructor, which creates an empty **ComboBox**. The second lets you specify the entries in the list. It is shown here:

ComboBox(ObservableList<T> *list*)

Here, *list* specifies a list of the items that will be displayed. It is an object of type **ObservableList**. As previously explained, **ObservableList** defines a list of observable objects. It inherits **java.util.List**. As also previously explained, an easy way to create an

ObservableList is to use the factory method **observableArrayList( )**, which is a static method defined by the **FXCollections** class.

A **ComboBox** generates an action event when its selection changes. It will also generate a change event. Alternatively, it is also possible to ignore events and simply obtain the current selection when needed.

You can obtain the current selection by calling **getValue( )**, shown here:

final T getValue( )

If the value of a combo box has not yet been set (by the user or under program control), **getValue( )** will return null. To set the value of a **ComboBox** under program control, call **setValue( )**:

final void setValue(T *newVal*)

Here, *newVal* becomes the new value.

The following program demonstrates a combo box by reworking the previous **ListView** example. It handles action events generated by the combo box.

```
// Demonstrate a combo box.

import javafx.application.*;
import javafx.scene.*;
import javafx.stage.*;
import javafx.scene.layout.*;
import javafx.scene.control.*;
import javafx.geometry.*;
import javafx.collections.*;
import javafx.event.*;


public class ComboBoxDemo extends Application {

  ComboBox<String> cbApple;
  Label response;

  public static void main(String[] args) {

    // Start the JavaFX application by calling launch().
    launch(args);
  }

  // Override the start() method.
  public void start(Stage myStage) {

    // Give the stage a title.
    myStage.setTitle("ComboBox Demo");
```

```
// Use a FlowPane for the root node. In this case,
// vertical and horizontal gaps of 10.
FlowPane rootNode = new FlowPane(10, 10);

// Pad top of window.
rootNode.setPadding(new Insets(10, 0, 0, 0));

// Center the control at top of the scene.
rootNode.setAlignment(Pos.TOP_CENTER);

// Create a scene.
Scene myScene = new Scene(rootNode, 240, 120);

// Set the scene on the stage.
myStage.setScene(myScene);

// Create a label.
response = new Label();

// Create an ObservableList of entries for the combo box.
ObservableList<String> appleTypes =
  FXCollections.observableArrayList("Winesap", "Cortland", "Gala",
                                    "Golden Delicious", "Fuji",
                                    "Jonathan");

// Create a combo box.
cbApple = new ComboBox<String>(appleTypes);

// Set the default value.
cbApple.setValue("Winesap");

// Set the response label to indicate the default selection.
response.setText("Selected apple is " + cbApple.getValue());

// Listen for action events on the combo box.
cbApple.setOnAction(new EventHandler<ActionEvent>() {
  public void handle(ActionEvent ae) {
    response.setText("Selected apple is " + cbApple.getValue());
  }
});

// Add the label and combo box to the scene graph.
rootNode.getChildren().addAll(cbApple, response);

// Show the stage and its scene.
myStage.show();
  }
}
```

Sample output is shown here:

One other point: Like **ListView**, you can set the size of a **ComboBox** by use of **setPrefWidth( )**, **setPrefHeight( )**, or **setPrefSize( )**, but often the default size is appropriate.

Enable ComboBox Editing

As mentioned, **ComboBox** can be configured to allow the user to edit a selection. Assuming that it contains only entries of type **String**, it is easy to enable the editing capabilities. Simply call **setEditable( )**, shown here:

final void setEditable(boolean *enable*)

If *enable* is **true**, editing is enabled. Otherwise, it is disabled. To see the effects of editing, add this line to the preceding program:

```
cbApple.setEditable(true);
```

After making this addition, you will be able to edit the selection.

Once you have enabled editing, here is an interesting experiment that you can try. Add the following statements to the action event handler in **ComboBoxDemo**:

```
// Add the modified item to the end of the list.
int i = cbApple.getSelectionModel().getSelectedIndex();
if(!appleTypes.get(i).equals(cbApple.getValue())) {
  appleTypes.add(cbApple.getValue());
}
```

Now, when the user edits a selection and then confirms the edit (such as by pressing ENTER), the edited version of the selection is added to the end of the list. Notice how the index of the selection is obtained from the selection model.

Show the Drop-Down List Under Program Control

Usually, the user will activate the drop-down list, but it is possible to cause the list to be shown under program control. To do this, call **show( )** on the combo box. It is shown here:

    void show( )

To try **show( )**, add the following code to the **ComboBoxDemo**:

```
Button btnShow = new Button("Show List");

btnShow.setOnAction(new EventHandler<ActionEvent>() {
  public void handle(ActionEvent ae) {
    cbApple.show();
  }
});
```

This adds the Show List button and its action event handler. Notice that the handler calls **show( )** on the **cbApple** combo box. Next, add **btnShow** to the scene graph. After making these changes, each time you press the Show List button, the list will be shown.

It is also possible to hide the drop-down list under program control. You do this by calling **hide( )**.

ComboBox supports many additional features and functionality beyond those mentioned here. You might find it interesting to explore further. Also, an alternative to a combo box in some cases is the **ChoiceBox** control, described next.

ChoiceBox

Another variation on the list control is **ChoiceBox**. **ChoiceBox** is somewhat like a **ComboBox** but without the editing capabilities. It lets the user select an option from a drop-down list. The selection is shown as checked in the list. Only single selection is supported. This makes **ChoiceBox** a useful alternative to radio buttons when space is an issue.

ChoiceBox is a generic class that is declared like this:

    class ChoiceBox<T>

Here, **T** specifies the type of entries. As with the other list controls, these are often entries of type **String**.

ChoiceBox defines two constructors. The first is the default constructor, which creates an empty **ChoiceBox**. The second lets you specify the list of entries. It is shown here:

    ChoiceBox(ObservableList<T> *list*)

Here, *list* specifies a list of the items that will be displayed. It is an object of type **ObservableList**. As previously explained, **ObservableList** defines a list of observable objects, and an easy way to create an **ObservableList** is to use the factory method **observableArrayList( )**, defined by the **FXCollections** class.

A **ChoiceBox** is managed much like a **ListView**. For example, you can monitor the list for changes by registering a change listener on the selection model in much the same way as shown for **ListView**. Doing so lets you respond each time the user changes a selection in the list. To listen for change events, you must first obtain the selection model. This is done by calling **getSelectionModel( )** on the **ChoiceBox**. It is shown here:

```
final SingleSelectionModel<T> getSelectionModel( )
```

It returns a reference to the model. **SingleSelectionModel** is a class that defines the model used for single selections. As mentioned, **ChoiceBox** supports only single selection. (If you need multiple selection, consider using a **ListView**.) Next, add the change listener to the object returned by **selectedItemProperty( )** when called on the selection model.

You can set the current value of the control by calling **setValue( )**. You can obtain the value by calling **getValue( )**.

Often, the default size of the control is appropriate, but you can set the size explicitly by use of **setPrefWidth( )**, **setPrefHeight( )**, or **setPrefSize( )**.

The following program demonstrates **ChoiceBox** by reworking the **ListViewDemo** example shown earlier so that it uses a choice box instead of a list view:

```java
// Demonstrate a choice box.

import javafx.application.*;
import javafx.scene.*;
import javafx.stage.*;
import javafx.scene.layout.*;
import javafx.scene.control.*;
import javafx.geometry.*;
import javafx.beans.value.*;
import javafx.collections.*;

public class ChoiceBoxDemo extends Application {

  Label response;

  ChoiceBox<String> cbApple;

  public static void main(String[] args) {

    // Start the JavaFX application by calling launch().
```

```
    launch(args);
}

// Override the start() method.
public void start(Stage myStage) {

  // Give the stage a title.
  myStage.setTitle("ChoiceBox Demo");

  // Use a FlowPane for the root node. In this case,
  // vertical and horizontal gaps of 10.
  FlowPane rootNode = new FlowPane(10, 10);

  // Center the controls in the scene.
  rootNode.setAlignment(Pos.CENTER);

  // Create a scene.
  Scene myScene = new Scene(rootNode, 220, 140);

  // Set the scene on the stage.
  myStage.setScene(myScene);

  // Create a label.
  response = new Label("Select Your Apple");

  // Create an ObservableList of entries for the choice box.
  ObservableList<String> appleType =
    FXCollections.observableArrayList("Winesap", "Cortland", "Gala",
                                      "Golden Delicious", "Fuji",
                                      "Jonathan");

  // Create the choice box.
  cbApple = new ChoiceBox<String>(appleType);

  // Set the initial selection.
  cbApple.setValue("Winesap");

  // Get the choice box selection model.
  SingleSelectionModel<String> cbSelModel =
                                  cbApple.getSelectionModel();

  // Use a change listener to watch for changes to the selection.
  cbSelModel.selectedItemProperty().addListener(
                                  new ChangeListener<String>() {
    public void changed(ObservableValue<? extends String> changed,
                    String oldVal, String newVal) {
      response.setText("Selected apple: " + newVal);
```

```
      }
   });

   // Add the label and choice box to the scene graph.
   rootNode.getChildren().addAll(cbApple, response);

   // Show the stage and its scene.
   myStage.show();
   }
}
```

Sample output is shown here:

Adding Tooltips

Here, we will look at a very popular element in the modern GUI: the *tooltip*. A tooltip is a short message that is displayed when the mouse hovers over a control. In JavaFX, a tooltip can easily be added to any control. Frankly, because of the benefits that tooltips offer and the ease by which they can be incorporated into your GUI, there is virtually no reason not to use them where appropriate.

To add a tooltip, you will call the **setTooltip( )** method defined by **Control**. (Recall that **Control** is a base class for all controls.) The **setTooltip( )** method is shown here:

final void setTooltip(Tooltip *tip*)

Here, *tip* is an instance of **Tooltip**, which specifies the tooltip. Once a tooltip has been set, it is automatically displayed when the mouse hovers over the control. No other action is required on your part.

The **Tooltip** class encapsulates a tooltip. The constructor that we will use is shown here:

Tooltip(String *str*)

Here, *str* specifies the message that will be displayed by the tooltip.

To see tooltips in action, try adding the following statements to the **RadioButtonDemo** program shown earlier.

```
rbKeyboard.setTooltip(new Tooltip("Use keyboard as primary input."));
rbMouse.setTooltip(new Tooltip("Use Mouse as primary input."));
rbTouchScreen.setTooltip(new Tooltip("Use Touch Screen as primary input."));
```

After these additions, the tooltips will be displayed for each radio button.

Before moving on, you might want to try adding tooltips to the other controls demonstrated in this chapter. As you will find, they are a simple way to enhance your GUI. They are also an element that users have come to expect.

Use a Visual Separator

The last control we will look at in this chapter is **Separator**. The **Separator** class creates a line, which can be either vertical or horizontal. Its purpose is to create visual separation between other GUI elements. In general, **Separator** helps visually organize the layout of controls. It is both easy to use and effective.

Separator defines two constructors. The first is the default constructor, which creates a horizontal line. The second, shown here, lets you specify the separator's orientation.

Separator(Orientation *how*)

The value of *how* determines the orientation. It can be either **Orientation.VERTICAL** or **Orientation.HORIZONTAL**. The **Orientation** enumeration is packaged in **javafx.geometry**.

You can specify the width and/or height of a **Separator** by use of **setPrefWidth( )**, **setPrefHeight( )**, or **setPrefSize( )**. You can also specify various alignment options by use of **setValignment( )** and **setHalignment( )**, shown next:

final void setValignment(VPos *vHow*)
final void setHalignment(HPos *hHow*)

For **setValignment( )**, *vHow* specifies the vertical alignment for a horizontal separator. It must be one of these values: **VPos.CENTER**, **VPos.TOP**, **VPos.BOTTOM**, or **VPos.BASELINE**. For **setHalignment( )**, *hHow* specifies the horizontal alignment for a vertical separator. It must be one of these values: **HPos.CENTER**, **HPos.LEFT**, or **HPos.RIGHT**. Both **VPos** and **HPos** are packaged in **javafx.geometry**.

To see an example of **Separator** in action, add the following statements to the **ListViewDemo** program shown earlier in this chapter:

```
Separator separator = new Separator();

separator.setValignment(VPos.BOTTOM);
```

```
separator.setPrefWidth(160);
separator.setPrefHeight(10);
```

Next, add **separator** to the scene graph, as shown here:

```
rootNode.getChildren().addAll(lvApple, separator, response);
```

Now, when you run the program, the window will look like this:

CHAPTER
4

Exploring JavaFX
Controls, Part Two

This chapter continues the exploration of the JavaFX controls begun in the preceding chapter. The controls discussed here are

- TextField
- TextArea
- PasswordField
- ScrollPane
- Slider
- TreeView
- TableView

The chapter also explains how to disable a control.

Text Controls

JavaFX provides controls that let you enter text. Such controls are important to a GUI because they let the user enter a string of his or her own choosing, rather than selecting a predefined option. For example, a text control might be used to obtain a filename, a search string, or an e-mail address. Whatever the reason, text controls provide a solution to a wide array of input situations.

JavaFX supports three forms of text controls. They are **TextField**, which allows one line of text to be entered; **TextArea**, which supports multiline text; and **PasswordField**, which can be used to input passwords because what is typed is not shown. All three controls inherit **TextInputControl**, which defines much of the text control's functionality. The text control we will focus on is **TextField**, but the other controls work in similar ways.

TextField defines two constructors. The first is the default constructor, which creates an empty text field that has the default size. The second lets you specify the initial contents of the field. Here, we will use the default constructor.

Although the default size is sometimes adequate, often you will want to specify a **TextField**'s size. This is done by calling **setPrefColumnCount( )**, shown here:

    final void setPrefColumnCount(int *columns*)

The *columns* value is used by **TextField** to determine its size.

You can set the text in a text field by calling **setText( )**. You can obtain the current text by calling **getText( )**. They are shown here:

    final void setText(String *str*)

    final string getText( )

In addition to these fundamental operations, **TextField** supports several other capabilities. For example, the keyboard commands for cut, copy, and paste are automatically supported by **TextField**. You can also perform a number of operations under program control, such as deleting and inserting text. You can obtain the position of the caret by calling **getCaretPosition( )**. When text is selected, you can obtain the *anchor* (the starting point of the selection) by calling **getAnchor( )**. You can clear the content of a text field by calling **clear( )**.

One especially useful **TextField** option is the ability to set a prompting message that is displayed inside the text field when the user attempts to use a blank field. To do this, call **setPromptText( )**, shown here:

final void setPromptText(String *str*)

Here, *str* is the string displayed in the text field when no text has been entered. It is displayed using low intensity (such as gray tone).

When the user presses ENTER while inside a **TextField**, an action event is generated. Although handling this event is often helpful, in some cases, your program will simply obtain the text when it is needed, rather than handling action events. Both approaches are demonstrated by the following program. It creates a text field that requests a string. When the user presses ENTER while the text field has input focus or presses the Get String button, the string is obtained and displayed. Notice that a prompting message is also included. When the user presses Reverse, the string in the text field is reversed, and then the reversed string is shown inside the text field.

```java
// Demonstrate a text field.

import javafx.application.*;
import javafx.scene.*;
import javafx.stage.*;
import javafx.scene.layout.*;
import javafx.scene.control.*;
import javafx.event.*;
import javafx.geometry.*;

public class TextFieldDemo extends Application {

  TextField tf;
  Label response;

  Button btnGetText;
  Button btnReverse;

  public static void main(String[] args) {

    // Start the JavaFX application by calling launch().
    launch(args);
  }
```

```
// Override the start() method.
public void start(Stage myStage) {

  // Give the stage a title.
  myStage.setTitle("Demonstrate a TextField");

  // Use a FlowPane for the root node. In this case,
  // vertical and horizontal gaps of 10.
  FlowPane rootNode = new FlowPane(10, 10);

  // Center the controls in the scene.
  rootNode.setAlignment(Pos.CENTER);

  // Create a scene.
  Scene myScene = new Scene(rootNode, 230, 140);

  // Set the scene on the stage.
  myStage.setScene(myScene);

  // Create a label that will display the string.
  response = new Label("String: ");

  // Create button that gets the text.
  btnGetText = new Button("Get String");

  // Create button that reverses the text.
  btnReverse = new Button("Reverse");

  // Create a text field
  tf = new TextField();

  // Set the prompt.
  tf.setPromptText("Enter a String");

  // Set preferred column count.
  tf.setPrefColumnCount(15);

  // Handle action events for the text field. Action
  // events are generated when ENTER is pressed while
  // the text field has input focus. In this case, the
  // text in the field is obtained and displayed.
  tf.setOnAction(new EventHandler<ActionEvent>() {
    public void handle(ActionEvent ae) {
      response.setText("String: " + tf.getText());
    }
  });

  // Get text from the text field when the button is pressed
```

```
    // and display it.
    btnGetText.setOnAction(new EventHandler<ActionEvent>() {
      public void handle(ActionEvent ae) {
        response.setText("String: " + tf.getText());
      }
    });

    // Get text from the text field when the button is pressed,
    // reverse it using a StringBuilder, and then display it.
    btnReverse.setOnAction(new EventHandler<ActionEvent>() {
      public void handle(ActionEvent ae) {
        StringBuilder str = new StringBuilder(tf.getText());
        tf.setText(str.reverse().toString());
      }
    });

    // Use a separator to better organize the layout.
    Separator separator = new Separator();
    separator.setPrefWidth(200);

    // Add controls to the scene graph.
    rootNode.getChildren().addAll(tf, btnGetText, btnReverse,
                                  separator, response);

    // Show the stage and its scene.
    myStage.show();
  }
}
```

Sample output is shown here:

The **PasswordField** control works like **TextField**, except that the characters are not shown when they are typed by the user. You can see this effect by substituting **PasswordField** for **TextField** in the preceding program. (Of course, in a real program, additional security measures are required to protect a password, which include clearing the password from the control as soon as possible. The topic of security is beyond the scope of this book. Before using **PasswordField** in a real application, you must be confident that you have taken the appropriate measures to secure your application.)

TextArea is also used much like **TextField**, except it does not generate an action event when ENTER is pressed. The reason for this is easy to understand: because **TextArea** supports multiline editing, ENTER is used to advance the caret to the next line. Normally, you will simply retrieve the text from a **TextArea** when you need it. A **TextArea** will have a default size, but you can set the size explicitly by using the **setPrefColumnCount( )** and **setPrefRowCount( )** methods. You can try **TextArea** by substituting it for **TextField** in the previous example and setting the row count to 5 and column count to 10. Also, remove the action event handler. Here is an example:

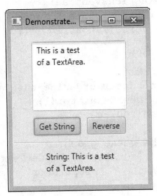

One other point: if the text inside a **TextArea** exceeds its width or height, scroll bars are added as needed.

NOTE
*Another JavaFX text-related control is **HTMLEditor**, packaged in **javafx.scene.web**. You may want to explore it on your own.*

ScrollPane

When designing the GUI for an application, it is not uncommon to find that screen space is at a premium. Often, one of the challenges of GUI design is the need to pack as much functionality as you can into as small a space as possible, but without sacrificing ease of use or effectiveness. Some controls, such as the **ListView**, **ComboBox**, and **TextArea**, address this need by automatically adding scroll bars when their contents exceed their dimensions. In other cases, you will need to deal with the situation on your own. Here are two examples: a large graphics image, such as a photo, may not fit within reasonable boundaries, or the text in a label is longer than will fit within the size allotted for it. Whatever the reason, JavaFX makes it easy to provide scrolling capabilities to any node in a scene graph. This is accomplished by wrapping the node in a **ScrollPane**. When a **ScrollPane** is used, scroll bars are automatically implemented that scroll the contents of the wrapped node. No further action is required on your part. Because of the versatility of **ScrollPane**, you will seldom need to use individual scroll bar controls.

ScrollPane defines two constructors. The first is the default constructor. The second lets you specify a node that you want to scroll. It is shown here:

ScrollPane(Node *content*)

Here, *content* specifies the information to be scrolled. When using the default constructor, you will add the node to be scrolled by calling **setContent( )**. It is shown here:

final void setContent(Node *content*)

After you have set the content, add the scroll pane to the scene graph. When displayed, the content can be scrolled.

NOTE
*You can also use **setContent( )** to change the content being scrolled by the scroll pane. Thus, what is being scrolled can be changed during the execution of your program.*

Although a default size is provided, as a general rule, you will want to set the dimensions of the *viewport*. The viewport is the viewable area of a scroll pane. It is the area in which the content being scrolled is displayed. Thus, the viewport displays the visible portion of the content. The scroll bars scroll the content through the viewport. Thus, by moving a scroll bar, you change what part of the content is visible.

You can set the viewport dimensions by using these two methods:

final void setPrefViewportHeight(double *height*)

final void setPrefViewportWidth(double *width*)

Here, *width* specifies the width of the viewport and *height* specifies the height. You can obtain the current viewport height and width by calling **getPrefViewportHeight( )** and **getPrefViewportWidth( )**. Each returns the indicated value.

In its default behavior, a **ScrollPane** will dynamically add or remove a scroll bar as needed. For example, if the component is taller than the viewport, a vertical scroll bar is added. If the component will completely fit within the viewport, the scroll bars are removed.

ScrollPane offers the ability to pan its contents by dragging the mouse. By default, this feature is off. To turn it on, use **setPannable( )**, shown here:

final void setPannable(boolean *enable*)

If *enable* is **true**, then panning is allowed. Otherwise, it is disabled. Panning is such a pleasing feature that you will often want to turn it on.

You can set the value of a scroll bar under program control by using **setHvalue( )** or **setVvalue( )**. The value determines the position of the scroll bar's thumb. These methods are shown here:

final void setHvalue(double *newHval*)

final void setVvalue(double *newVval*)

The new horizontal position is specified by *newHval*, and the new vertical position is specified by *newVval*. By default, scroll bar positions start at zero.

ScrollPane supports various other options. For example, it is possible to set the minimum and maximum scroll bar positions. You can also specify when and if the scroll bars are shown by setting a scroll bar policy. The current position of the scroll bars can be obtained by calling **getHvalue( )** and **getVvalue( )**.

The following program demonstrates **ScrollPane** by using one to scroll the contents of a multiline label. Notice that it also enables panning.

```
// Demonstrate a scroll pane.
// This program scrolls the contents of a multiline
// label, but any other type of Node can be scrolled.

import javafx.application.*;
import javafx.scene.*;
import javafx.stage.*;
import javafx.scene.layout.*;
import javafx.scene.control.*;
import javafx.event.*;
import javafx.geometry.*;

public class ScrollPaneDemo extends Application {

  ScrollPane scrlPane;

  Button btnReset;

  public static void main(String[] args) {

    // Start the JavaFX application by calling launch().
    launch(args);
  }

  // Override the start() method.
  public void start(Stage myStage) {

    // Give the stage a title.
    myStage.setTitle("Demonstrate a ScrollPane");

    // Use a FlowPane for the root node.
    FlowPane rootNode = new FlowPane(10, 10);
```

```java
      // Center the controls in the scene.
      rootNode.setAlignment(Pos.CENTER);

      // Create a scene.
      Scene myScene = new Scene(rootNode, 200, 200);

      // Set the scene on the stage.
      myStage.setScene(myScene);

      // Create a label that will be scrolled.
      Label scrlLabel = new Label(
                       "ScrollPane streamlines the process of\n" +
                       "adding scroll bars to a Node whose\n" +
                       "contents exceed the allotted space.\n" +
                       "It also enables a control to fit in a\n" +
                       "smaller space than it otherwise would.\n" +
                       "Because of its ease-of-use, ScrollPane\n" +
                       "offers an elegant solution to a wide range\n" +
                       "of user interface design challenges.");

      // Create a scroll pane, setting scrlLabel as the content.
      scrlPane = new ScrollPane(scrlLabel);

      // Set the viewport width and height.
      scrlPane.setPrefViewportWidth(130);
      scrlPane.setPrefViewportHeight(80);

      // Enable panning.
      scrlPane.setPannable(true);

      // Create a reset button.
      btnReset = new Button("Reset Scroll Bar Positions");

      // Handle action events for the reset button.
      btnReset.setOnAction(new EventHandler<ActionEvent>() {
        public void handle(ActionEvent ae) {
          // Set the scroll bars to their zero position.
          scrlPane.setVvalue(0);
          scrlPane.setHvalue(0);
        }
      });

      // Add the scroll pane and button to the scene graph.
      rootNode.getChildren().addAll(scrlPane, btnReset);

      // Show the stage and its scene.
      myStage.show();
   }
}
```

Sample output is shown here:

It is important to point out that you can add any type of node to a **ScrollPane**. This includes nodes that hold other nodes. For example, you can create an instance of **FlowPane** that contains several controls. Then you can add the **FlowPane** to a **ScrollPane**. Finally, you can add the **ScrollPane** to the root node of the scene graph. Doing this would let you scroll through a group of controls. You will want to experiment with this on your own.

Slider

A control that has become a popular part of the modern GUI is the *slider*. A slider presents a track on which an indicator, usually called the *thumb,* runs. Most often, the track is labeled with numbers that indicate the range of the slider and with tick marks that help indicate the position of the thumb. You have almost certainly seen sliders in action because they are frequently used to set the value of some attribute within a range, such as the volume, treble, and bass controls for an audio system. In JavaFX, the slider is supported by the **Slider** control.

Slider defines two constructors. The first is the default constructor. The second is shown here:

Slider(double *minVal*, double *maxVal*, double *initVal*)

This constructor creates a horizontal **Slider** that ranges from *minVal* to *maxVal,* inclusive. It sets the initial value to *initVal*. The slider produced by this constructor is fully functional but displays only the track and thumb.

Although the default slider may be sufficient in some situations, in most cases, you will want to configure the slider to provide a more pleasant and useful user experience. Two options that you will most often need are tick marks and labels. We will begin with tick marks. *Tick marks* are small lines that provide a rule. There are two types of tick marks: major and minor. Major tick marks show large divisions in the track and will have a label on them if labels are enabled. For example, if the slider runs from 0 to 100, then having major tick marks every 10 units would be a common approach. Minor tick marks indicate subdivisions between the major tick marks. Tick marks are off by default. To turn on tick marks, use the **setShowTickMarks( )** method, shown here:

final void setShowTickMarks(boolean *on*)

If *on* is **true**, the tick marks are shown. Otherwise, they are hidden.

After turning on tick marks, you will want to set the major tick mark units and the number of minor tick marks between major tick marks. To set the major tick mark units, use **setMajorTickUnit( )**, shown here:

final void setMajorTickUnit(double *val*)

Here, *val* specifies the number of units between major tick marks. For example, if the slider range is 0 to 100 and you set the major tick mark units to 25, then the major tick marks will be at 0, 25, 50, 75, and 100.

To set the minor tick mark spacing, use **setMinorTickCount( )**:

final void setMinorTickCount(int *val*)

Here, *val* specifies the number of minor tick marks between major tick marks. For example, if the major tick mark unit is 5, then setting the minor tick count to 4 causes the minor tick marks to align with the whole number values between major tick marks.

Labels can be added to a slider by calling **setShowTickLabels( )**, shown here:

final void setShowTickLabels(boolean *on*)

If *on* is **true**, the labels will be shown. Otherwise, they are hidden. The labels show values that indicate the range of the slider and the value of the major tick marks.

Another option that is often useful is the "snap-to-ticks" feature. When snap-to-ticks is enabled, after the slider is dragged to a new setting, its value is automatically adjusted to equal that of the nearest tick mark. This feature can be especially helpful when a slider represents integer values. Recall that the value of a slider is represented by a **double**. By moving the value to the nearest tick mark, you can cause the slider to produce only integer values. (Of course, this works only if the tick marks are on whole number intervals.) To enable snap-to-ticks, call **setSnapToTicks( )**, shown here:

final void setSnapToTicks(boolean *on*)

When *on* is **true**, the snap-to-ticks feature is enabled. Otherwise, it is disabled.

You can control how far the slider moves each time its position is changed by pressing an arrow key on the keyboard by setting the *block increment*. To set this value, call **setBlockIncrement( )**, shown here:

final void setBlockIncrement(boolean *val*)

The value for the block increment is specified by *val*.

As mentioned, by default, a slider is horizontal, but you can change this by using **setOrientation( )**, shown here:

final void setOrientation(Orientation *how*)

The value passed to *how* sets the orientation. It must be either **Orientation.VERTICAL** or **Orientation.HORIZONTAL**. **Orientation** is an enumeration packaged in **javafx.geometry**.

You can observe changes to the value of a slider by registering a change listener on the slider's value property. The value property is obtained by calling **valueProperty( )**, shown here:

final DoubleProperty valueProperty( )

Among many other interfaces, **DoubleProperty** implements **ObservableValue<Number>**. Thus, you can register a change listener for numeric values on the instance returned.

At any time, you can obtain the current value of the slider by calling **getValue( )**. You can set the value of a slider by calling **setValue( )**.

The following program demonstrates **Slider** by creating two controls, one horizontal and the other vertical. Tick marks and labels are displayed; snap-to-ticks is enabled; and the block increment is set. Each time a slider is moved, its value is displayed in a label. Notice how change events are handled. Also notice how the slider positions are reset to their defaults when the Reset button is pressed.

```
// Demonstrate a Slider

import javafx.application.*;
import javafx.scene.*;
import javafx.stage.*;
import javafx.scene.layout.*;
import javafx.scene.control.*;
import javafx.event.*;
import javafx.geometry.*;
import javafx.beans.value.*;

public class SliderDemo extends Application {

  Slider sldrHorz;
  Slider sldrVert;

  Button btnReset;

  Label lblValueHorz;
  Label lblValueVert;

  public static void main(String[] args) {

    // Start the JavaFX application by calling launch().
    launch(args);
  }
```

```java
// Override the start() method.
public void start(Stage myStage) {

  // Give the stage a title.
  myStage.setTitle("Demonstrate a Slider");

  // Use a FlowPane for the root node.
  FlowPane rootNode = new FlowPane(10, 10);

  // Center the controls in the scene.
  rootNode.setAlignment(Pos.CENTER);

  // Create a scene.
  Scene myScene = new Scene(rootNode, 250, 250);

  // Set the scene on the stage.
  myStage.setScene(myScene);

  // Create labels that will show the slider values.
  lblValueHorz = new Label("Horizontal value: ");
  lblValueVert = new Label("Vertical value: ");

  // Create horizontal slider.
  sldrHorz = new Slider(0.0, 10.0, 0.0);

  // Configure the horizontal slider.
  sldrHorz.setShowTickMarks(true);
  sldrHorz.setShowTickLabels(true);
  sldrHorz.setBlockIncrement(1.0);
  sldrHorz.setSnapToTicks(true);
  sldrHorz.setMajorTickUnit(5.0);
  sldrHorz.setMinorTickCount(4);

  // Create vertical slider.
  sldrVert = new Slider(0.0, 20.0, 10.0);
  sldrVert.setOrientation(Orientation.VERTICAL);

  // Configure the vertical slider.
  sldrVert.setShowTickMarks(true);
  sldrVert.setShowTickLabels(true);
  sldrVert.setBlockIncrement(2.0);
  sldrVert.setSnapToTicks(true);
  sldrVert.setMajorTickUnit(4.0);
  sldrVert.setMinorTickCount(3);

  // Create the reset button.
  btnReset = new Button("Reset Sliders");

  // Handle action events for the button.
  btnReset.setOnAction(new EventHandler<ActionEvent>() {
```

```
    public void handle(ActionEvent ae) {
      sldrHorz.setValue(0.0);
      sldrVert.setValue(10.0);
    }
  });

  // Handle change events on the slider's value.
  sldrHorz.valueProperty().addListener(new ChangeListener<Number>() {
    public void changed(ObservableValue<? extends Number> changed,
                        Number oldVal, Number newVal) {

      // Display the slider's current value.
      lblValueHorz.setText("Current value is " + newVal);
    }
  });

  sldrVert.valueProperty().addListener(new ChangeListener<Number>() {
    public void changed(ObservableValue<? extends Number> changed,
                        Number oldVal, Number newVal) {

      // Display the slider's current value.
      lblValueVert.setText("Current value is " + newVal);
    }
  });

  // Add the sliders, label, and button to the scene graph.
  rootNode.getChildren().addAll(sldrHorz, sldrVert, lblValueHorz,
                                lblValueVert, btnReset);

  // Show the stage and its scene.
  myStage.show();
  }
}
```

Sample output is shown here:

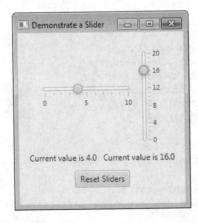

TreeView

One of JavaFX's most powerful controls is the **TreeView**. It presents a hierarchical view of data in a tree-like format. In this context, the term *hierarchical* means some items are subordinate to others. For example, a tree is commonly used to display the contents of a file system. In this case, the individual files are subordinate to the directory that contains them. In a **TreeView**, branches can be expanded or collapsed on demand by the user. This allows hierarchical data to be presented in a compact, yet expandable form. Although **TreeView** supports many customization options, you will often find the default tree style and capabilities are suitable. Therefore, even though **TreeView** supports a sophisticated structure, it is still quite easy to work with.

TreeView implements a conceptually simple, tree-based data structure. A tree begins with a single *root node* that indicates the start of the tree. Under the root are one or more *child nodes*. There are two types of child nodes: *leaf nodes* (also called *terminal nodes*), which have no children, and *branch nodes*, which form the root nodes of *subtrees*. A subtree is simply a tree that is part of a larger tree. The sequence of nodes that leads from the root to a specific node is called a *path*.

One very useful feature of **TreeView** is that it automatically provides scroll bars when the size of the tree exceeds the dimensions of the view. Although a fully collapsed tree might be quite small, its expanded form may be quite large. By automatically adding scroll bars as needed, **TreeView** lets you use a smaller space than would ordinarily be possible.

TreeView is a generic class that is defined like this:

    class TreeView<T>

Here, **T** specifies the type of value held by an item in the tree. Often, this will be of type **String**. **TreeView** defines two constructors. The first is the default constructor. The second is shown here:

    TreeView(TreeItem<T> rootNode)

Here, *rootNode* specifies the root of the tree. Since all nodes descend from the root, it is the only one that needs to be passed to **TreeView**.

The items that form the tree are objects of type **TreeItem**. At the outset, it is important to state that **TreeItem** does not inherit **Node**. Thus, **TreeItem**s are not general-purpose objects. They can be used in a **TreeView**, but not as stand-alone controls. **TreeItem** is a generic class, as shown here:

    class TreeItem<T>

Here, **T** specifies the type of value held by the tree item. **TreeItem** supplies three constructors. The one we will use is shown here:

    TreeItem(T val)

Here, *val* specifies the item represented by an instance of **TreeItem**.

Before you can use a **TreeView**, you must construct the tree that it will display. To do this, you must first create the root. Next, you will add other nodes to that root. This is done by calling either **add( )** or **addAll( )** on the list returned by **getChildren( )**. These other nodes can be leaf nodes or subtrees. After the tree has been constructed, you create the **TreeView** by passing the root node to its constructor.

You can handle selection events in the **TreeView** through the use of a change listener. The process is similar to that used by other selection controls that generate change events. First obtain the selection model by calling **getSelectionModel( )**. Then, call **selectedItemProperty( )** to obtain the property for the selected item. On that return value, call **addListener( )** to add a change listener. Each time a selection is made, a reference to the new selection will be passed to the **changed( )** handler as the new value.

By default, **TreeView** allows only one item to be selected at any one time. To obtain a reference to the selected item in a tree, call **getSelectedItem( )** on the selection model. This method is shown here:

T getSelectedItem( )

A reference to the selected item is returned. Thus, you don't need to handle tree selection events if your program obtains the selection only when it is needed.

NOTE
*TreeView also allows you to enable multiple selection. The process is similar to that used to enable multiple selection in a **ListView**, described in the previous chapter. Here, we will use only single selection. You might want to experiment with multiple **TreeView** selections on your own.*

You can obtain the value of a **TreeItem** by calling **getValue( )**. It is shown here:

final T getValue( )

You can also follow the tree path of an item in either the forward or backward direction. To obtain the parent, call **getParent( )**. To obtain the children, call **getChildren( )**. They are shown next:

final TreeItem<T> getParent( )

ObservableList<TreeItem<T>> getChildren( )

As explained earlier, **ObservableList** is a list collection that can be monitored for changes. It is, of course, not necessary to watch the list for changes to simply obtain the child nodes.

Normally, a branch is expanded or collapsed by the user, but it is also possible to do this under program control by use of **setExpanded( )**, which is defined by **TreeItem**. It is shown here:

final void setExpanded(boolean *expand*)

If *expand* is **true**, the branch is expanded. If *expand* is **false**, the branch is collapsed. Of course, this method only affects those tree items that have children. You can determine if a branch under a **TreeItem** is expanded by calling **isExpanded( )** on the item. It returns **true** if the branch is expanded and **false** otherwise.

The following example shows how to build and use a **TreeView**. The tree presents a hierarchy of food. The type of items stored in the tree are strings. The root is labeled Food. Under it are three direct descendent nodes: Fruit, Vegetables, and Nuts. Each of these constitutes a subtree. For example, under Fruit are three child nodes: Apples, Pears, and Oranges; and under Apples, are three leaf nodes: Fuji, Winesap, and Jonathan. Each time a selection is made, the name of the item is displayed. Also, the path from the root to the item is shown. This is done by the repeated use of **getParent( )**. The Expand/Collapse button demonstrates how a branch can be expanded or collapsed under program control. If the currently selected item has children, then pressing the button will reverse its expanded state. That is, if the branch was collapsed, it will be expanded, and vice versa.

```
// Demonstrate a TreeView

import javafx.application.*;
import javafx.scene.*;
import javafx.stage.*;
import javafx.scene.layout.*;
import javafx.scene.control.*;
import javafx.event.*;
import javafx.beans.value.*;
import javafx.geometry.*;

public class TreeViewDemo extends Application {

  Label response;

  TreeView<String> tvFood;

  Button btnExpand;

  public static void main(String[] args) {

    // Start the JavaFX application by calling launch().
    launch(args);
  }

  // Override the start() method.
  public void start(Stage myStage) {
```

```
// Give the stage a title.
myStage.setTitle("Demonstrate a TreeView");

// Use a FlowPane for the root node. In this case,
// vertical and horizontal gaps of 10.
FlowPane rootNode = new FlowPane(10, 10);

// Center the controls in the scene.
rootNode.setAlignment(Pos.CENTER);

// Create a scene.
Scene myScene = new Scene(rootNode, 310, 520);

// Set the scene on the stage.
myStage.setScene(myScene);

// Create a label that will report the state of the
// selected tree item.
response = new Label("No Selection");

// Create tree items, starting with the root.
TreeItem<String> tiRoot = new TreeItem<>("Food");

// Now add subtrees, beginning with fruit.
TreeItem<String> tiFruit = new TreeItem<>("Fruit");

// Construct the Apple subtree.
TreeItem<String> tiApples = new TreeItem<>("Apples");

// Add child nodes to the Apple node.
tiApples.getChildren().add(new TreeItem<>("Fuji"));
tiApples.getChildren().add(new TreeItem<>("Winesap"));
tiApples.getChildren().add(new TreeItem<>("Jonathan"));

// Add varieties to the fruit node.
tiFruit.getChildren().add(tiApples);
tiFruit.getChildren().add(new TreeItem<>("Pears"));
tiFruit.getChildren().add(new TreeItem<>("Oranges"));

// Finally, add the fruit node to the root.
tiRoot.getChildren().add(tiFruit);

// Now, add vegetables subtree, using the same general process.
TreeItem<String> tiVegetables = new TreeItem<>("Vegetables");
tiVegetables.getChildren().add(new TreeItem<>("Corn"));
tiVegetables.getChildren().add(new TreeItem<>("Peas"));
tiVegetables.getChildren().add(new TreeItem<>("Broccoli"));
tiVegetables.getChildren().add(new TreeItem<>("Beans"));
tiRoot.getChildren().add(tiVegetables);

// Likewise, add nuts subtree.
TreeItem<String> tiNuts = new TreeItem<>("Nuts");
```

```java
tiNuts.getChildren().add(new TreeItem<>("Walnuts"));
tiNuts.getChildren().add(new TreeItem<>("Peanuts"));
tiNuts.getChildren().add(new TreeItem<>("Pecans"));
tiRoot.getChildren().add(tiNuts);

// Create tree view using the tree just created.
tvFood = new TreeView<String>(tiRoot);

// Get the tree view selection model.
MultipleSelectionModel<TreeItem<String>> tvSelModel =
                                tvFood.getSelectionModel();

// Use a change listener to respond to a selection within
// a tree view
tvSelModel.selectedItemProperty().addListener(
                    new ChangeListener<TreeItem<String>>() {
  public void changed(
              ObservableValue<? extends TreeItem<String>> changed,
                  TreeItem<String> oldVal, TreeItem<String> newVal) {

    // Display the selection and its complete path from the root.
    if(newVal != null) {
      // Construct the entire path to the selected item.
      String path = newVal.getValue();
      TreeItem<String> tmp = newVal.getParent();
      while(tmp != null) {
        path = tmp.getValue() + " -> " + path;
        tmp = tmp.getParent();
      }

      // Display the selection and the entire path.
      response.setText("Selection is " + newVal.getValue() +
                    "\nComplete path is " + path);
    }
  }
});

// Create the expand/collapse button.
btnExpand = new Button("Expand/Collapse");

// Handle action events for the button.
btnExpand.setOnAction(new EventHandler<ActionEvent>() {
  public void handle(ActionEvent ae) {
    TreeItem<String> tmp =
      tvFood.getSelectionModel().getSelectedItem();

    if(tmp.isExpanded())
      tmp.setExpanded(false);
    else
      tmp.setExpanded(true);
  }
});
```

```
        Separator separator = new Separator();
        separator.setPrefWidth(260);

        // Add controls to the scene graph.
        rootNode.getChildren().addAll(tvFood, response, separator, btnExpand);

        // Show the stage and its scene.
        myStage.show();
    }
}
```

Sample output is shown here:

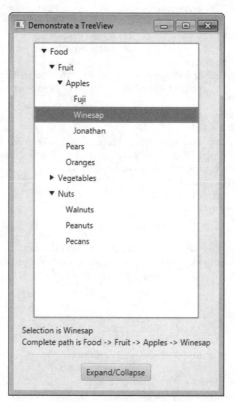

There are two things to pay special attention to in this program. First, notice how the tree is constructed. First, the root node is created by this statement:

```
TreeItem<String> tiRoot = new TreeItem<>("Food");
```

Next, the nodes under the root are constructed. These nodes consist of the root nodes of subtrees: one for fruit, one for vegetables, and one for nuts. Next, the leaves are added to these subtrees. However, one of these, the fruit subtree, consists of another subtree that contains varieties of apples. The point here is that each branch in a tree leads either to a leaf or to the root of a subtree. After all of the nodes have been constructed, the root nodes of each subtree are added to the root node of the tree. This is done by calling **add( )** on the root node. For example, this is how the nuts subtree is added to **tiRoot**.

```
tiRoot.getChildren().add(tiNuts);
```

The process is the same for adding any child node to its parent node.

The second thing to notice in the program is the way the path from the root to the selected node is constructed within the change event handler. It is shown here:

```
String path = newVal.getValue();
TreeItem<String> tmp = newVal.getParent();
while(tmp != null) {
  path = tmp.getValue() + " -> " + path;
  tmp = tmp.getParent();
}
```

The code works like this: First, the value of the newly selected node is obtained. In this example, the value will be a string, which is the node's name. This string is assigned to the **path** string. Then, a temporary variable of type **TreeItem<String>** is created and initialized to refer to the parent of the newly selected node. If the newly selected node does not have a parent, then **tmp** will be null. Otherwise, the loop is entered, within which each parent's value (which is its name in this case) is added to **path**. This process continues until the root node of the tree (which has no parent) is found.

Although the preceding shows the basic mechanism required to handle a **TreeView**, it is important to point out that several customizations and options are supported. **TreeView** is a powerful control that you will want to examine fully on your own.

TableView

TableView is a sophisticated, full-featured control that creates, displays, and manages tables of information. Tables are especially important to many applications because they display data in an easy-to-use format. For example, a table offers a convenient way to display a list of e-mail messages, name and address information, employee ID numbers, department names, or order status, to name just a few. Whatever the use, tables are an important part of many JavaFX GUIs.

TableView is a bit more complicated to use than the controls previously discussed, but don't be intimidated by this fact. As you will see, simple tables are quite easily constructed and managed. The key is to properly construct the data that will go inside them. Of course, the more sophisticated the table, the more hands-on control and customization that will be required. Fortunately, for many uses, the default table is exactly what you want.

TableView is a generic class that is declared like this:

class TableView<S>

Here, **S** specifies the type of items represented in the table. In general, this will be a class that encapsulates the data, in the form of properties, to be displayed, along with getter and setter methods to access those properties. Typically, setter methods are needed only when cell editing is allowed.

TableView provides two constructors. The first is the default constructor. The second is shown here:

TableView(ObservableList<S> *list*)

Here, *list* specifies a list of the items to display.

At its core, **TableView** is conceptually simple. It is a control that consists of columns of information. At the top of each column is a heading. In addition to describing the data in a column, the heading provides the mechanism by which the user can change the size of a column or change the location of a column within the table.

The information within the table is contained in *cells*. Cells are created by a *cell factory*. To construct a table view, you will specify a cell factory for each column in the table. The factory is then responsible for providing the information for that cell. Thus, it is the cell factory that determines how information is displayed. A cell factory can also support cell editing, but we won't be making use of that feature here.

TableView can be used to simply display data. It can also be used to enable the user to select a portion of that data. By default, **TableView** supports single selection, but this can be changed to multiple selection. To handle selection events, you must register a change listener on the selection model, much as you have done with other controls described earlier. When a selection occurs, you can obtain the selected row by use of **getSelectedIndex( )** on the selection model. The selection model used by **TableView** is **TableView.TableViewSelectionModel<S>**, which inherits **TableSelectionModel<T>**, **MultipleSelectionModel<T>**, and **SelectionModel<T>**, so it supports all forms of selection relating to tables.

NOTE
*By default, row selection is used, but it is possible to enable cell selection. When cell selection is enabled, you can obtain the selected cell(s) by use of **getSelectedCells( )**.*

The easiest way to create a **TableView** is to display objects that support properties. Recall that properties support getter and setter methods. These methods have this basic form: **getX( )** and **setX( )**, where **X** is the name of the property. For example, the getter for a property called **size** is **getSize( )**. **TableView** uses a property's getter method to obtain the information to display.

A good way to understand the basics of **TableView** is to work through an example. To begin, we need a class that defines the type of objects that the table will display. In this example, the table will show information about a programming project. Each row will display the name of a programmer, the package on which he or she is working, the status of the package, and its size. This information is encapsulated within the **ProjectEntry** class, shown here:

```
// A class that contains project information.

import javafx.beans.property.*;

public class ProjectEntry {
  // Declare properties.
  private SimpleStringProperty programmer;
  private SimpleStringProperty packageName;
  private SimpleStringProperty status;
  private SimpleIntegerProperty size;

  // Constructor
  ProjectEntry(String prog, String pName, String st, int sz) {
    programmer = new SimpleStringProperty(prog);
    packageName = new SimpleStringProperty(pName);
    status = new SimpleStringProperty(st);
    size = new SimpleIntegerProperty(sz);
  }

  // Getters and setters for the properties.
  public String getProgrammer() { return programmer.get(); }
  public void setProgrammer(String prog) { programmer.set(prog); }

  public String getPackageName() { return packageName.get(); }
  public void setPackageName(String pName) { packageName.set(pName); }

  public String getStatus() { return status.get(); }
  public void setStatus(String st) { status.set(st); }

  public int getSize() { return size.get(); }
  public void setSize(int sz) { size.set(sz); }
}
```

Let's look at two important aspects of this class. First, notice that getter and setter methods are provided for each property. Although we don't actually need the setters in the example that follows, they are included for completeness.

Second, notice how the properties themselves are declared. For example, here is the declaration for **programmer**:

```
private SimpleStringProperty programmer;
```

Here, the type of the property is **SimpleStringProperty**. **SimpleStringProperty** is one of several classes in **javafx.beans.property** that encapsulates a value in a property. It implements several interfaces, including **Property** and **Observable**. It inherits several classes, including **StringPropertyBase**. An instance of some form of **Property** is required so that **TableView** can access its value through the use of **get( )** and **set( )** methods, defined by **StringPropertyBase**.

As mentioned, JavaFX supplies a number of properties that simplify working with table data. They are shown here. Their names describe the type of value they encapsulate.

SimpleBooleanProperty	SimpleDoubleProperty	SimpleFloatProperty
SimpleIntegerProperty	SimpleListProperty<E>	SimpleLongProperty
SimpleMapProperty<K, V>	SimpleObjectProperty<T>	SimpleSetProperty<E>
SimpleStringProperty		

In **ProjectEntry**, notice that the **size** property is of type **SimpleIntegerProperty** because it will hold an integer value.

Once you have defined the data type, you can create a **TableView**. The process involves these steps:

1. Create an **ObservableList** of the data to be displayed in the table. One way to do this is to use **FXCollections.observableArrayList( )**, as described earlier in this book.

2. Create a **TableView** instance, passing in the list of items to display.

3. Define a **TableColumn** instance for each column in the table, specifying the name of the column.

4. Set the cell factory for each **TableColumn**.

5. Add each column to the **TableView** instance.

Steps 1 and 2 are self-explanatory. Let's look closely at steps 3, 4, and 5.

Each column in the table is defined by a **TableColumn** instance. **TableColumn** is a generic class that is declared like this:

```
TableColumn<S, T>
```

Here, **S** specifies the type of data in the **TableView** and **T** specifies the type of element shown in the column. **TableColumn** defines two constructors. The first is the default constructor. The second is shown here:

TableColumn(String *heading*)

Here, *heading* specifies the heading of the column. In general, the heading describes the contents of the column.

Once you have a **TableColumn** instance, you must then set its cell factory. The cell factory obtains the data that will be displayed in each cell of a column. The cell factory is set by calling **setCellValueFactory( )** on the column, passing in a reference to a **Callback** method that returns the value. Although you can create your own **Callback** instances, often you can obtain one by use of **PropertyValueFactory**, packaged in **javafx.scene.control.cell**. It is designed expressly for this purpose. It is a generic class declared like this:

class PropertyValueFactory<S, T>

Here, **S** specifies the type of data in the **TableView** and **T** specifies the type of the element shown in the column. Here is the **PropertyValueFactory** constructor:

PropertyValueFactory(String *propertyName*)

Here, *propertyName* specifies the property that will be displayed in the column. The name must match the name of the property in the data. For example, for the **size** property in **ProjectEntry**, pass "size" to the **PropertyValueFactory** constructor.

Once you have set the heading and property factory, you can add the column to the **TableView** by calling **add( )** on the list of columns returned by **getColumns( )** called on the **TableView** instance.

One other point: if needed, you can set the dimensions of the table by use of **setPrefWidth( )**, **setPrefHeight( )**, or **setPrefSize( )**.

The following program puts the preceding discussion into action. Notice that it uses the **ProjectEntry** class shown earlier. Each time the selection in the table changes, the index of the selected row is displayed.

```
// Demonstrate TableView.

import javafx.application.*;
import javafx.scene.*;
import javafx.stage.*;
import javafx.scene.layout.*;
import javafx.scene.control.*;
import javafx.beans.value.*;
import javafx.geometry.*;
import javafx.collections.*;
import javafx.scene.control.cell.*;
```

```java
public class TableViewDemo extends Application {

  Label response;
  Label heading;

  TableView<ProjectEntry> tvProject;

  public static void main(String[] args) {

    // Start the JavaFX application by calling launch().
    launch(args);
  }

  // Override the start() method.
  public void start(Stage myStage) {

    // Give the stage a title.
    myStage.setTitle("Demonstrate a TableView");

    // Use a FlowPane for the root node. In this case,
    // vertical and horizontal gaps of 10.
    FlowPane rootNode = new FlowPane(10, 10);

    // Center the controls in the scene.
    rootNode.setAlignment(Pos.CENTER);

    // Create a scene.
    Scene myScene = new Scene(rootNode, 400, 400);

    // Set the scene on the stage.
    myStage.setScene(myScene);

    // Create a label that will report the state of the
    // selected row.
    response = new Label("");

    // Create a heading.
    heading = new Label("Project Organizer");

    // Create data that will be displayed.
    ObservableList<ProjectEntry> projEntries =
     FXCollections.observableArrayList(
       new ProjectEntry("Jessica", "myapp.audio", "Completed", 14028),
       new ProjectEntry("Jon", "myapp.video", "On Schedule", 33077),
       new ProjectEntry("Adam", "myapp.archive", "Delayed", 183255),
       new ProjectEntry("Rachel", "myapp.dbase", "On Schedule", 65890),
       new ProjectEntry("Josselyn", "myapp.cloudstore", "Completed", 19890),
       new ProjectEntry("Chris", "myapp.filter", "In Testing", 69770),
       new ProjectEntry("Sasha", "myapp.stats", "In Code Review", 85290)
     );
```

```java
    // Create the table view.
    tvProject = new TableView<ProjectEntry>(projEntries);

    // Add headings and specify cell factories.
    TableColumn<ProjectEntry, String> progName =
      new TableColumn<>("Programmer");
    progName.setCellValueFactory(new PropertyValueFactory<>("programmer"));
    tvProject.getColumns().add(progName);

    TableColumn<ProjectEntry, String> packName =
      new TableColumn<>("Package Name");
    packName.setCellValueFactory(new PropertyValueFactory<>("packageName"));
    tvProject.getColumns().add(packName);

    TableColumn<ProjectEntry, String> status =
      new TableColumn<>("Status");
    status.setCellValueFactory(new PropertyValueFactory<>("status"));
    tvProject.getColumns().add(status);

    TableColumn<ProjectEntry, Integer> size =
      new TableColumn<>("Size");
    size.setCellValueFactory(new PropertyValueFactory<>("size"));
    tvProject.getColumns().add(size);

    // Size the table view.
    tvProject.setPrefWidth(360);
    tvProject.setPrefHeight(196);

    // Get the TableView selection model.
    TableView.TableViewSelectionModel<ProjectEntry> tvSelModel =
                                tvProject.getSelectionModel();

    // Use a change listener to respond to a change of selection within
    // the table view.
    tvSelModel.selectedIndexProperty().addListener(
                               new ChangeListener<Number>() {
      public void changed(ObservableValue<? extends Number> changed,
                      Number oldVal, Number newVal) {

        // Display the index of the selection.
        response.setText("Selected row is " + newVal);
      }
    });

    // Add controls to the scene graph.
    rootNode.getChildren().addAll(heading, tvProject, response);

    // Show the stage and its scene.
    myStage.show();
  }
}
```

Sample output is shown here:

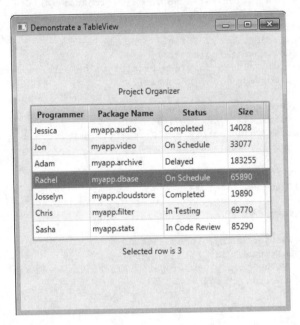

It is important to emphasize that this introduction describes what is, essentially, **TableView**'s simplest form. **TableView** supports far more options and functionality than described here. It is definitely a control that you will want to explore fully on your own.

Disabling a Control

Before concluding our discussion of controls, it is useful to point out that any control can be disabled under program control. To disable a control, use **setDisable( )**, defined by **Node**. It is shown here:

final void setDisable(boolean *disable*)

Here, if *disable* is **true**, the control is disabled; otherwise, it is enabled. Thus, using **setDisable( )**, you can disable a control and then enable it later.

You can determine if a control is disabled by calling **isDisabled( )**. It returns **true** if the control is disabled and **false** otherwise.

Other Controls to Explore

In addition to the controls introduced by this and the preceding chapters, JavaFX supports several others. You are now at the point at which you should be able to explore other controls on your own. Here are a few that you might find interesting to start with:

Accordion

ProgressBar

ProgressIndicator

TitledPane

SplitPane

TabPane

In addition to general-purpose controls, JavaFX also defines several special-purpose ones, including

DatePicker

ColorPicker

FileChooser

HTMLEditor

These controls offer easy-to-use solutions to what are sometimes challenging user-input situations.

CHAPTER
5

Work with Images, Fonts, and Layouts

This chapter discusses three elements that have a significant effect on the user interface: images, fonts, and layouts. *Images* are graphical elements, such as photos and icons. *Fonts* determine the precise look of text. *Layouts* organize the content of a scene. Because images, fonts, and layouts are visual elements that influence the overall appearance of a user interface, it makes sense to look at them together here.

Use Image and ImageView

Images are widely used in the modern GUI. In some cases, images are employed in a stand-alone fashion, such as when a photo is displayed. In other cases, an image might be added to a control. For example, in addition to text, a button or label might include an image or, in some cases, display only an image without any text at all. In such cases, the image displays an icon that indicates the purpose of the control. Whatever the use, JavaFX provides substantial support for images, making it easy to incorporate them into your program.

At the foundation of JavaFX's support for images are two classes: **Image** and **ImageView**. **Image** encapsulates the image itself, and **ImageView** manages the display of an image. Both classes are packaged in **javafx.scene.image**.

The **Image** class loads an image from either an **InputStream**, a URL, or a path to the image file. **Image** defines several constructors; the one we will use is shown here:

Image(String *url*)

Here, *url* specifies a URL or a path to a file that supplies the image. The argument is assumed to refer to a path if it does not constitute a properly formed URL. Otherwise, the image is loaded from the URL. The examples that follow will load images from files on the local file system. Other constructors let you specify various options, such as the image's width and height, or request background loading. One other point: **Image** is not derived from **Node**. Thus, it cannot, itself, be part of a scene graph.

Once you have an **Image**, you will use **ImageView** to display it. **ImageView** is derived from **Node**, which means that it can be part of a scene graph. **ImageView** defines three constructors. The first one we will use is shown here:

ImageView(Image *image*)

This constructor creates an **ImageView** that uses *image* for its image.

Putting the preceding discussion into action, here is a program that loads an image of a woodland setting and displays it via **ImageView**. The image is contained in a file called **woodland.png**, which is assumed to be in the local directory.

```
// Load and display an image.

import javafx.application.*;
```

```
import javafx.scene.*;
import javafx.stage.*;
import javafx.scene.layout.*;
import javafx.geometry.*;
import javafx.scene.image.*;


public class ImageDemo extends Application {

  public static void main(String[] args) {

    // Start the JavaFX application by calling launch().
    launch(args);
  }

  // Override the start() method.
  public void start(Stage myStage) {

    // Give the stage a title.
    myStage.setTitle("Display an Image");

    // Use a FlowPane for the root node.
    FlowPane rootNode = new FlowPane();

    // Use center alignment.
    rootNode.setAlignment(Pos.CENTER);

    // Create a scene.
    Scene myScene = new Scene(rootNode, 300, 200);

    // Set the scene on the stage.
    myStage.setScene(myScene);

    // Create an image.
    Image imgWoodland = new Image("woodland.png");

    // Create an image view that uses the image.
    ImageView ivWoodland = new ImageView(imgWoodland);

    // Add the image to the scene graph.
    rootNode.getChildren().add(ivWoodland);

    // Show the stage and its scene.
    myStage.show();
  }
}
```

Sample output from the program is shown here:

In the program, pay close attention to the following sequence that loads the image and then creates an **ImageView** that uses the image:

```
// Create an image.
Image imgWoodland = new Image("woodland.png");

// Create an image view that uses the image.
ImageView ivWoodland = new ImageView(imgWoodland);
```

As explained, an image by itself cannot be added to the scene graph. It must first be embedded in an **ImageView**.

In cases in which you won't make further use of the image, you can specify a URL or filename when creating an **ImageView**. In this case, there is no need to explicitly create an **Image.** Instead, an **Image** instance containing the specified image is constructed automatically and embedded in the **ImageView**. Here is the **ImageView** constructor that does this:

ImageView(String *url*)

Here, *url* specifies the URL or the path to a file that contains the image. For example, the **ImageView** in the preceding program could have been created with the following statement, thus eliminating the need to create a separate **Image** instance:

```
ImageView ivWoodland = new ImageView("woodland.png");
```

Scale Images

One important feature provided by **Image** is its ability to scale an image. Scaling is accomplished by specifying a bounding rectangle when the **Image** instance is constructed. **Image** supplies three constructors that support scaling. The one we will use is shown here:

Image(String *url*, double *width*, double *height*, boolean *aspRatio*, boolean *hiQ*)

As before, *url* specifies a URL or a path to a file that supplies the image. The desired width and height are specified by *width* and *height*. To preserve the aspect ratio, set *aspRatio* to **true**. For the best quality scaling, set *hiQ* to **true**. When it is set to **false**, the scaling is optimized for speed.

To see the effect of scaling, replace the line in the preceding program that constructs the image with the one shown here:

```
Image imgWoodland = new Image("woodland.png", 100, 100, true, true);
```

When you run the program, the window will now look like this:

Wrap an ImageView in a ScrollPane

In cases in which you want to display a large image in a small space, consider wrapping the **ImageView** in a **ScrollPane**. This way, scroll bars are automatically added that let the user scroll through the image. You can try this by adding the following statements to the previous program:

```
ScrollPane sp = new ScrollPane(ivWoodland);
sp.setPrefViewportHeight(300);
sp.setPrefViewportWidth(300);
```

Next, add **sp**, rather than **ivWoodland** to the scene. You will also need to import **javafx.scene.control.***. After making these changes, the image can be scrolled. Here is sample output:

Add Images to a Label

As explained in Chapter 1, the **Label** class encapsulates a label. So far, we have used it to display only text, but it can also display an image, or both text and an image. It is easy to add an image to a label. One way is to use this form of **Label**'s constructor:

    Label(String *str*, Node *image*)

Here, *str* specifies the text and *image* specifies the image. Notice that the image is of type **Node**. This allows great flexibility in the type of image added to the label, but for our purposes, the image type will be **ImageView**.

Here is a program that demonstrates a label that includes a graphic. It creates a label that displays the string "Woodland" and shows a scaled image of a woodland scene that is loaded from the **woodland.png** file.

```
// Demonstrate an image in a label.

import javafx.application.*;
import javafx.scene.*;
```

```java
import javafx.stage.*;
import javafx.scene.layout.*;
import javafx.scene.control.*;
import javafx.geometry.*;
import javafx.scene.image.*;

public class LabelImageDemo extends Application {

  public static void main(String[] args) {

    // Start the JavaFX application by calling launch().
    launch(args);
  }

  // Override the start() method.
  public void start(Stage myStage) {

    // Give the stage a title.
    myStage.setTitle("Use an Image in a Label");

    // Use a FlowPane for the root node.
    FlowPane rootNode = new FlowPane();

    // Use center alignment.
    rootNode.setAlignment(Pos.CENTER);

    // Create a scene.
    Scene myScene = new Scene(rootNode, 300, 200);

    // Set the scene on the stage.
    myStage.setScene(myScene);

    // Create a scaled image.
    Image imgWoodland = new Image("woodland.png", 100, 100, true, true);

    // Create an image view that uses the image.
    ImageView ivWoodland = new ImageView(imgWoodland);

    // Create a label that contains both an image and text.
    Label imageLabel = new Label("Woodland", ivWoodland);

    // Add the label to the scene graph.
    rootNode.getChildren().add(imageLabel);

    // Show the stage and its scene.
    myStage.show();
  }
}
```

Here is the window produced by the program:

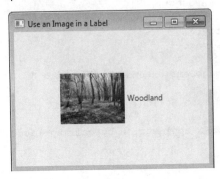

As you can see, both the image and the text are displayed.

In the output just shown, notice that the text is to the right of the image. This is the default position. You can change the relative positions of the image and text by calling **setContentDisplay( )** on the label. This method is specified by **Labeled**, which is inherited by **Label**. It is shown here:

    final void setContentDisplay(ContentDisplay *position*)

The value passed to *position* determines how the text and image are displayed. It must be one of these values, which are defined by the **ContentDisplay** enumeration:

BOTTOM	CENTER
TOP	LEFT
RIGHT	GRAPHIC_ONLY
TEXT_ONLY	

With the exception of **TEXT_ONLY** and **GRAPHIC_ONLY**, the values specify the location of the image. For example, if you add this line to the preceding program:

```
imageLabel.setContentDisplay(ContentDisplay.TOP);
```

the image will be above the text, as shown here:

The other two values let you display either just the text or just the image. This might be useful if you want to use an image at some times and not at others, for example. (If you want only an image, you can simply display it without the use of a label, as described in the previous section.)

You can also add an image to a label after it has been constructed by using the **setGraphic( )** method. It is shown here:

```
final void setGraphic(Node image)
```

Here, *image* specifies the image to add. This method is also specified by **Labeled**, which is inherited by **Label**. Thus, you can use it to add an image to any control that inherits **Labeled**.

Use an Image with a Button

A popular and effective use for images is with buttons. Up to now, we have only been using text inside a button, but you are not limited to this approach because you can include an image. You can also use only the image if you choose. The procedure for adding an image to a button is similar to that used to add an image to a label, as just described. First, obtain an **ImageView** of the image, and then add it to the button.

In general, an image can be added to any type of button, including **Button**, **ToggleButton**, **CheckBox**, and **RadioButton**. Because all are derived from **ButtonBase**, which is derived from **Labeled**, all support the use of a graphical image. In some cases, you can specify an image when you construct an instance. For example, **Button** includes the following constructor:

```
Button(String str, Node image)
```

Here, *str* specifies the text that is displayed within the button and *image* specifies the image. In other cases, you will need to specify the image separately, via a call to **setGraphic( )**, described in the previous section. In either case, you can specify the position of the image relative to the text by using **setContentDisplay( )** in the same way as just described for **Label**. Because all buttons inherit **Labeled**, all have access to **Labeled**'s functionality, including its support for images.

The following example adds images to a group of radio buttons. The radio buttons represent different kinds of timepieces, from which the user must select one. The radio buttons each display text, which is specified when they are created, and a graphics image that depicts the timepiece. The images are added with calls to **setGraphic( )**.

```
// Use images with radio buttons.

import javafx.beans.value.*;
import javafx.application.*;
import javafx.scene.*;
import javafx.stage.*;
```

```
import javafx.scene.layout.*;
import javafx.scene.control.*;
import javafx.event.*;
import javafx.geometry.*;
import javafx.scene.image.*;

public class ImageRadioButtonDemo extends Application {

  Label response;
  Label prompt;

  RadioButton rbAnalog;
  RadioButton rbHourglass;
  RadioButton rbStopwatch;

  ToggleGroup tg;

  public static void main(String[] args) {

    // Start the JavaFX application by calling launch().
    launch(args);
  }

  // Override the start() method.
  public void start(Stage myStage) {

    // Give the stage a title.
    myStage.setTitle("Use Images with Radio Buttons");

    // Use a FlowPane for the root node. In this case,
    // vertical gap of 10.
    FlowPane rootNode = new FlowPane(Orientation.VERTICAL, 0, 10);

    // Center the controls vertically, left-align them horizontally.
    rootNode.setAlignment(Pos.CENTER_LEFT);

    // Set a padding value of 10 on the left for the flow pane.
    rootNode.setPadding(new Insets(0, 0, 0, 10));

    // Create a scene.
    Scene myScene = new Scene(rootNode, 220, 240);

    // Set the scene on the stage.
    myStage.setScene(myScene);

    // Create the prompting label.
    prompt = new Label("Select Timepiece");
```

```java
    // Create a label that will report the selection.
    response = new Label("");

    // Create the radio buttons.
    rbAnalog = new RadioButton("Analog Clock");
    rbHourglass = new RadioButton("Hourglass");
    rbStopwatch = new RadioButton("Stopwatch");

    // Add images to the buttons.
    rbAnalog.setGraphic(new ImageView("analog.png"));
    rbHourglass.setGraphic(new ImageView("hourglass.png"));
    rbStopwatch.setGraphic(new ImageView("stopwatch.png"));

    // Create a toggle group.
    tg = new ToggleGroup();

    // Add each radio button to a toggle group.
    rbAnalog.setToggleGroup(tg);
    rbHourglass.setToggleGroup(tg);
    rbStopwatch.setToggleGroup(tg);

    // Use a change listener to respond to a radio button selection.
    tg.selectedToggleProperty().addListener(new ChangeListener<Toggle>() {
      public void changed(ObservableValue<? extends Toggle> changed,
                          Toggle oldVal, Toggle newVal) {

        // Cast newVal to RadioButton.
        RadioButton rb = (RadioButton) newVal;

        // Display the selected timepiece.
        response.setText("You selected " + rb.getText());
      }
    });

    // Select the first button.
    rbAnalog.setSelected(true);

    // Add controls to the scene graph.
    rootNode.getChildren().addAll(prompt, rbAnalog, rbHourglass,
                                  rbStopwatch, response);

    // Show the stage and its scene.
    myStage.show();
  }
}
```

Sample output produced by this program is shown here:

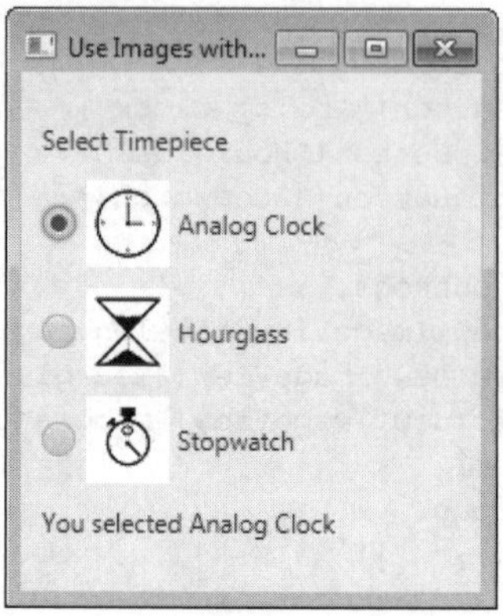

If you want a button that contains only the image, pass a null string for the text when constructing the button and then call **setContentDisplay( )**, passing in the parameter **ContentDisplay.GRAPHIC_ONLY**.

Introducing Fonts

In the preceding example that uses images with radio buttons, notice that the height of the image is significantly larger than the height of the text next to the image. In many cases, this may be acceptable (or even desirable), but in other cases, you might want the two heights to be more compatible. Fortunately, in JavaFX it is easy to adjust the size of a font. It is also easy to change fonts.

Fonts are represented by the **Font** class, which is packaged in **javafx.scene.text**. Any control that is derived from **Labeled** provides a means of setting or obtaining the current font. Thus, it is simple to set the font for any label or button. For these controls, you can set the current font by calling **setFont( )**. You can obtain the current font by calling **getFont( )**. They are shown here:

final Font getFont( )

final void setFont(Font *font*)

Here, *font* specifies the new font.

You can create a font in two ways. First, you can use one of **Font**'s constructors. They are shown here:

Font(double *size*)

Font(String *fontName*, double *size*)

In both cases, *size* specifies the size of the font. For the first constructor, the system font is used. The system font is the default font for labeled controls if no other font has been specified. Thus, it is the font used by all of the preceding examples. For the second constructor, the font specified by *fontName* is used. In this case, the font name must match one that is available on the system.

The second way to obtain a font is to use one of **Font**'s factory methods. For example, this one lets you specify the font's name, size, style, and weight:

static Font font(String *fontFamily*, FontWeight *fontWeight*,
                FontPosture *style,* double *size*)

Here, *fontFamily* specifies the family name of a font, such as Courier or Arial. The weight of the font, such as normal or bold, is passed in *fontWeight*. **FontWeight** is an enumeration in **javafx.scene.text** that defines several font weights. They are shown here:

BLACK	BOLD	EXTRA_BOLD
EXTRA_LIGHT	LIGHT	MEDIUM
NORMAL	SEMI_BOLD	THIN

The style, which will be either regular or italic, is passed in *style*. It must be one of the values defined by **FontPosture**, which are **ITALIC** and **REGULAR**. The size of the font is specified by *size*. This method attempts to return a font that is a close match to that which is specified. Thus, it should not be used to obtain a specific font when its name is known.

You can obtain a list of all fonts supported by the execution environment by calling **getFontNames( )**, as shown here:

static List<String> getFontNames( )

This method returns a list of specific font names, such as Times New Roman Italic or Courier New Bold.

Sometimes it is more useful to obtain a list of the font families, such as when you want to use a font factory method to construct a font. You can obtain a list of the available font families with **getFamilies( )**, shown next:

static List<String> getFamilies( )

It returns a list of the font families, such as Courier New, Times New Roman, and Arial. You can obtain a list of fonts associated with a family by using this version of **getFontNames( )**:

static List<String> getFontNames(String *fontFamily*)

This method returns a list of specific font names for the specified font family. For example, if you specify Courier New, you will likely see Courier New, Courier New Bold, Courier New Italic, and Courier New Bold Italic.

To put the preceding discussion into action, try adding the following lines to the **ImageRadioButtonDemo** example in the previous section. They set the font size of each radio button label to 30. For the first button, the default system font is used. For the second, Times New Roman is explicitly specified. For the third, Courier New Italic is constructed by the **font( )** factory method.

```
rbAnalog.setFont(new Font(30));
rbHourglass.setFont(new Font("Times New Roman Italic",30));
rbStopwatch.setFont(Font.font("Courier New", FontWeight.NORMAL,
                FontPosture.ITALIC, 30));
```

Also, import **javafx.scene.text.***. After making these changes, the output will now look like this:

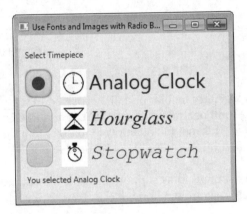

You can confirm that a font or family is available before using it by searching the list returned by one of the methods just described. For example, the following sequence obtains the list of available fonts and then confirms that Times New Roman Italic is available before attempting to use it:

```
List<String> fontList = Font.getFontNames();
if(fontList.contains("Times New Roman Italic"))
   rbHourglass.setFont(new Font("Times New Roman Italic",30));
```

In general, it is a good idea to confirm the availability of a font before attempting to use it.

Explore Layout Panes

As explained in Chapter 1, the layout of components on the screen is managed by a layout pane. So far, we have been using only one: **FlowPane**. It lays out its visual contents line by line, wrapping as needed. Thus, it is easy to use, making it excellent for most of the examples in this book. However, **FlowPane** gives you only limited control over the precise placement of visual elements, and the layout can change when the pane is resized. Fortunately, **FlowPane** is only one of eight general-purpose layout panes supported by JavaFX. The layout panes are packaged in **javafx.scene.layout** and are shown here:

AnchorPane	BorderPane	FlowPane
GridPane	HBox	StackPane
TilePane	VBox	

Each of these layouts inherits the base class **Pane**. They also inherit **Region**, which provides foundational support for controls and layouts. Each of the layouts is introduced here.

Before beginning, it is important to state that the layout panes are powerful elements of JavaFX, and they all support more features than discussed in this chapter. You will want to study their capabilities in depth. Simply put, mastery over the layout panes helps you produce professional GUIs.

FlowPane

FlowPane lays out content line by line, with lines wrapping as needed. By default, a horizontal flow is used, but it is possible to specify a vertical flow. You are already familiar with **FlowPane** because it has been used by the preceding examples in this book. However, a few additional points of interest are mentioned here.

One feature that you might find especially useful is the ability to specify the *wrap length*. This is the length at which the next element will be wrapped to the next line. You can set this length by calling **setPrefWrapLength( )**. It is shown here:

    final void setPrefWrapLength(double *len*)

Here, *len* specifies the preferred length. Here is an example. It uses two **FlowPanes**. One is the root pane. The other, called **labelPane**, holds 9 labels, and its preferred length is set to 150, which (in this case) results in 3 columns of 3 labels each. The **labelPane** is then added as a child of the root node.

```
// Demonstrate FlowPane preferred length.

import javafx.application.*;
import javafx.scene.*;
import javafx.stage.*;
import javafx.scene.layout.*;
import javafx.scene.control.*;

public class FlowPaneWidthDemo extends Application {
```

```java
public static void main(String[] args) {

  // Start the JavaFX application by calling launch().
  launch(args);
}

// Override the start() method.
public void start(Stage myStage) {

  // Give the stage a title.
  myStage.setTitle("Demonstrate FlowPane Length");

  Label one = new Label("Label 1");
  Label two = new Label("Label 2");
  Label three = new Label("Label 3");
  Label four = new Label("Label 4");
  Label five = new Label("Label 5");
  Label six = new Label("Label 6");
  Label seven = new Label("Label 7");
  Label eight = new Label("Label 8");
  Label nine = new Label("Label 9");

  // Create a FlowPane that holds nine labels.
  FlowPane labelPane = new FlowPane(10, 10);
  labelPane.getChildren().addAll(one, two, three, four, five,
                                 six, seven, eight, nine);

  // Set the preferred length to 150, which will result
  // in three columns of three labels, each.
  labelPane.setPrefWrapLength(150);

  // Create the root node of the scene graph and add
  // the label pane to it.
  FlowPane rootNode = new FlowPane();
  rootNode.getChildren().add(labelPane);

   // Create a scene.
  Scene myScene = new Scene(rootNode, 230, 140);

  // Set the scene on the stage.
  myStage.setScene(myScene);

  // Show the stage and its scene.
  myStage.show();
  }
}
```

The output is shown here:

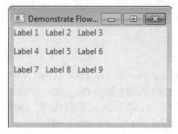

It is important to point out that in cases in which the **FlowPane** is resized, the preferred length may be ignored.

Beginning with JavaFX 8, several new constructors were added to **FlowPlane** that enable you to specify an initial list of child nodes. Here are two examples:

FlowPane(Node ... *childNodes*)

FlowPane(double *hGap*, double *vGap*, Node ... *childNodes*)

Here, *childNodes* specifies the child nodes that will descend from the **FlowPane** in the scene graph. When using one of the new constructors, it may not be necessary in some cases to add child nodes using the traditional approach, which explicitly calls **getChildren( )** followed by **add( )** or **addAll( )**. For example, beginning with JavaFX 8, this sequence

```
FlowPane rootNode = new FlowPane(10, 10);
// ...
Button btnAlpha = new Button("Alpha");
Button btnBeta = new Button("Beta");
TextField tf = new TextField();
rootNode.getChildren().addAll(tf, btnAlpha, btnBeta);
```

can be replaced with this sequence:

```
Button btnAlpha = new Button("Alpha");
Button btnBeta = new Button("Beta");
TextField tf = new TextField();
FlowPane rootNode = new FlowPane(10, 10, tf, btnAlpha, btnBeta);
```

Although specifying an initial list of child nodes when constructing a **FlowPane** can be helpful in some cases, the traditional approach offers flexibility because the child nodes do not need to be available at the time the **FlowPane** is created.

In general, this book will use the traditional approach, which uses **getChildren( )**, because it clearly illustrates and emphasizes the scene graph mechanism that is a fundamental aspect of JavaFX. It also enables the code to be run with earlier versions of JavaFX, which will be useful to readers who will be maintaining legacy code. Of course, in your own code, either approach is valid, based on the dictates of your specific situation.

HBox and VBox

Two simple but effective layout panes are **HBox** and **VBox**. **HBox** organizes its contents into a horizontal line. **VBox** lays out its contents in a vertical column. A principal advantage of **HBox** and **VBox** is that their contents will not be reorganized when the pane's size is changed. Thus, the contents will not reflow as they do in a **FlowPane**, for example.

Both **HBox** and **VBox** provide several constructors, including the default constructor. Here are the ones we will use:

HBox(double *hGap*)

VBox(double *vGap*)

Here, *hGap* specifies the horizontal space between elements and *vGap* specifies the vertical gap. When the default constructor is used, the gap is zero in both cases. Beginning with JavaFX 8, both **HBox** and **VBox** provide constructors that let you specify a list of nodes that will be contained within the pane. You might find this useful in some cases.

To see the effect of an **HBox**, replace this line:

```
FlowPane rootNode = new FlowPane(Orientation.VERTICAL, 0, 10);
```

with this line:

```
HBox rootNode = new HBox(10);
```

in the **ImageRadioButtonDemo** program, shown earlier. The output will now look like this:

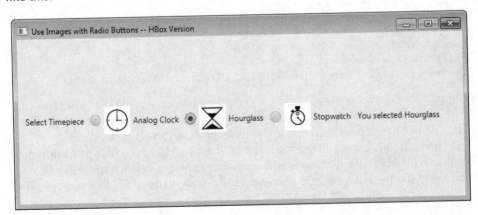

As you can see, all of the controls are now in one horizontal line.

To try **VBox**, substitute the following line in the **ImageRadioButtonDemo** program:

```
VBox rootNode = new VBox(10);
```

Now, all of the controls will be laid out vertically, as shown here:

The difference between this layout and the one produced originally by **FlowPane** is that the controls are kept in a vertical column no matter how the pane is resized. Thus, they will not move around, as they do with **FlowPane**.

Although **HBox** and **VBox** are sometimes useful as a root pane, they are often the most effective when they hold a group of controls that are added to the root pane. Doing so lets you create a control group that can be handled as a unit. To see the effect of this, first substitute the following line that creates the root pane into the **ImageRadioButtonDemo** program:

```
FlowPane rootNode = new FlowPane(Orientation.VERTICAL, 10, 10);
```

Next, add the following statements, which create a **VBox** and then add the radio buttons to it:

```
// Create a VBox that will hold the radio buttons.
VBox rbPane = new VBox(10);
// Add the controls to the VBox.
rbPane.getChildren().addAll(rbAnalog, rbHourglass, rbStopwatch);
```

Finally, substitute this line for the original:

```
rootNode.getChildren().addAll(prompt, rbPane, response);
```

After making these changes, no matter how the window is resized, the group of radio buttons will remain in a column as a unit. For example, here is the window after its dimensions have been changed:

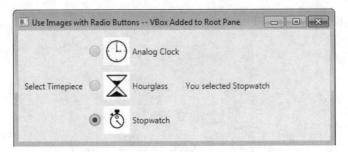

As with all of the layout panes, you can set the preferred height and width by calling **setPrefHeight( )** and **setPrefWidth( )**, respectively. You can also specify maximum and minimum values by use of methods such as **setMaxHeight( )** or **setMinWidth( )**. It is also possible to set a "grow" priority for one or more items in an **HBox** or **VBox** by use of static methods defined by these classes. Doing so enables extra space to be allocated for these elements if the pane is enlarged beyond its preferred size. These methods are **setHgrow( )** and **setVgrow( )**, respectively. You can set the alignment of items within a **VBox** or **HBox** by use of **setAlignment( )**.

BorderPane

One of the more popular layouts is **BorderPane**. It implements a layout style that defines five locations to which an item can be added. The first is the center. The other four are the sides (i.e., borders): top, bottom, left, and right. **BorderPane** is quite useful when you want to organize a window that has a header and footer, content, and various controls on the left and/or right.

BorderPane defines three constructors. The first is the default constructor. When using the default constructor, you can assign a node to a location by use of the following methods:

    final void setCenter(Node *item*)

    final void setTop(Node *item*)

    final void setBottom(Node *item*)

    final void setLeft(Node *item*)

    final void setRight(Node *item*)

In all cases, the node to add is specified by *item*.

The other two **BorderPane** constructors are shown here:

BorderPane(Node *centerPos*)

BorderPane(Node *centerPos*, Node *topPos*, Node *rightPos*,
　　　　Node *bottomPos*, Node *leftPos*)

These constructors let you assign a node to the indicated positions. Although these constructors are useful, often it is more natural to use the default constructor and then call the appropriate *set* method to add elements to the desired locations. In all cases, a location can be null. Thus, you have to set only those locations you need.

You can set the alignment used in a location by calling the static method **setAlignment( )**, shown here:

static void setAlignment(Node *what*, Pos *how*)

Here, *what* specifies the element being aligned and *how* specifies the alignment. As previously explained, **Pos** is an enumeration that specifies alignment constants, such as **Pos.CENTER**, **Pos.BOTTOM_RIGHT**, and **Pos.TOP_LEFT**. It is packaged in **javafx.geometry**.

When using a **BorderPane**, you will often want to set the margins around a node. The margins provide a gap between the edges of the node and the edges of a border position, thus preventing the two from crashing. To set the margins, call the static method **setMargin( )**, shown next:

static void setMargin(Node *what*, Insets *margin*)

Here, *what* specifies the node for which the margin specified by *margin* is set.

The following is an example that shows **BorderPane** in action: it puts labels into the top and bottom locations, a text field in the center, a slider on the right, and a **VBox** on the left.

```
// Demonstrate BorderPane.

import javafx.application.*;
import javafx.scene.*;
import javafx.stage.*;
import javafx.scene.layout.*;
import javafx.scene.control.*;
import javafx.geometry.*;

public class BorderPaneDemo extends Application {

  public static void main(String[] args) {

    // Start the JavaFX application by calling launch().
    launch(args);
  }
```

```java
// Override the start() method.
public void start(Stage myStage) {

  // Give the stage a title.
  myStage.setTitle("Demonstrate BorderPane");

  // Use a BorderPane
  BorderPane rootNode = new BorderPane( );

  // Create a scene.
  Scene myScene = new Scene(rootNode, 340, 200);

  // Set the scene on the stage.
  myStage.setScene(myScene);

  // Create controls and put them into the five BorderPane locations.

  // Center
  TextField tfCenter =  new TextField("This text field is in the center");
  BorderPane.setAlignment(tfCenter, Pos.CENTER);
  rootNode.setCenter(tfCenter);

  // Right
  Slider sldrRight = new Slider(0.0, 100.0, 50.0);
  sldrRight.setOrientation(Orientation.VERTICAL);
  sldrRight.setPrefWidth(60);
  sldrRight.setShowTickLabels(true);
  sldrRight.setShowTickMarks(true);
  BorderPane.setAlignment(sldrRight, Pos.CENTER);
  rootNode.setRight(sldrRight);

  // Left
  Button btnAlpha = new Button("Alpha");
  Button btnBeta = new Button("Beta");
  Button btnGamma = new Button("Gamma");
  btnAlpha.setPrefWidth(60);
  btnBeta.setPrefWidth(60);
  btnGamma.setPrefWidth(60);

  Label vbLabel = new Label("Vbox on left");

  VBox vbLeft = new VBox(10);
  vbLeft.getChildren().addAll(vbLabel, btnAlpha, btnBeta, btnGamma);
  vbLeft.setAlignment(Pos.CENTER);
  rootNode.setLeft(vbLeft);
  BorderPane.setAlignment(vbLeft, Pos.CENTER);

  // Set margin for left location.
  BorderPane.setMargin(vbLeft, new Insets(10, 10, 10, 10));
```

```
  // Top
  Label lblTop = new Label("This label is displayed along the top.");
  BorderPane.setAlignment(lblTop, Pos.CENTER);
  rootNode.setTop(lblTop);

  // Bottom
  Label lblBottom =
    new Label("This label is displayed along the bottom.");
  BorderPane.setAlignment(lblBottom, Pos.CENTER);
  rootNode.setBottom(lblBottom);

  // Show the stage and its scene.
  myStage.show();
  }
}
```

Here is the window produced by the program:

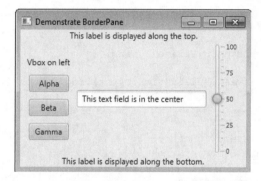

Perhaps the most important aspect of this example is the use of the **VBox** in the left location. The **VBox** contains a label and three buttons. Although each location in a **BorderPane** can hold only one node, you can put multiple controls into a location by containing them in another layout pane. Thus, by putting the buttons and label into a **VBox**, and then assigning the **VBox** instance to the left location, multiple items can be displayed. This technique can be used with any location in a **BorderPane** and is not uncommon.

One last point: in Chapter 7, you will see an example that makes good use of a **BorderPane** with menus and toolbars.

StackPane

One of the more interesting layouts is **StackPane** because its layout is based on the Z-order, with one node placed on top of another, in a stack-like fashion. This layout can be very useful when you want to overlay one control with another. For example, you might want to link a text field with the label that describes it. You can accomplish this with **StackPane**.

StackPane provides two constructors. The one we will use is the default constructor. The second, added by JavaFX 8, lets you specify a list of child nodes. You can set the alignment of each node in a **StackPane** by use of the static **setAlignment( )** method, in the same way as shown for **BorderPane**, previously discussed.

The following program demonstrates **StackPane**. It creates a text field and two labels. The labels are positioned at the top and bottom of the pane, with the text field in the center.

```java
// Demonstrate StackPane.

import javafx.application.*;
import javafx.scene.*;
import javafx.stage.*;
import javafx.scene.layout.*;
import javafx.scene.control.*;
import javafx.geometry.*;

public class StackPaneDemo extends Application {

  public static void main(String[] args) {

    // Start the JavaFX application by calling launch().
    launch(args);
  }

  // Override the start() method.
  public void start(Stage myStage) {

    // Give the stage a title.
    myStage.setTitle("Demonstrate StackPane");

    // Create a text field and two labels.
    TextField tf =  new TextField();
    tf.setMaxWidth(120);

    Label lblTop = new Label("Enter your name.");
    Label lblBottom = new Label("Name required for forum access.");

    // Create the StackPane.
    StackPane rootNode = new StackPane();

    // By default, nodes are centered. The following aligns
    // the labels to the top and bottom center.
    StackPane.setAlignment(lblTop, Pos.TOP_CENTER);
    StackPane.setAlignment(lblBottom, Pos.BOTTOM_CENTER);

    // Add the labels and text field to the scene graph.
    rootNode.getChildren().addAll(tf, lblTop, lblBottom);
```

```
   // Create a scene.
   Scene myScene = new Scene(rootNode, 200, 120);

   // Set the scene on the stage.
   myStage.setScene(myScene);

   // Show the stage and its scene.
   myStage.show();
  }
}
```

Sample output is shown next. As you can see, all three controls overlay the same space.

GridPane

Sometimes you will want to lay out controls using a row/column format. To handle this type of layout, JavaFX provides the **GridPane**. When using **GridPane**, you specify the row and column indices in which you want a control to be placed. Thus, **GridPane** gives you a way to position controls at specific locations within a two-dimensional grid.

GridPane provides only the default constructor. The location at which a child node is added to the grid is specified by setting its row and column indices. There are various ways to do this. For example, you can use the static method **setConstraints( )**, shown here:

static void setConstraints(Node *what*, int *column*, int *row*)

Here, *what* is the node affected and *column*, *row* specifies its location in the grid. The row and column can also be specified individually by use of the **setRowIndex( )** and **setColumnIndex( )**.

Another way to specify the row and column position is to use this form of **add( )** defined by **GridPane**:

void add(Node *child*, int *column*, int *row*)

Using this method, the row and column position is set on *child* when it is added to the **GridPane**.

You can set the vertical or horizontal gap around a control by use of the **setVgap( )** and **setHgap( )** methods, respectively. They are shown here:

final void setVgap(double *gap*)

final void setHgap(double *gap*)

In both cases, *gap* specifies the space between controls. You can set the padding within the pane by use of **setPadding( )**.

Here is an example that demonstrates **GridPane**. It creates three labels and three text fields. It uses the grid to organize the layout so each label is linked with its text field.

```
// Demonstrate GridPane.

import javafx.application.*;
import javafx.scene.*;
import javafx.stage.*;
import javafx.scene.layout.*;
import javafx.scene.control.*;
import javafx.geometry.*;

public class GridPaneDemo extends Application {

  public static void main(String[] args) {

    // Start the JavaFX application by calling launch().
    launch(args);
  }

  // Override the start() method.
  public void start(Stage myStage) {

    // Give the stage a title.
    myStage.setTitle("Demonstrate GridPane");

    // Create text fields and labels.
    TextField tfName =  new TextField();
    tfName.setMaxWidth(120);
    TextField tfPhone =  new TextField();
    tfPhone.setMaxWidth(120);
    TextField tfEMail =  new TextField();
    tfEMail.setMaxWidth(120);

    Label lblName = new Label("Enter your name:");
    Label lblPhone = new Label("Enter your phone number:");
    Label lblEMail = new Label("Enter e-mail address: ");
```

```
// Create the GridPane.
GridPane rootNode = new GridPane();
rootNode.setPadding(new Insets(10, 10, 10, 10));

// Set vertical and horizontal gaps between controls.
rootNode.setVgap(10);
rootNode.setHgap(20);

// Add first column.
rootNode.add(lblName, 0, 0);
rootNode.add(lblPhone, 0, 1);
rootNode.add(lblEMail, 0, 2);

// Add second column.
rootNode.add(tfName, 1, 0);
rootNode.add(tfPhone, 1, 1);
rootNode.add(tfEMail, 1, 2);

// Create a scene.
Scene myScene = new Scene(rootNode, 300, 120);

// Set the scene on the stage.
myStage.setScene(myScene);

// Show the stage and its scene.
myStage.show();
    }
}
```

Sample output is shown here:

Although the default features of **GridPane** are often appropriate, making it easy to use, several customizations are possible. Here are some examples. When a grid is enlarged past its preferred dimensions, it is possible to set the priority that a row or column will receive with regard to its new size. This is done by use of the **setVgrow( )** and **setHgrow( )** methods. You can have a control span more than one column or row by use of **setColumnSpan( )** or **setRowSpan( )**. You can request that lines that define the grid be displayed by calling **setGridLinesVisible( )**.

TilePane

Although quite simple, **TilePane** is quite effective when you want to create evenly spaced rows and columns. **TilePane** lays its contents out line by line, wrapping to the next line as needed. The key attribute of **TilePane** is that each control occupies the same amount of vertical and horizontal space. Thus, unlike in a **GridPane**, each tile in a **TilePane** is the same size. **TilePane**s are horizontal, by default, but you can specify a vertical orientation if desired.

TilePane defines several constructors, which parallel those used by **FlowPane**. In addition to the default constructor, there are constructors that let you specify the orientation and/or the vertical and horizontal gap between components. Beginning with JavaFX 8, there are also constructors that let you specify the initial set of child nodes.

The key to using **TilePane** is the **setPrefColumns( )** and **setPrefRows( )** methods. For a horizontal pane, **setPrefColumns( )** determines the preferred number of columns that will be displayed before content wraps to the next line. For a vertical pane, **setPrefRows( )** specifies the preferred number of rows that will be displayed before content wraps to the next column. These methods are shown here:

final void setPrefColumns(int *num*);

final void setPrefRows(int *num*);

Here, *num* specifies the preferred number of columns or rows. By default, the size of a tile is that of the largest node in the **TilePane**.

TilePane is especially useful when you want to display columns of information. The following program provides a simple demonstration. It uses a **TilePane** to display the numbers 1 through 9, along with their squares and cubes.

```
// Demonstrate a TilePane.

import javafx.application.*;
import javafx.scene.*;
import javafx.stage.*;
import javafx.scene.layout.*;
import javafx.scene.control.*;
import javafx.geometry.*;

public class TilePaneDemo extends Application {

  public static void main(String[] args) {
```

```
    // Start the JavaFX application by calling launch().
    launch(args);
  }

  // Override the start() method.
  public void start(Stage myStage) {

    // Give the stage a title.
    myStage.setTitle("Demonstrate TilePane");

    // Create a TilePane.
    TilePane sqrsCubesPane = new TilePane(10, 10);

    // Add three labels that will act as column headings.
    sqrsCubesPane.getChildren().add(new Label("Value"));
    sqrsCubesPane.getChildren().add(new Label("Square"));
    sqrsCubesPane.getChildren().add(new Label("Cube"));

    // Add labels that display a value, its square, and cube.
    for(int i=1; i < 10; i++) {
      sqrsCubesPane.getChildren().add(new Label(i+""));
      sqrsCubesPane.getChildren().add(new Label(i*i + ""));
      sqrsCubesPane.getChildren().add(new Label(i*i*i + ""));
    }

    sqrsCubesPane.setPrefColumns(3);

    // Create the root node of the scene graph and add
    // the tile pane to it.
    FlowPane rootNode = new FlowPane();
    rootNode.getChildren().add(sqrsCubesPane);

    // Create a scene.
    Scene myScene = new Scene(rootNode, 200, 280);

    // Set the scene on the stage.
    myStage.setScene(myScene);

    // Show the stage and its scene.
    myStage.show();
  }
}
```

The output is shown here:

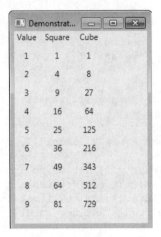

AnchorPane

AnchorPane is an interesting layout option. It allows you to anchor a node at a specific location, based on its distance from one or more of the four sides of the pane. Depending on the configuration, you can have the node automatically resize when the **AnchorPane** is resized or have it retain its preferred size. **AnchorPane** offers an excellent way to position controls in the same location even when the pane is resized. For example, you might use it to anchor left and right arrow buttons on the side for navigation through a document.

AnchorPane provides two constructors. The first is the default constructor. The second, added by JavaFX 8, lets you specify a list of the initial children.

The anchoring process is governed by these four methods:

static void setTopAnchor(Node *child*, Double *inset*)

static void setBottomAnchor(Node *child*, Double *inset*)

static void setLeftAnchor(Node *child*, Double *inset*)

static void setRightAnchor(Node *child*, Double *inset*)

In all cases, *child* is the node for which the location is being specified and *inset* specifies the amount that the node is inset from the specified side.

When an **AnchorPane** is resized, a node will be automatically resized horizontally if both the left and right anchors are set. The node will be automatically resized vertically if both the top and bottom anchors are set. The node will be automatically resized in both directions if all anchors are set.

The following program provides a simple illustration of how **AnchorPane** works. It defines four buttons, one for each location in the pane. The ones on the top and bottom will resize horizontally if the pane's width is changed. The left button will resize vertically when the pane's height is changed. The right button will not resize because it is anchored on the top and right.

```
// Demonstrate AnchorPane.

import javafx.application.*;
import javafx.scene.*;
import javafx.stage.*;
import javafx.scene.layout.*;
import javafx.scene.control.*;
import javafx.geometry.*;

public class AnchorPaneDemo extends Application {

  public static void main(String[] args) {

    // Start the JavaFX application by calling launch().
    launch(args);
  }

  // Override the start() method.
  public void start(Stage myStage) {

    // Give the stage a title.
    myStage.setTitle("Demonstrate AnchorPane");

    // Create the AnchorPane.
    AnchorPane rootNode = new AnchorPane();
    rootNode.setPadding(new Insets(10, 10, 10, 10));

    // Create four buttons, one for each location.
    Button btnTop = new Button("Top");
    Button btnBottom = new Button("Bottom");
    Button btnLeft = new Button("Left");
    Button btnRight = new Button("Right");

    // Top button will resize horizontally.
    AnchorPane.setTopAnchor(btnTop, 10.0);
    AnchorPane.setLeftAnchor(btnTop, 60.0);
    AnchorPane.setRightAnchor(btnTop, 60.0);

    // Bottom button will resize horizontally.
    AnchorPane.setBottomAnchor(btnBottom, 10.0);
    AnchorPane.setLeftAnchor(btnBottom, 60.0);
    AnchorPane.setRightAnchor(btnBottom, 60.0);
```

```
    // Left button will resize vertically.
    AnchorPane.setTopAnchor(btnLeft, 50.0);
    AnchorPane.setLeftAnchor(btnLeft, 10.0);
    AnchorPane.setBottomAnchor(btnLeft, 50.0);

    // The button on the right will NOT resize.
    AnchorPane.setTopAnchor(btnRight, 50.0);
    AnchorPane.setRightAnchor(btnRight, 10.0);

    rootNode.getChildren().addAll(btnTop, btnBottom, btnLeft,
btnRight);

    // Create a scene.
    Scene myScene = new Scene(rootNode, 300, 250);

    // Set the scene on the stage.
    myStage.setScene(myScene);

    // Show the stage and its scene.
    myStage.show();
  }
}
```

Sample output is shown here. Notice how the top, bottom, and left buttons resize as determined by their anchors. However, the right button does not because only one side is anchored.

CHAPTER
6

Effects and Transforms

A principal advantage of JavaFX is its ability to alter the appearance of a node in the scene graph through the application of an *effect* and/or a *transform*. Both effects and transforms help give your GUI the sophisticated, modern look that users have come to expect. Furthermore, transforms can be applied to both two-dimensional (2-D) and three-dimensional (3-D) objects, which enables powerful graphics operations, such as changing the size of a button or rotating a cube in space. As you will see, the ease with which these features can be used in JavaFX is one of its strongest points. Also introduced in this chapter is JavaFX's support for both two-dimensional and three-dimensional shapes.

Effects

Effects are supported by the abstract **Effect** class and its concrete subclasses, which are packaged in **javafx.scene.effect**. Using these effects, you can customize the way a node in a scene graph looks. Several built-in effects are provided. Here is a sampling:

Effect	Description
Bloom	Increases the brightness of the brighter parts of a node.
BoxBlur	Blurs a node.
DropShadow	Displays a shadow that appears behind the node.
Glow	Produces a glowing effect.
InnerShadow	Displays a shadow inside a node.
Lighting	Creates effects associated with a light source.
Reflection	Displays a reflection.

These effects, and the others, are easy to use and are available for use by any **Node**, including controls. Of course, depending on the control, some effects will be more appropriate than others.

To set an effect on a node, call **setEffect( )** which is defined by **Node**. It is shown here:

    final void setEffect(Effect *effect*)

Here, *effect* is the effect that will be applied. To specify no effect, pass **null**. Thus, to add an effect to a node, first create an instance of that effect and then pass it to **setEffect( )**. Once this has been done, the effect will be used whenever the node is rendered (as long as the effect is supported by the environment).

NOTE

Effects (and several other JavaFX features) are listed as conditional features, *which means they may not be supported in all environments. In general, you won't have any trouble using these features or running the examples in this chapter in a typical desktop environment. When a conditional feature is not supported by an environment, often that feature has no effect. For information about the JavaFX conditional features, see the API documentation for the* **ConditionalFeature** *enumeration.*

To demonstrate the power of effects, we will use three of them: **Reflection**, **BoxBlur**, and **Glow**. However, the process of adding an effect is essentially the same no matter what effect you choose.

BoxBlur blurs the node on which it is used. It is called **BoxBlur** because it uses a blurring technique based on adjusting pixels within a rectangular region. The amount of blurring is under your control. To use a blur effect, you must first create a **BoxBlur** instance. **BoxBlur** supplies two constructors. Here is the constructor we will use:

BoxBlur(double *width,* double *height,* int *iterations*)

Here, *width* and *height* specify the size of box into which a pixel will be blurred. These values must be between 0 and 255, inclusive. Typically, these values are at the lower end of this range. The number of times that the blur effect is applied is specified by *iterations,* which must be between 0 and 3, inclusive. A default constructor is also supported, which sets the width and height to 5.0 and the iterations to 1.

After a **BoxBlur** instance has been created, the width and height of the box can be changed by using **setWidth( )** and **setHeight( )**, shown here:

final void setWidth(double *width*)

final void setHeight(double *height*)

The number of iterations can be changed by calling **setIterations( )**:

final void setIterations(int *iterations*)

By using these methods, you can change the blur effect during the execution of your program.

Reflection produces an effect that simulates a reflection of the node on which it is called. It is particularly useful on text, such as that contained in a label. **Reflection** gives you significant control over how the reflection will look. For example, you can set the opacity of both the top and the bottom of the reflection. You can also set the space between the image and its reflection and the amount reflected. These can be set by the following **Reflection** constructor:

Reflection(double *offset*, double *fraction*, double *topOpacity*,
   double *bottomOpacity*)

Here, *offset* specifies the distance between the bottom of the image and its reflection. The amount of the reflection that is shown is specified as a fraction, specified by *fraction*. It must be between zero and 1.0. The top and bottom opacity is specified by *topOpacity* and *bottomOpacity*. Both must be between 0 and 1.0. A default constructor is also supplied, which sets the offset to 0, the amount to 0.75, the top opacity to 0.5, and the bottom opacity to 0.

The offset, amount shown, and opacities can also be changed during program execution. For example, the opacities are set using **setTopOpacity( )** and **setBottomOpacity( )**, shown here:

final void setTopOpacity(double *opacity*)

final void setBottomOpacity(double *opacity*)

The offset is changed by calling **setTopOffset( )**:

final void setTopOffset(double *offset*)

The amount of the reflection displayed can be set by calling **setFraction( )**:

final void setFraction(double *amount*)

These methods let you adjust the reflection during program execution.

Glow produces an effect that gives a node a glowing appearance. The amount of glow is under your control. To use a glow effect, you must first create a **Glow** instance. The constructor that we will use is shown here:

Glow(double *glowLevel*)

Here, *glowLevel* specifies the amount of glowing, which must be a value between 0.0 and 1.0.

After a **Glow** instance has been created, the glow level can be changed by use of **setLevel( )**, shown here:

final void setLevel(double *glowLevel*)

As before, *glowLevel* specifies the glow level, which must be between 0.0 and 1.0.

The following program demonstrates **BoxBlur**, **Reflection**, and **Glow**. It does so by creating two buttons and a label. The buttons are called Blur and Glow. Each time one of these buttons is pressed, the corresponding effect is applied to the button. Specifically, each time you press Blur, the button is progressively blurred. Each time you press Glow, the button's glow value is progressively increased. The label illustrates the reflection effect. When you examine the program, you will see how easy it is to customize the look of your GUI by using effects. You might find it interesting to experiment, either trying different effects or trying the effects on different types of nodes.

```
// Demonstrate BoxBlur, Glow, and Reflection.

import javafx.application.*;
import javafx.scene.*;
import javafx.stage.*;
import javafx.scene.layout.*;
import javafx.scene.control.*;
import javafx.event.*;
import javafx.geometry.*;
import javafx.scene.effect.*;

public class EffectsDemo extends Application {

  double blurVal = 1.0;
  double glowVal = 0.0;

  Reflection reflection;
  BoxBlur blur;
  Glow glow;

  Button btnBlur;
  Button btnGlow;;

  Label reflect;

  public static void main(String[] args) {

    // Start the JavaFX application by calling launch().
    launch(args);
  }

  // Override the start() method.
  public void start(Stage myStage) {

    // Give the stage a title.
    myStage.setTitle("Effects Demo");

    // Use a FlowPane for the root node. In this case,
    // vertical and horizontal gaps of 20 are used.
    FlowPane rootNode = new FlowPane(20, 20);
```

```
// Center the controls in the scene.
rootNode.setAlignment(Pos.CENTER);

// Create a scene.
Scene myScene = new Scene(rootNode, 340, 120);

// Set the scene on the stage.
myStage.setScene(myScene);

// Create the effects.
reflection = new Reflection();
blur = new BoxBlur(1.0, 1.0, 1);
glow = new Glow(0.0);

// Create push buttons.
btnBlur = new Button("Blur off");
btnGlow = new Button("Glow");

// Set the blur and glow effects.
btnGlow.setEffect(glow);
btnBlur.setEffect(blur);

// Create the reflection label.
reflect = new Label("Reflection Adds Visual Sparkle");

// Set the reflection effect on the reflection label.
reflection.setTopOpacity(0.7);
reflection.setBottomOpacity(0.3);
reflect.setEffect(reflection);

// Handle the action events for the Blur button.
btnBlur.setOnAction(new EventHandler<ActionEvent>() {
  public void handle(ActionEvent ae) {
    // Each time button is pressed, its blur status is changed.
    if(blurVal == 10.0) {
      blurVal = 1.0;
      btnBlur.setText("Blur off");
    } else {
      blurVal++;
      btnBlur.setText("Blur on");
    }
    // Set the blur rectangle to the new dimensions.
    blur.setWidth(blurVal);
    blur.setHeight(blurVal);
  }
});
```

```
     // Handle the action events for the Glow button.
     btnGlow.setOnAction(new EventHandler<ActionEvent>() {
       public void handle(ActionEvent ae) {
         // Each time button is pressed, its glow value is changed.
         glowVal += 0.1;
         if(glowVal > 1.0) glowVal = 0.0;

         // Set the new glow value.
         glow.setLevel(glowVal);
       }
     });

     // Add the label and buttons to the scene graph.
     rootNode.getChildren().addAll(btnBlur, btnGlow, reflect);

     // Show the stage and its scene.
     myStage.show();
   }
}
```

Sample output is shown here:

Transforms

Transforms are supported by the abstract **Transform** class, which is packaged in
javafx.scene.transform. Four of its concrete subclasses are **Rotate**, **Scale**, **Shear**, and
Translate. Each does what its name suggests. (Another subclass is **Affine**, but typically
you will use one or more of the preceding transform classes.) It is possible to perform
more than one transform on a node. For example, you could rotate it and scale it.
Transforms are supported by the **Node** class as described next.

As you will see later in this chapter, JavaFX supports 3-D graphics. As a result, the
transforms also support three dimensions. This makes them quite powerful. However,
you can still use the transforms on two-dimensional objects because when the
Z coordinate is not specified, it simply defaults to zero. Therefore, if you want to
transform a button, for example, you can use a two-dimensional transform. The
Z-axis will be ignored.

One way to add a transform to a node is to add it to the list of transforms maintained by the node. This list is obtained by calling **getTransforms( )**, which is defined by **Node**. It is shown here:

    final ObservableList<Transform> getTransforms( )

It returns a reference to the list of transforms. To add a transform, simply add it to this list by calling **add( )**. You can clear the list by calling **clear( )**. You can use **remove( )** to remove a specific element.

In some cases, you can specify a transform directly by setting one of **Node**'s properties. For example, you can set the rotation angle of a node, with the pivot point being at the center of the node, by calling **setRotate( )**, passing in the desired angle. You can set a scale by using **setScaleX( )**, **setScaleY( )**, and **setScaleZ( )**. You can translate a node by using **setTranslateX( )**, **setTranslateY( )**, and **setTranslateZ( )**. (Of course, the Z-axis methods are not needed for 2-D transformations.) These transforms are applied after those in the transforms list. As a general rule, adding transforms to the list returned by **getTransforms( )** offers the greatest flexibility, and that is the approach demonstrated here.

We will divide our discussion of transforms into two sections. The first describes how to use two-dimensional transforms. The second section demonstrates transforms in three dimensions.

2-D Transformations

It is very easy to apply a two-dimensional transform. To do so, simply use a two-dimensional version of **Rotate**, **Scale**, and **Translate.** The **Shear** transform affects only the X and Y axes, so the same instance will work in both 2-D and 3-D. Each transform class is briefly described here.

Rotate rotates a node through a specified angle around a specified point. These values can be set when a **Rotate** instance is created. **Rotate** defines constructors that let you create either a 2-D or a 3-D rotation. Here is one of its 2-D constructors:

    Rotate(double *angle*, double *x*, double *y*)

Here, *angle* specifies the number of degrees to rotate. The center of rotation, called the *pivot point,* is specified by *x* and *y*. In this case, the Z coordinate defaults to zero, thus creating a 2-D transform.

It is also possible to use the default constructor and set the rotation values after a **Rotate** object has been created, which is what the following demonstration program will do. This is done by using the **setAngle( )**, **setPivotX( )**, and **setPivotY( )** methods, shown here:

    final void setAngle(double *angle*)

    final void setPivotX(double *x*)

    final void setPivotY(double *y*)

As before, *angle* specifies the number of degrees to rotate, and *x* and *y* specify the center of rotation. Using these methods, you can rotate a node during program execution, creating a dramatic effect.

Scale scales a node as specified by a scale factor. Thus, it changes a node's size. **Scale** defines several constructors, which support both 2-D and 3-D scaling. Here is the 2-D version that we will use:

Scale(double *xFactor*, double *yFactor*)

Here, *xFactor* specifies the scaling factor applied to the node's width and *yFactor* specifies the scaling factor applied to the node's height. It scales the node around the pivot point 0,0. (Another constructor lets you specify the pivot point.) The scale factors can be changed after a **Scale** instance has been created by using **setX( )** and **setY( )**, shown here:

final void setX(double *xFactor*)

final void setY(double *yFactor*)

As before, *xFactor* specifies the scaling factor applied to the node's width and *yFactor* specifies the scaling factor applied to the node's height. You might use these methods to change the size of a control during program execution, possibly to draw attention to it.

Translate performs a coordinate translation on an object. That is, it moves each point in the object to a new location. Thus, the object will look the same but be in a different position in the coordinate space. Both 2-D and 3-D translations are supported. For a two-dimensional translation, use the following constructor:

Translate(double *xDistance*, double *yDistance*)

Here, *xDistance* and *yDistance* specify the amount to move each point in the specified direction. Of course, these values can be positive or negative, depending on the direction of the move. These values can also be set after the fact by calling **setX( )** or **SetY( )**.

Shear tilts an object. It does this by using a factor that is applied to the coordinates of the X and/or Y axis. **Shear** provides three constructors. The one we will use is shown here:

Shear(double *xFactor*, double *yFactor*)

Here, *xFactor* specifies the amount by which to multiply the X coordinates and *yFactor* specifies the amount by which to multiply the Y coordinates. These values can also be set after the fact by calling **setX( )** or **SetY( )**. By default, the pivot point of the shear is at 0,0, but you can set it, either through the use of another of **Shear**'s constructors or by calling the **setPivotX( )** and **setPivotY( )** methods. For our purposes, having the pivot point at 0,0 is appropriate.

A 2-D Transformation Example

The following program demonstrates the transforms in two dimensions. In this example, the target of the transforms are buttons, but they work with other types of objects. The program creates four buttons labeled Rotate, Scale, Shear, and Translate. Each time one of the buttons is pressed, the indicated transform is applied to the button, itself.

```
// Demonstrate rotation, scaling, translation, and shear.

import javafx.application.*;
import javafx.scene.*;
import javafx.stage.*;
import javafx.scene.layout.*;
import javafx.scene.control.*;
import javafx.event.*;
import javafx.geometry.*;
import javafx.scene.transform.*;

public class TransformsDemo extends Application {

  Shear shear;
  Rotate rotate;
  Scale scale;
  Translate translate;

  double angle = 0.0;
  double scaleFactor = 0.4;
  double xShearFactor = 0.0;

  boolean trans = true;

  Button btnRotate;
  Button btnScale;
  Button btnShear;
  Button btnTranslate;

  public static void main(String[] args) {

    // Start the JavaFX application by calling launch().
    launch(args);
  }

  // Override the start() method.
  public void start(Stage myStage) {

    // Give the stage a title.
    myStage.setTitle("Transforms Demo");
```

```
// Use a FlowPane for the root node. In this case,
// vertical and horizontal gaps of 40 are used.
FlowPane rootNode = new FlowPane(40, 40);

// Center the controls in the scene.
rootNode.setAlignment(Pos.CENTER);

// Create a scene.
Scene myScene = new Scene(rootNode, 500, 200);

// Set the scene on the stage.
myStage.setScene(myScene);

// Create transforms.
rotate = new Rotate();
scale = new Scale(scaleFactor, scaleFactor);
shear = new Shear();
translate = new Translate();

// Create transform push buttons.
btnRotate = new Button("Rotate");
btnScale = new Button("Scale");
btnShear = new Button("Shear");
btnTranslate = new Button("Translate");

// Add rotation to the transform list for the Rotate button.
btnRotate.getTransforms().add(rotate);

// Add scaling to the transform list for the Scale button.
btnScale.getTransforms().add(scale);

// Add shear to the transform list for the Shear button.
btnShear.getTransforms().add(shear);

// Add translation to the transform list for the Translate button.
btnTranslate.getTransforms().add(translate);

// Handle the action events for the Rotate button.
btnRotate.setOnAction(new EventHandler<ActionEvent>() {
  public void handle(ActionEvent ae) {
    // Each time button is pressed, it is rotated 15 degrees
    // around its center.
    angle += 15.0;

    rotate.setAngle(angle);
    rotate.setPivotX(btnRotate.getWidth()/2);
    rotate.setPivotY(btnRotate.getHeight()/2);
  }
});
```

```java
    // Handle the action events for the Scale button.
    btnScale.setOnAction(new EventHandler<ActionEvent>() {
      public void handle(ActionEvent ae) {
        // Each time button is pressed, the button's scale is changed.
        scaleFactor += 0.1;
        if(scaleFactor > 2.0) scaleFactor = 0.4;

        scale.setX(scaleFactor);
        scale.setY(scaleFactor);
      }
    });

    // Handle the action events for the Shear button.
    btnShear.setOnAction(new EventHandler<ActionEvent>() {
      public void handle(ActionEvent ae) {
        // Each time button is pressed, the button's shear is changed.
        xShearFactor += 0.1;
        if(xShearFactor > 2.0) xShearFactor = 0.0;

        shear.setX(xShearFactor);
      }
    });

    // Handle the action events for the Translate button.
    btnTranslate.setOnAction(new EventHandler<ActionEvent>() {
      public void handle(ActionEvent ae) {
        // Each time button is pressed, the button is moved.
        if(trans) {
          translate.setX(50);
          translate.setY(50);
        }
        else {
          translate.setX(0);
          translate.setY(0);
        }

        // Flip the translation state.
        trans = !trans;
      }
    });

    // Add the label and buttons to the scene graph.
    rootNode.getChildren().addAll(btnRotate, btnScale, btnShear, btnTranslate);

    // Show the stage and its scene.
    myStage.show();
  }
}
```

Sample output is shown here:

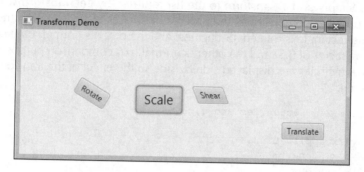

Transforming 2-D Shapes

Although the preceding example applied transforms to buttons, their use is certainly not limited in this regard. For example, an effective use for the 2-D transformations is found when they are applied to the 2-D shapes packaged in **javafx.scene.shape**. These include **Line**, **Circle**, **Arc**, and **Rectangle**, among others. Each of these is a subclass of the **Shape** class, which inherits **Node**. Thus, these items can be added as child nodes in a scene graph. To demonstrate transforms on 2-D shapes, we will use the **Rectangle** and **Circle** classes.

NOTE
*JavaFX also supplies drawing primitives for lines, rectangles, and so on, in the **GraphicsContext** class in **javafx.scene.canvas**. An overview is found in Chapter 9.*

Rectangle defines four constructors. The one we will use is shown here:

Rectangle(double *width*, double *height*)

This creates a filled rectangle with the specified width and height. By default, the fill color is black.

Circle defines five constructors. The one we will use is shown here:

Circle(double *radius*)

This creates a filled circle with the specified *radius*. By default, the fill color is black.

Because the 2-D shapes inherit **Node**, they support the use of transforms as just described. Simply add a transform to the list returned by **getTransforms( )**. The following program demonstrates the process. It creates two rectangles and two circles. One rectangle is rotated 45 degrees, and the other is normal. One circle is sheared by a factor of 0.3, and the other is normal. For comparison purposes, both rectangles and circles are displayed side by side so the effect of the transforms can be easily seen.

```
// Transform 2-D rectangles and circles.

import javafx.application.*;
import javafx.scene.*;
import javafx.stage.*;
import javafx.scene.layout.*;
import javafx.geometry.*;
import javafx.scene.transform.*;
import javafx.scene.shape.*;

public class TransformShapesDemo extends Application {

  public static void main(String[] args) {

    // Start the JavaFX application by calling launch().
    launch(args);
  }

  // Override the start() method.
  public void start(Stage myStage) {

    // Give the stage a title.
    myStage.setTitle("Transform 2-D Shapes");

    // Use a FlowPane for the root node. In this case,
    // vertical and horizontal gaps of 40 are used.
    FlowPane rootNode = new FlowPane(40, 40);

    // Center the controls in the scene.
    rootNode.setAlignment(Pos.CENTER);

    // Create a scene.
    Scene myScene = new Scene(rootNode, 500, 200);

    // Set the scene on the stage.
    myStage.setScene(myScene);
```

```
      // Create two equivalent rectangles.
      Rectangle rectA = new Rectangle(100, 50);
      Rectangle rectB = new Rectangle(100, 50);

      // Rotate rectB 45 degrees around its center.
      rectB.getTransforms().add(new Rotate(45, rectB.getWidth()/2,
                                           rectB.getHeight()/2));

      // Create two equivalent circles.
      Circle circleA = new Circle(20);
      Circle circleB = new Circle(20);

      // Shear circleB by a factor 0.3 on the X axis.
      circleB.getTransforms().add(new Shear(0.3, 0));

      // Add the rectangles and circles to the scene graph.
      rootNode.getChildren().addAll(rectA, rectB, circleA, circleB);

      // Show the stage and its scene.
      myStage.show();
    }
  }
```

The output is shown here:

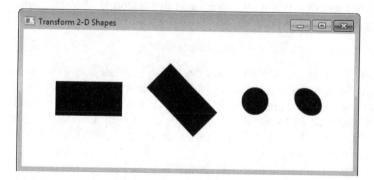

As you might expect, the 2-D shapes support a significant amount of functionality and options beyond those described here. They are a part of JavaFX that you will definitely want to explore fully. You will also want to experiment with the **Text** class, which inherits **Shape**. Packaged in **javafx.scene.text**, **Text** creates a node that consists of text. Because it is a node, the text can be easily manipulated as a unit and effects and transforms can be applied. As you will see in the next section, the 2-D shapes are just one part of JavaFX's support for graphics programming. The other part supports the use of 3-D.

3-D Transformations

One of the more powerful aspects of JavaFX's support for graphics is its ability to manage three-dimensional objects. Not only can you display 3-D shapes, but also you can apply 3-D transformations to them. For example, you can rotate a 3-D object. Although working with three dimensions is a bit more complicated than using only two, the results can be stunning—and well worth the effort. The following discussion will help you get started with this exciting aspect of JavaFX.

Working with 3-D requires the use of 3-D versions of the transforms described in the previous section. It also requires the use of several features not yet discussed. These are the camera, **SubScene**, **Group**, and **Shape3D**. Each is examined, in turn.

NOTE
3-D features may not be supported by all environments.

3-D Versions of the Transforms

As a general rule, to perform transformations on 3-D objects in three-dimensional space, you will need to use 3-D versions of the transforms. The exception is **Shear** because it shears output along the X and Y axes and it works the same in both 2-D and 3-D situations. For the others, you will need to specify a Z-axis component. The easiest way to do this is when you construct the transform.

Here is the 3-D constructor for **Rotate** that we will use:

Rotate(double *angle*, Point3D *axisOfRotation*)

Here, *angle* specifies the angle of rotation and *axisOfRotation* specifies the axis around which the rotation takes place. **Point3D** defines a three-dimensional point or a vector. As it is used here, it defines the axis of rotation, which will be either **X_AXIS**, **Y_AXIS**, or **Z_AXIS**, which are fields defined by **Rotate**. The pivot point (center of rotation) is located at 0,0,0. (Another **Rotate** constructor lets you specify the pivot point, if needed.)

Here is the 3-D constructor for **Scale** that we will use:

Scale(double *xFactor*, double *yFactor*, double *zFactor*)

Here, *xFactor* specifies the scaling factor applied to the width, *yFactor* specifies the scaling factor applied to the height, and *zFactor* specifies the scaling factor applied to the depth. The pivot point (center of the scaling) is located at 0,0,0. (Another **Scale** constructor lets you specify the pivot point, if needed.)

Here is the 3-D constructor for **Translate** that we will use:

Translate(double *xDistance*, double *yDistance*, double *zDistance*)

Here, *xDistance*, *yDistance*, and *zDistance* specify the amount to move each point in the specified direction. Of course, these values can be positive or negative, depending on the direction of the move.

Cameras

In general, the camera attached to a scene determines how the contents of that scene are rendered. The default camera attached to a scene supports 2-D, not 3-D. In order to view a scene in three dimensions, the scene must use a *perspective camera*. A perspective camera is an instance of the **PerspectiveCamera** class. It inherits the class **Camera**, which is the base class for all cameras. It also inherits **Node**.

To create a **PerspectiveCamera**, you will normally use this constructor:

PerspectiveCamera(boolean *fixedEye*)

Here, *fixedEye* specifies whether the "eye" of the camera is in a fixed location at 0,0,0 or if the "eye" can move. For 3-D graphics, this value will normally be set to **true**.

PerspectiveCamera offers a number of configuration options. The two we will use set the field of view and the far clipping distance.

By default, **PerspectiveCamera** has a field of view of 30 degrees. Often this is sufficient, but you can change it to best fit your needs. To do so, call

final void setFieldOfView(double *angle*)

Here, *angle* specifies the field of view, in degrees.

The far clipping distance specifies the point at which no output is rendered. It is set by the **setFarClip( )** method, shown here:

final void setFarClip(double *distance*)

Here, *distance* specifies the clipping distance. By default, the far clipping distance is 100. As a point of interest, it is also possible to set the near clipping distance, but we won't be doing so here.

Once you have a perspective camera, you can set it on a scene. To do this, call **setCamera( )**, which is defined by both the **Scene** class and the **SubScene** class, discussed shortly. It is shown here:

final void setCamera(Camera *newCam*)

Here, *newCam* specifies the camera that will be attached to the scene. It is important to understand that a camera instance can be attached to one and only one scene. Thus, if two different scenes need a camera, you will need to create two camera instances. Because cameras are nodes, one can also be added to a scene graph.

You can add transformations to a camera in just the same way you would to any other node, by adding them to the list obtained from **getTransforms( )**. In the examples that follow, you will see how it is possible to perform 3-D transformations in two different ways. One way is to transform the camera. The other is to transform an individual 3-D object, itself. Each is appropriate, depending on the situation.

SubScene

When working with 3-D objects, it is often useful to contain them in a scene of their own. This way, when a transformation is applied to the scene's camera, the transformation applies to the entire scene, not just a specific object. In such a situation, it may not be desirable to mix 2-D objects, such as controls, with 3-D objects. For example, if you want to rotate a 3-D box by 15 degrees each time a button is pressed, then you will usually want the button displayed in 2-D, but the box rendered in 3-D. To handle this type of situation, JavaFX 8 added the **SubScene** class. **SubScene** is a node that provides a scene that can then become part of another scene, such as the primary scene of the application. Thus, with **SubScene**, you can create a 3-D workspace that is embedded in a 2-D main scene.

   SubScene provides two constructors. Here is the one we will use:

   SubScene(Parent *subSceneRoot*, double *width*, double *height*,
          boolean *depthBuffer*, SceneAntialiasing *how*)

Here, *subSceneRoot* is the root node of the subscene. The width and height of the subscene are passed in *width* and *height*. To enable a depth buffer, pass **true** to *depthBuffer*. By using a depth buffer, you enable one object in the scene to be behind another object as it relates to the Z axis. This is particularly helpful when 3-D scenes are rotated. In general, you will want to use a depth buffer when handling 3-D images. The value of *how* can be either **SceneAntialiasing.DISABLED** or **SceneAntialiasing.BALANCED**. We will use the former.

   After a subscene is constructed, you might want to set its fill color. Doing so is one way to let the boundaries of the subscene be visible. The fill color is set with **setFill( )**, shown here:

   final void setFill(Paint *fill*)

Here, *fill* specifies the background, which can be one of the **Color** static field values, such as **Color.BLUE** or **Color.RED**, or any other type of **Paint** instance. **Paint** and **Color** are packaged in **javafx.scene.paint**.

   As mentioned earlier, to set a camera on an instance of **SubScene**, call **setCamera( )**. Once you have done this, the subscene can render 3-D graphics.

Group

When working with 3-D graphics, it can be useful to hold the shapes in an instance of **Group**. A **Group** contains a list of child nodes. When a group is rendered, the child nodes are rendered in list order. Thus, **Group** is not a layout pane. Rather, it is simply a way to treat two or more nodes as a unit. The advantage of using a **Group** with 3-D transformations is that the output is not affected by a layout mechanism.

Group supplies three constructors. In the examples that follow, we will use the default constructor. Nodes are added to a **Group** in the same way as with the layout panes: add them to the list obtained by calling **getChildren( )**.

Shape3D

Shape3D is, in essence, the three-dimensional version of **Shape** described earlier. It is packaged in **javafx.scene.shape**. Only objects of type **Shape3D** can be properly rendered in three dimensions. It is an abstract class that is inherited by four concrete 3-D classes: **Box**, **Sphere**, **Cylinder**, and **MeshView**. **MeshView** is used to construct arbitrary 3-D shapes. The other three create the shapes suggested by their names.

In the examples that follow, we will use two 3-D shapes: a box and a cylinder. To make these objects, the **Box** and **Cylinder** classes are employed. Here are the constructors we will use:

Box(double *width*, double *height*, double *depth*)

Cylinder(double *radius*, double *height*)

The names of the parameters describe their meaning.

Before using any of the 3-D shapes, you will probably want to set the *material*. This property defines, among other attributes, the color of the object. By default, the material is light gray. You can set the material by calling **setMaterial( )**, shown here:

final void setMaterial(Material *material*)

Here, *material* specifies the material. **Material** is an abstract class that has one concrete subclass called **PhongMaterial** (which supports the Phong shading model). This material provides a realistic 3-D view. Both **Material** and **PhongMaterial** are packaged in **javafx.scene.paint**.

The **PhongMaterial** constructor we will use is shown here:

PhongMaterial(Color *color*)

Here, *color* specifies the diffuse color of the material.

By default, 3-D shapes are displayed as solids. However, you can change this to line mode by calling **setDrawMode( )**, defined by **Shape3D**. It is shown here:

final void setDrawMode(DrawMode *mode*)

Here, *mode* specifies the drawing mode, which must be either **DrawMode.LINE** or **DrawMode.FILL**. When line mode is selected, the objects are rendered by connecting lines between vertices rather than filling areas. The examples use the default fill mode, but you might want to experiment with line mode on your own.

A 3-D Transformation Example

The following example puts the preceding theory into practice. It creates a box and a cylinder, puts them into a group, and puts that group into a subscene. It then creates an application that supports the following operations:

- Rotate horizontally

- Rotate vertically

- Shear

- Scale

- Zoom in

- Zoom out

The first four demonstrate the rotation, shear, and scale transformations. The last two demonstrate translation as applied to the Z axis. The program accomplishes these actions by applying transforms to the camera rather than individual objects. Thus, these transforms affect the camera, not the contents in a scene. In the case of rotation, the effect is that of moving the camera around the scene.

```java
// Use a perspective camera in a 3-D scene.

import javafx.application.*;
import javafx.scene.*;
import javafx.stage.*;
import javafx.scene.layout.*;
import javafx.scene.control.*;
import javafx.event.*;
import javafx.geometry.*;
import javafx.scene.transform.*;
import javafx.scene.paint.*;
import javafx.scene.shape.*;

public class Transforms3DDemo extends Application {

  Rotate hRot;
  Rotate vRot;
  Translate zTrans;
  Shear shear;
  Scale scale;

  double angleH = 0;
  double angleV = 0;
```

```
double zPos = -60;
double shearVal = 0;
double scaleVal = 1;

boolean trans = true;

Button btnRotateH;
Button btnRotateV;
Button btnZoomOut;
Button btnZoomIn;
Button btnScale;
Button btnShear;

Box box;
Cylinder cylinder;

PerspectiveCamera pCamera;

public static void main(String[] args) {

  // Start the JavaFX application by calling launch().
  launch(args);
}

// Override the start() method.
public void start(Stage myStage) {

  // Give the stage a title.
  myStage.setTitle("3-D Transforms Demo");

  // Use a FlowPane for the root node. In this case,
  // vertical and horizontal gaps of 10 are used.
  FlowPane rootNode = new FlowPane(10, 10);

  // Center nodes in the scene.
  rootNode.setAlignment(Pos.CENTER);

  // Create a scene.
  Scene myScene = new Scene(rootNode, 380, 440);

  // Set the scene on the stage.
  myStage.setScene(myScene);

  // Create push buttons for transforms.
  btnRotateH = new Button("Horizontal Rotate");
  btnRotateV = new Button("Vertical Rotate");
  btnZoomOut = new Button("Zoom Out");
  btnZoomIn = new Button("Zoom In");
```

```
btnScale = new Button("Scale");
btnShear = new Button("Shear");

// Create Rotate transforms.
hRot = new Rotate(0, Rotate.Y_AXIS);
vRot = new Rotate(0, Rotate.X_AXIS);

// Create Z translation.
zTrans = new Translate(0, 0, zPos);

// Create shear.
shear = new Shear(shearVal, shearVal);

// Create scale.
scale = new Scale(scaleVal, 1, 1);

// Create the camera.
pCamera = new PerspectiveCamera(true);

// Add transforms to the camera.
pCamera.getTransforms().addAll(hRot, vRot, zTrans, shear, scale);

// Set the camera's field of view and far clip.
pCamera.setFieldOfView(45);
pCamera.setFarClip(120);

// Create a 3-D box and cylinder.
box = new Box(10, 20, 30);
box.setMaterial(new PhongMaterial(Color.LIGHTSTEELBLUE));

cylinder = new Cylinder(5, 20);
cylinder.setMaterial(new PhongMaterial(Color.GREEN));

// Rotate the cylinder 90 degrees so that it is horizontal.
// Translate the cylinder 10 units down so that it is half
// out of the box.
// Note: These transforms apply to the cylinder, itself,
// and not the camera.
cylinder.getTransforms().add(new Rotate(90,0,0));
cylinder.getTransforms().add(new Translate(10, 0, 0));

// Create a group that will hold the box and cylinder.
Group shapesGroup = new Group();
shapesGroup.getChildren().addAll(box, cylinder);

// Create subscene to manage the group. Notice that a
// depth buffer is enabled.
```

```
SubScene shapesSub = new SubScene(shapesGroup, 340, 340, true,
                                  SceneAntialiasing.DISABLED);
shapesSub.setFill(Color.AZURE);

// Set the camera on the subscene.
shapesSub.setCamera(pCamera);

// Handle rotation buttons by changing camera's angle.
btnRotateH.setOnAction(new EventHandler<ActionEvent>() {
  public void handle(ActionEvent ae) {
    angleH +=15;
    hRot.setAngle(angleH);
    if(angleH == 360) angleH = 0;
  }
});

btnRotateV.setOnAction(new EventHandler<ActionEvent>() {
  public void handle(ActionEvent ae) {
    angleV += 15;
    vRot.setAngle(angleV);
    if(angleV == 360) angleV = 0;
  }
});

// Handle zoom in by incrementing the Z coordinate.
btnZoomIn.setOnAction(new EventHandler<ActionEvent>() {
  public void handle(ActionEvent ae) {
    if(zPos < -30) zPos++;;
    zTrans.setZ(zPos);
  }
});

// Handle zoom out by decrementing the Z coordinate.
btnZoomOut.setOnAction(new EventHandler<ActionEvent>() {
  public void handle(ActionEvent ae) {
    if(zPos > -100) zPos--;
    zTrans.setZ(zPos);
  }
});

// Shear the X axis.
btnShear.setOnAction(new EventHandler<ActionEvent>() {
  public void handle(ActionEvent ae) {
    shearVal += 0.1;
    if(shearVal > 0.5) shearVal = 0;
    shear.setX(shearVal);
  }
});
```

```
// Scale the X axis, which makes things look narrower.
btnScale.setOnAction(new EventHandler<ActionEvent>() {
  public void handle(ActionEvent ae) {
    scaleVal += 0.1;
    if(scaleVal > 1.5) scaleVal = 1;
    scale.setX(scaleVal);
  }
});

rootNode.getChildren().addAll(shapesSub, btnRotateH, btnRotateV,
                        btnZoomIn,btnZoomOut, btnScale,
                        btnShear);

// Show the stage and its scene.
myStage.show();
  }
}
```

Sample output is shown here:

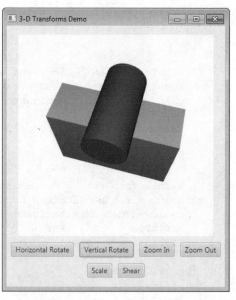

There are a few important points to make about this program. First, notice how the camera has a list of transforms added to it by this line:

```
pCamera.getTransforms().addAll(hRot, vRot, zTrans, shear, scale);
```

As mentioned, the program applies the 3-D transforms controlled by the buttons to the camera, not the objects, themselves.

A second key point is that the objects in the **shapesGroup** are rendered by use of a depth buffer. As mentioned, by using a depth buffer, you enable one object to be behind another in the scene. Thus, in the example, when the camera is rotated, portions of the box or cylinder are hidden when one is in front of the other. If a depth buffer had not been used, then the objects in the scene would have been rendered in the order in which they were added to the group. In that case, since the cylinder was added after the box, it would always be the last thing drawn. Thus, it would always overlay the box and be visible, even if the rotations would normally hide a portion of it. You can confirm this effect for yourself by changing the **SubScene** constructor so depth buffering is not used. As you will see, the effect of not using a depth buffer produces counterintuitive results.

Finally, notice that **cylinder** has two 3-D transforms added to itself. These rotate the cylinder 90 degrees, so it is horizontal, rather than vertical, and translate it so it is a bit lower than the box. The key point here is that 3-D transforms can be applied to a **Shape3D** object, a camera, or both. This offers a great deal of flexibility when designing 3-D scenes.

Although the preceding introduction is sufficient to get you started with 3-D graphics, it only scratches the surface of this powerful subsystem. Other topics relating to 3-D graphics include lighting and materials. If graphics programming is in your future, you will definitely want to study this topic in greater detail and depth.

CHAPTER
7

Animation

This chapter introduces one of the most impressive features incorporated into JavaFX: animation. Animation lets you change aspects of a node in the scene graph over a span of time. For example, you can create an animation that moves, resizes, rotates, or scales a node during the execution of a program. Thus, animation enables you to put into motion the transforms discussed in the preceding chapter. You can animate more than just those transforms, however. For example, a node can be faded and a shape can have its fill color changed. Additionally, the JavaFX animation system lets you define your own animation timeline that can change any write-enabled property during execution. Despite the power of the animation system, it is incredibly easy to use. You can animate a button, for example, with just a few minutes' worth of work. Simply put: with JavaFX you can now make your GUIs move.

Animation Basics

At the core of JavaFX's support for animation is the abstract **Animation** class, which is a superclass for all concrete animation classes. There are two direct subclasses of **Animation**. One is **Transition**, which is the superclass for all transition-based animations, such as **RotateTransition** and **ScaleTransition**. The transition-based classes provide predefined animations in which JavaFX handles many of the details, making them very easy to use. The second subclass of **Animation** is **Timeline**. The **Timeline** class gives you a way to define your own animation, based on key frames and key values. Before looking at any specific animation class, it will be helpful to examine several core methods in **Animation** because they are common to all animations and are used by the examples in this chapter.

The **play( )** method begins execution of an animation. In other words, **play( )** runs the animation. It is shown here:

    void play( )

If the animation has not yet been run, or if it has been run and finished, then calling **play( )** causes the animation to proceed from the start. If the animation has been paused, then calling **play( )** causes the animation to resume from the pause point. A call to **play( )** on a currently running animation is ignored.

To pause an animation, call **pause( )**. It is shown here:

    void pause( )

A call to **pause( )** on a stopped animation is ignored. To completely stop an animation, call **stop( )**:

    void stop( )

Like **pause( )**, a call to **stop( )** on a stopped animation is ignored.

Sometimes it is useful to know if an animation is currently running, stopped, or paused. To do this, call **getStatus( )**, shown here:

final Animation.Status getStatus( )

The status is returned as a value defined by the **Animation.Status** enumeration. The possible values are

PAUSED	The animation is paused.
RUNNING	The animation is running.
STOPPED	The animation is stopped, including when it has finished normally or has not yet begun.

Notice that the **STOPPED** value indicates the animation is stopped. This will be the case after it is explicitly stopped via a call to **stop( )**, it has finished normally, or it has not yet begun.

You can specify the number of times you want an animation to run by calling **setCycleCount( )**, shown here:

final void setCycleCount(int *cycles*)

Here, *cycles* specifies the number of times to run the animation. If you want the animation to repeat until you stop it, specify the value **INDEFINITE**. Be aware, however, that if you specify **INDEFINITE**, then you must be sure to stop the animation because forgetting to do so can result in a memory leak.

It is often useful to have an animation automatically reverse direction. For example, you might animate a button so it rotates clockwise and then counterclockwise as a special effect. To do this, you need only define the clockwise rotation and then simply request that the animation automatically reverse. To request auto-reversal, call **setAutoReverse( )**, shown here:

final void setAutoReverse(boolean *autoRev*)

If *autoRev* is **true**, then when the animation has concluded in the forward direction, it will automatically run in the reverse direction. It is important to understand that the forward direction constitutes one cycle and the reverse direction constitutes another. Therefore, if you want the animation to run one time in both the forward and reverse direction, you must specify two cycles in the call to **setCycleCount( )**.

One particularly useful feature of **Animation** is its ability to notify you when an animation has finished. To receive a notification at the end of an animation, register an event handler by calling **setOnFinished( )**, shown next:

final void setOnFinished(EventHandler<ActionEvent> *handler*)

Here, *handler* specifies the event handler that will be executed when the animation concludes.

In addition to the methods just described, **Animation** supplies many others. For example, you can run the animation from a specific play point by the use of the **playFrom( )** and **playFromStart( )** methods. You can have the animation move to a specific location by calling the **jumpTo( )** method. The rate of play can be set by calling **setRate( )**. The rate determines both the speed and direction. A positive rate animates forward; a negative rate animates in reverse. By default, the rate is 1. Values with an absolute value greater than 1 increase the rate.

As mentioned, from **Animation** are derived two types of animations. The first are the built-in ones based on **Transition**. The second are user-defined animations based on **Timeline**. We will begin with the transitions.

Transitions

Transitions are predefined animations that handle many of the details for you. This makes them very easy to use. Furthermore, they are quite powerful. Even though they do not offer as much flexibility as timeline-based animations, they will be appropriate for a wide range of your animation needs. Frankly, the built-in transitions make animation so easy, it is hard to justify not using one when the situation calls for it.

Transitions are subclasses of the abstract class **Transition**. At the time of this writing, JavaFX defines the concrete transition classes shown in Table 7-1. Notice that two of the classes, **ParallelTransition** and **SequentialTransition**, are used to combine multiple animations into a single instance. They make it possible to construct sophisticated animations with ease. The others provide the animations described by their names. Because **Transition** is a subclass of **Animation**, all transitions have access to the core animation methods defined by **Animation**.

Transition Class	Description
FadeTransition	Fades a **Node**
FillTransition	Changes the fill color of a **Shape**
ParallelTransition	Runs two or more animation sequences at the same time
PathTransition	Moves a **Node** through a path
PauseTransition	Pauses execution for a specified time
RotateTransition	Rotates a **Node**
ScaleTransition	Scales a **Node**
SequentialTransition	Runs two or more animation sequences, one after another
StrokeTransition	Changes the stroke (outline) color of a **Shape**
TranslateTransition	Translates a **Node**

TABLE 7-1. *The Concrete Transition Classes*

Throughout the course of this chapter, we will use the following transitions: **RotateTransition**, **ScaleTransition**, and **TranslateTransition**. Once you understand the operation of these transitions, you can easily learn to use the other transitions. We will also demonstrate the use of **ParallelTransition** and **SequentialTransition** to manage groups of transitions.

A First Example of Transitions

Although the specifics vary, all transitions work in the same general way. You create an instance of the transition and then specify values that define the way the transition will take place. Once you have defined a transition, it can be controlled by the core animation methods defined by **Animation**, described earlier. For example, to run the transition, call **play( )**; to stop it, call **stop( )**; to set the number of cycles, use **setCycleCount( )**; and so on. Of course, each transition defines methods of its own that affect aspects specific to the transition.

The best way to understand the general procedure of using a transition and controlling animation is to work through an example. Here, we will use **RotateTransition**, which rotates a **Node** through a specified angle. **RotateTransition** specifies three constructors. The one we will use is shown here:

RotateTransition(Duration *timeSpan*, Node *what*)

Here, *timeSpan* specifies the time over which the rotation will occur and *what* specifies the node upon which the rotation is applied. It is also possible to set these two values after a **RotateTransition** has been created by use of **setDuration( )** and **setNode( )**.

Duration is a class in **javafx.util** that defines a span of time. Its constructor is shown here:

Duration(double *milliseconds*)

It constructs an object whose duration is specified by the number of milliseconds passed to *milliseconds*. **Duration** also supplies a number of factory methods that construct time spans specified in minutes, hours, seconds, and milliseconds. It also has various methods that let you manipulate a **Duration**. All of the transitions require a **Duration** that specifies the span of time over which the transition will occur.

One way to set the angle through which the rotation will occur is by calling **setByAngle( )**, shown here:

final void setByAngle(double *angle*)

The angle of rotation is specified in degrees by *angle*. The rotation begins with the current value of the **rotate** property of the node being rotated. It stops after *angle* degrees of rotation have taken place. Thus, the current orientation of the node will define the starting point. Based on the value of *angle*, **RotateTransition** will automatically construct a set of frames through which the node is rotated over the given time span. This makes **RotateTransition** very easy to use. (And, indeed, all of the transitions are equally easy to use because they all use the same basic approach to supplying the animation.) One other point: **RotateTransition** also supports an alternative way to specify the rotation in which you define a start and end angle for the rotation, but often the angle set by **setByAngle( )** is easier to use.

The following program uses **RotateTransition** to rotate a button through an arc of 360 degrees during a span of 2 seconds. The animation is auto-reversed, and the number of cycles is set to 4. The program defines two buttons that control the animation. The first is Start, which starts the animation when it is pressed. When the animation runs, it rotates this button. The second button is called Pause/Resume. It alternates between pausing and resuming the animation. When the animation is finished, a message is displayed to that effect by the handler set by **setOnFinished( )**.

```java
// Demonstrate a RotateTransition.

import javafx.application.*;
import javafx.scene.*;
import javafx.stage.*;
import javafx.scene.layout.*;
import javafx.scene.control.*;
import javafx.event.*;
import javafx.geometry.*;
import javafx.animation.*;
import javafx.util.*;

public class RotateTransitionDemo extends Application {

  Label response;
  Button btnStart;
  Button btnPauseResume;

  public static void main(String[] args) {

    // Start the JavaFX application by calling launch().
    launch(args);
  }

  // Override the start() method.
  public void start(Stage myStage) {

    // Give the stage a title.
    myStage.setTitle("RotateTransition Demo");

    // Use a VBox for the root node.
    VBox rootNode = new VBox(30);

    // Center the controls in the scene.
    rootNode.setAlignment(Pos.CENTER);
```

```
// Create a scene.
Scene myScene = new Scene(rootNode, 300, 180);

// Set the scene on the stage.
myStage.setScene(myScene);

// Create a label.
response = new Label("Push the Start button.");

// Create buttons.
btnStart = new Button("Start");
btnPauseResume = new Button("Pause/Resume");
btnPauseResume.setDisable(true); // initially disable the button.

// Create a RotateTransition that rotates the Start button
// through a 2 second period.
RotateTransition myRotate =
        new RotateTransition(new Duration(2000), btnStart);

// Cycle 4 times, auto-reverse, and rotate through 360 degrees.
myRotate.setAutoReverse(true);
myRotate.setCycleCount(4);
myRotate.setByAngle(360);

// Handle the action events for the Start button.
btnStart.setOnAction(new EventHandler<ActionEvent>() {
  public void handle(ActionEvent ae) {

    // If animation is not currently running, then run it.
    if(myRotate.getStatus() == Animation.Status.STOPPED) {
      response.setText("Rotating");

      // Enable the Pause/Resume button.
      btnPauseResume.setDisable(false);

      // Play the animation.
      myRotate.play();
    } else { // Otherwise, wait.
      response.setText("Rotation Already In Progress");
    }
  }
});

// Handle the action events for the Pause/Resume button.
btnPauseResume.setOnAction(new EventHandler<ActionEvent>() {
  public void handle(ActionEvent ae) {

    // If animation is running, then pause it.
    if(myRotate.getStatus() == Animation.Status.RUNNING) {
      response.setText("Rotation Paused");
```

```
          myRotate.pause();
      } else { // Otherwise, resume play.
        if(myRotate.getStatus() == Animation.Status.PAUSED) {
          response.setText("Rotation Resumed");
          myRotate.play();
        }
      }
    }
  });

  // Handle animation-finish events.
  myRotate.setOnFinished(new EventHandler<ActionEvent>() {
    public void handle(ActionEvent ae) {
      response.setText("Rotation Finished");

      // Disable the Pause/Resume button.
      btnPauseResume.setDisable(true);
    }
  });

  // Add the label and buttons to the scene graph.
  rootNode.getChildren().addAll(btnStart, btnPauseResume, response);

  // Show the stage and its scene.
  myStage.show();
  }
}
```

The following output shows the rotation of the button in two positions:

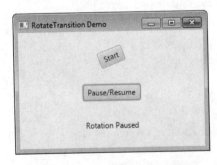 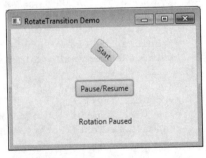

Let's look closely at how the transition in the program works.

A **RotateTransition** called **myRotate** is created by the following line:

```
RotateTransition myRotate =
        new RotateTransition(new Duration(2000), btnStart);
```

This constructs a **RotateTransition** that spans 2 seconds and operates on the Start button. Thus, when the rotation takes place, it will rotate the Start button over a period of 2 seconds.

Next, auto-reverse is set to **true** by this line:

```
myRotate.setAutoReverse(true);
```

As mentioned, when auto-reverse is **true**, the animation direction is automatically reversed at the end. In other words, the animation will alternate between running forward and backward. This is often very effective.

Next, the cycle count is set to four:

```
myRotate.setCycleCount(4);
```

This causes the rotation to occur four times: twice in the forward direction and twice in the reverse direction.

The angle through which the rotation takes place is set by this line:

```
myRotate.setByAngle(360);
```

In this case, the angle is 360 degrees.

When the program begins, the Pause/Resume button is disabled because the transition is not running. To start the rotation, push the Start button. When this occurs, the Pause/Resume button is enabled and the Start button begins to rotate. At that time, you can pause and then resume the rotation by pressing the Pause/Resume button. When the rotation is completed, the Pause/Resume button is once again disabled. These actions are handled by the button event handlers and the on-finished handler. Let's look closely at each.

When the Start button is pressed, the following handler is called:

```
btnStart.setOnAction(new EventHandler<ActionEvent>() {
  public void handle(ActionEvent ae) {

    // If animation is not currently running, then run it.
    if(myRotate.getStatus() == Animation.Status.STOPPED) {
      response.setText("Rotating");

      // Enable the Pause/Resume button.
      btnPauseResume.setDisable(false);

      // Play the animation.
      myRotate.play();
    } else { // Otherwise, wait.
      response.setText("Rotation Already In Progress");
    }
  }
});
```

This handler demonstrates several key aspects of using **RotateTransition** (and transitions in general). First, it obtains the current status of the rotation by calling **getStatus( )** on **myRotate**. If the current status is **STOPPED**, then the rotation is begun by calling **play( )** and the Pause/Resume button is enabled. Otherwise, a message is displayed that indicates that the rotation is already in progress. It is important to emphasize that it would not have been an error to call **play( )** during an ongoing rotation, but doing so would have had no effect. However, obtaining the status of **myRotate** allows the Pause/Resume button to be enabled only when a rotation is actually taking place.

Each time the Pause/Resume button is pressed, the rotation is toggled between a running and a paused state. The Pause/Resume button handler is shown here:

```
btnPauseResume.setOnAction(new EventHandler<ActionEvent>() {
  public void handle(ActionEvent ae) {

    // If animation is running, then pause it.
    if(myRotate.getStatus() == Animation.Status.RUNNING) {
      response.setText("Rotation Paused");
      myRotate.pause();
    } else { // Otherwise, resume play.
      if(myRotate.getStatus() == Animation.Status.PAUSED) {
        response.setText("Rotation Resumed");
        myRotate.play();
      }
    }
  }
});
```

Each time the button is pressed, the current status of the rotation is obtained. If the current state is **RUNNING**, the rotation is paused by calling **pause( )**. If the current state is **PAUSED**, the rotation is resumed by calling **play( )**. Recall that **play( )** will resume execution at the point at which **pause( )** was called.

When the animation completes, the on-finished event handler is called. It is shown here:

```
myRotate.setOnFinished(new EventHandler<ActionEvent>() {
  public void handle(ActionEvent ae) {
    response.setText("Rotation Finished");

    // Disable the Pause/Resume button.
    btnPauseResume.setDisable(true);
  }
});
```

This handler reports that the rotation has finished and then disables the Pause/Resume button.

At this point, you will want to run this program for yourself and observe its actions. You will also want to experiment a bit by changing various settings, such as the angle of rotation or the duration. You might also want to try setting the **rotate** property on the Start button by calling **setRotate( )**, passing in a value such as 45. This will cause the button to be initially rotated 45 degrees. When the rotation transition occurs, the button will still rotate through 360 degrees but will use the initial rotation as its starting point. You might also want to try stopping the animation with a call to **stop( )** and then restart it, observing the results.

Two More Transitions

At this point, it will be helpful to look at two more transition classes because we will be using them in the next section. As mentioned, the basic transition mechanism is the same for all transitions. Only the specifics change. Therefore, once you understand how to use one transition, it is easy to learn to use another. The two we will examine here are **ScaleTransition** and **TranslateTransition**.

To animate the scale (i.e., visual size) of a node, use **ScaleTransition**. Animating the scale can be quite effective in some situations. For example, you could repeatedly increase and decrease the size of a button. Pulsating a button in this manner draws attention to it. **ScaleTransition** defines three constructors. The one we will use is shown here:

ScaleTransition(Duration *timeSpan*, Node *what*)

Here, *timeSpan* specifies the time over which the transition will occur, and *what* specifies the node upon which the transitions are applied. It is also possible to set these two values after the transition has been created by use of **setDuration( )** and **setNode( )**.

The scale will change according to the values specified for the X and Y scale factors. (You can also set the Z factor, but we won't be doing that here.) One way to set these factors is to use the methods **setByX( )** and **setByY( )**, shown here:

final void setByX(double *xFactor*)

final void setByY(double *yFactor*)

The scale transition begins with the current value of the node's **scaleX** and **scaleY** properties and stops when the target value has been reached. Thus, the current size of the node will define the animation's starting point. It is also possible to define a start and end scale factor for a **ScaleTransition**, rather than just the target value.

You can try **ScaleTransition** by substituting it for **RotateTransition** in the preceding program. Here is the code you can use:

```
// Create a ScaleTransition that scales the Start button
// for 2 seconds.
ScaleTransition myScale =
        new ScaleTransition(new Duration(2000), btnStart);

// Cycle 4 times, auto-reverse, and scale by a factor of 1.2.
myScale.setCycleCount(4);
myScale.setAutoReverse(true);
myScale.setByX(1.2);
myScale.setByY(1.2);
```

You will also need to change **myRotate** to **myScale** throughout the program. When you run this transition, the button will grow and shrink in size.

To animate a node's location (i.e., change its location on the screen), use **TranslateTransition**. Through the use of this transition, you can move a node about the screen in real time. For example, you could use **TranslateTransition** to "wiggle" a button up and down as a special effect. **TranslateTransition** defines three constructors. The one we will use is shown here:

TranslateTransition(Duration *timeSpan*, Node *what*)

Here, *timeSpan* specifies the time over which the transition will occur and *what* specifies the node upon which the transition is applied. It is also possible to set these two values after the transition has been created by use of **setDuration( )** and **setNode( )**.

You can define the motion in two ways, either by defining a starting and ending point, or by using the current location as the starting point and defining just the ending point. Once the motion has been defined, the animation will proceed from the start to the end point. Here, we will use the current location of the node as the starting point. To define the end point, we will use the **setByX( )** and **setByY( )** methods, shown here:

final void setByX(double *x*)

final void setByY(double *y*)

Here, the values of *x* and *y* specify the end point for the transition. (It is also possible to set the Z coordinate, but we won't do that here.) The motion begins with the current value of the node's **translateX** and **translateY** properties and stops when the target value has been reached.

You can try **TranslateTransition** by substituting it for **RotateTransition** in the preceding program. Here is the code you can use:

```
// Create a TranslateTransition that moves the Start button
// for 2 seconds.
TranslateTransition myTranslate =
        new TranslateTransition(new Duration(2000), btnStart);

// Cycle 4 times, auto-reverse, and translate by 50 units in each
// direction.
myTranslate.setCycleCount(4);
myTranslate.setAutoReverse(true);
myTranslate.setByX(50);
myTranslate.setByY(50);
```

Of course, you will also need to change **myRotate** to **myTranslate** throughout the program. When you run this transition, the Start button will move diagonally down and right at approximately a 45-degree angle and then return to its starting position.

Managing Groups of Transitions

It is possible to play two or more transitions on the same node at the same time. For example, assuming a rotation transition called **myRotate** and a scaling transition called **myScale** that both operate on the same node, you could run them at the same time by simply calling one after the other, as shown here:

```
myRotate.play();
myScale.play();
```

Although this works, JavaFX supplies a better way that uses either **ParallelTransition** or **SequentialTransition**. These classes let you combine two or more transitions into a single unit. The advantage of this approach is that you can manage the transitions as a group, rather than individually. For example, if **myRotate** and **myScale** are combined in a **ParallelTransition** instance called **myPTrans**, you can call **play( )** once on **myPTrans**, and both transitions will run. Calling **pause( )** on **myPTran** pauses both transitions. In general, this is much more convenient than trying to handle a group of transitions individually.

The difference between **ParallelTransition** and **SequentialTransition** is when the transitions in the group are executed. A **ParallelTransition** executes its transitions simultaneously (i.e., in parallel). Therefore, **ParallelTransition** enables you to run a group of transitions all at once. A **SequentialTransition** executes its transitions one after the other (i.e., in sequence). Thus, it lets you combine individual transitions into a single, longer sequence.

Both **ParallelTransition** and **SequentialTransition** define several constructors. The ones we will use are shown here:

ParallelTransition(Animation … *animations*)

SequentialTransition(Animation … *animations*)

In both cases, *animations* specify the transitions (or any other type of **Animation**) that will be managed by the instance.

Once you have created a **ParallelTransition** or **SequentialTransition**, it is controlled like the other transitions, using methods such as **play( )**, **pause( )**, **getStatus( )**, and **stop( )**.

The following program demonstrates **ParallelTransition** by adapting the previous program so it combines translation, scaling, and rotation into a single unit, and then uses all three simultaneously to animate the Start button:

```
// Demonstrate parallel transitions.

import javafx.application.*;
import javafx.scene.*;
import javafx.stage.*;
import javafx.scene.layout.*;
import javafx.scene.control.*;
import javafx.event.*;
import javafx.geometry.*;
```

```java
import javafx.animation.*;
import javafx.util.*;

public class ParallelTransitionDemo extends Application {

  Label response;
  Button btnStart;
  Button btnPauseResume;

  public static void main(String[] args) {

    // Start the JavaFX application by calling launch().
    launch(args);
  }

  // Override the start() method.
  public void start(Stage myStage) {

    // Give the stage a title.
    myStage.setTitle("ParallelTransition Demo");

    // Use a VBox for the root node.
    VBox rootNode = new VBox(90);

    // Center the controls in the scene.
    rootNode.setAlignment(Pos.CENTER);

    // Create a scene.
    Scene myScene = new Scene(rootNode, 300, 300);

    // Set the scene on the stage.
    myStage.setScene(myScene);

    // Create a label.
    response = new Label("Push the Start button.");

    // Create buttons.
    btnStart = new Button("Start");
    btnPauseResume = new Button("Pause/Resume");
    btnPauseResume.setDisable(true); // initially disable the button.

    // Create a TranslateTransition that moves the Start button
    // for 2 seconds
    TranslateTransition myTranslate =
            new TranslateTransition(new Duration(2000), btnStart);

    // Cycle 4 times, auto-reverse, and translate by 50 units in each
    // direction.
    myTranslate.setCycleCount(4);
    myTranslate.setAutoReverse(true);
    myTranslate.setByX(50);
    myTranslate.setByY(50);
```

```
// Create a ScaleTransition that scales the Start button
// for 2 seconds.
ScaleTransition myScale =
        new ScaleTransition(new Duration(2000), btnStart);

// Cycle 4 times, auto-reverse, and scale by a factor of 1.2.
myScale.setCycleCount(4);
myScale.setAutoReverse(true);
myScale.setByX(1.2);
myScale.setByY(1.2);

// Create a RotateTransition that rotates the Start button
// for 2 seconds.
RotateTransition myRotate =
        new RotateTransition(new Duration(2000), btnStart);

// Cycle 4 times, auto-reverse, and rotate through 360 degrees.
myRotate.setCycleCount(4);
myRotate.setAutoReverse(true);
myRotate.setByAngle(360);

// Create a ParallelTransition for rotation, translation, and scaling.
ParallelTransition myPTrans =
        new ParallelTransition(myScale, myRotate, myTranslate);

// Handle the action events for the Start button.
btnStart.setOnAction(new EventHandler<ActionEvent>() {
  public void handle(ActionEvent ae) {

    // If animation is not currently running, then run it.
    if(myPTrans.getStatus() == Animation.Status.STOPPED) {
      response.setText("Running");

      // Enable the Pause/Resume button.
      btnPauseResume.setDisable(false);

      // Play the animation.
      myPTrans.play();
    } else { // Otherwise, wait.
      response.setText("Animation Already In Progress");
    }
  }
});

// Handle the action events for the Pause/Resume button.
btnPauseResume.setOnAction(new EventHandler<ActionEvent>() {
  public void handle(ActionEvent ae) {

    // If animation is running, then pause it.
    if(myPTrans.getStatus() == Animation.Status.RUNNING) {
      response.setText("Animation Paused");
      myPTrans.pause();
```

```
        } else { // Otherwise, resume play.
          if(myPTrans.getStatus() == Animation.Status.PAUSED) {
            response.setText("Animation Resumed");
            myPTrans.play();
          }
        }
      }
    }
  });

  // Handle animation-finish events.
  myPTrans.setOnFinished(new EventHandler<ActionEvent>() {
    public void handle(ActionEvent ae) {
      response.setText("Animation Finished");

      // Disable the Pause/Resume button.
      btnPauseResume.setDisable(true);
    }
  });

  // Add the label and buttons to the scene graph.
  rootNode.getChildren().addAll(btnStart, btnPauseResume, response);

  // Show the stage and its scene.
  myStage.show();
  }
}
```

Sample output is shown here:

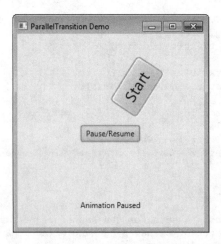

When you run the program, you will see that the Start button rotates, scales, and moves all at the same time. Furthermore, pressing the Pause/Resume button affects all three transitions. This is because they are managed by **myPTrans**, the **ParallelTransition** instance of which they are a part. Thus, they can be efficiently managed as a unit.

Let's look at the key points of this program. After the translation, rotation, and scaling transitions have been created, they are used to create the **ParallelTransition** instance called **myPTrans**, as shown here:

```
ParallelTransition myPTrans =
        new ParallelTransition(myScale, myRotate, myTranslate);
```

Now, **myPTrans** manages the execution of all three transitions. Thus, when **myPTrans.play( )** is called, it runs all three transitions. When **myPTrans.pause( )** is called, it pauses all three transitions. Furthermore, when **myPTrans.getStatus( )** is called, it returns the status of the **myPTrans**. Thus, it will not return **STOPPED** until all of the transitions that it manages have been stopped. This also means that the on-finished handler for **myPTrans** will not execute until all of its transitions have completed. You can prove this by increasing the number of cycles used by the rotation transition to 6, for example. Now, **myPTrans** will not complete until after the rotation has ended, which is 2 cycles more than the other transitions.

To see the effect of **SequentialTransition**, simply substitute it for **ParallelTransition** in the preceding program. As you will see, now all transitions will run one after the other, rather than at the same time.

Use Timeline Animation

Although the built-in transitions offer the easiest way to add animation to your program, and often provide the solution you are looking for, you are not limited to them because you can also define your own animation sequence. To do this, use the **Timeline** class. With **Timeline**, you can use any write-enabled property as a basis for the animation. For example, you can create a custom translation for any **Node** by use of **translateXProperty( )** and **translateYProperty( )**.

An animation based on **Timeline** makes use of three key classes. They are **Timeline**, **KeyFrame**, and **KeyValue**. Here is how they relate. **Timeline** is a subclass of **Animation** that manages the animation of **KeyFrame**s. A **KeyFrame** specifies the time span and the value or values being changed. The values are specified as objects of type **KeyValue**. A **KeyValue** specifies the property being changed and the target value. Once you have assembled all of the pieces into a **Timeline**, you can control the animation in just the same way as you did when using transitions. For example, to start a **Timeline** animation, call **play( )**. Now, let's look more closely at each class.

TimeLine provides several constructors. The one we will use is shown here:

Timeline(KeyFrame … *keyFrames*)

Here, the frames to be animated are specified by the list passed to *keyFrames*. When more than one frame is used, each frame is executed. Often, only one frame is required to achieve the desired animation. Another constructor lets you specify a frame rate. A default constructor is also available.

KeyFrame also supplies several constructors. Here is the one we will use:

KeyFrame(Duration *timeSpan*, KeyValue … *keyValues*)

Here, *timeSpan* specifies the time over which the animation will occur. The value or values being changed are passed via *keyValues*. When more than one key value is specified, the values are changed in parallel. Other constructors let you specify an event handler that is executed when the frame concludes and a name for the frame.

KeyValue encapsulates a value that will be changed during the animation. The constructor that we will use is shown here:

KeyValue(WritableValue<T> *what*, T *targetValue*)

Here, *what* specifies the writable value that is being affected and *targetValue* specifies the end point for the value. **WritableValue** is an interface defined in **javafx.beans.value**. It is implemented by several classes, including **BooleanProperty**, **DoubleProperty**, and **IntegerProperty**, to name just a few. For example, **scaleX** and **scaleY** defined by **Node** are of type **DoubleProperty**.

The following program demonstrates **Timeline** animation. Like the preceding programs, it provides a Start button and a Pause/Resume button. Each time you press Start, the animation is started. You can pause or resume the animation by pressing the Pause/Resume button. The difference in this example is that the animation is provided by an instance of **Timeline**, rather than a transition. In this case, the **Timeline** scales and rotates the Start button at the same time.

```
// Timeline animation demonstration.

import javafx.application.*;
import javafx.scene.*;
import javafx.stage.*;
import javafx.scene.layout.*;
import javafx.scene.control.*;
import javafx.event.*;
import javafx.geometry.*;
import javafx.animation.*;
import javafx.util.*;

public class TimelineDemo extends Application {

  Label response;
  Button btnStart;
  Button btnPauseResume;

  public static void main(String[] args) {

    // Start the JavaFX application by calling launch().
    launch(args);
  }
```

```
// Override the start() method.
public void start(Stage myStage) {

  // Give the stage a title.
  myStage.setTitle("Timeline Animation Demo");

  // Use a VBox for the root node.
  VBox rootNode = new VBox(30);

  // Center the controls in the scene.
  rootNode.setAlignment(Pos.CENTER);

  // Create a scene.
  Scene myScene = new Scene(rootNode, 300, 180);

  // Set the scene on the stage.
  myStage.setScene(myScene);

  // Create a label.
  response = new Label("Push the Start button.");

  // Create buttons.
  btnStart = new Button("Start");
  btnPauseResume = new Button("Pause/Resume");
  btnPauseResume.setDisable(true); // initially disable the button.

  // Create key values that affect the scale in both the X and Y
  // directions of btnStart.
  KeyValue kvScaleX = new KeyValue(btnStart.scaleXProperty(), 1.5);
  KeyValue kvScaleY = new KeyValue(btnStart.scaleYProperty(), 1.5);

  // Create a key value that affects the rotation of btnStart.
  KeyValue kvRotation = new KeyValue(btnStart.rotateProperty(), 180);

  // Create a key frame that uses the key values.
  KeyFrame kf = new KeyFrame(new Duration(1000),
                             kvScaleX, kvScaleY, kvRotation);

  // Create an animation timeline.
  Timeline myTL = new Timeline(kf);
  myTL.setCycleCount(4);
  myTL.setAutoReverse(true);

  // Add the key frame to the timeline.
  myTL.getKeyFrames().add(kf);

  // Handle the action events for the Start button.
  btnStart.setOnAction(new EventHandler<ActionEvent>() {
    public void handle(ActionEvent ae) {
```

```
      // If animation is not currently running, then run it.
      if(myTL.getStatus() == Animation.Status.STOPPED) {
        response.setText("Animation Started");

        // Enable the Pause/Resume button.
        btnPauseResume.setDisable(false);

        // Play the animation.
        myTL.play();
      } else { // Otherwise, wait.
        response.setText("Animation Already Running");
      }
    }
  });

  // Handle the action events for the Pause/Resume button.
  btnPauseResume.setOnAction(new EventHandler<ActionEvent>() {
    public void handle(ActionEvent ae) {

      // If animation is running, then pause it.
      if(myTL.getStatus() == Animation.Status.RUNNING) {
        response.setText("Animation Paused");
        myTL.pause();
      } else { // Otherwise, resume play.
        if(myTL.getStatus() == Animation.Status.PAUSED) {
          response.setText("Animation Resumed");
          myTL.play();
        }
      }
    }
  });

  // Handle animation-finish events.
  myTL.setOnFinished(new EventHandler<ActionEvent>() {
    public void handle(ActionEvent ae) {
      response.setText("Animation Finished");

      // Disable the Pause/Resume button.
      btnPauseResume.setDisable(true);
    }
  });

  // Add the label and buttons to the scene graph.
  rootNode.getChildren().addAll(btnStart, btnPauseResume, response);

  // Show the stage and its scene.
  myStage.show();
  }
}
```

When you run the program, the Start button will rotate and change size, as shown here:

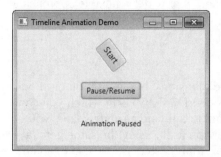

Let's look closely at portions of this program. First, notice how the key values are created. Here are the lines that construct the ones that specify the scale:

```
KeyValue kvScaleX = new KeyValue(btnStart.scaleXProperty(), 1.5);
KeyValue kvScaleY = new KeyValue(btnStart.scaleYProperty(), 1.5);
```

Notice that the properties are specified by **scaleXProperty( )** and **scaleYProperty( )**. These are defined by **Node** as shown here:

DoubleProperty scaleXProperty( )

DoubleProperty scaleYProperty( )

They return a reference to the **scaleX** and **scaleY** properties. These properties determine the scale factor for a **Node.** In previous chapters, we have been setting these values using the methods **setScaleX( )** and **setScaleY( )**, but **KeyValue** requires a reference to them. The same approach is used when the rotation key value is created, where the **rotate** property is specified by **rotateProperty( )**.

Once the key values are defined, they are used to create a key frame, as shown here:

```
KeyFrame kf = new KeyFrame(new Duration(1000),
                           kvScaleX, kvScaleY, kvRotation);
```

Here, the time span is set to 1 second and the values being animated are specified. All values will be animated in parallel when the timeline animation executes.

Finally, the **Timeline** is constructed:

```
Timeline myTL = new Timeline(kf);
myTL.setCycleCount(4);
myTL.setAutoReverse(true);
```

In this case, only one key frame, **kf**, forms the timeline. The timeline will cycle four times, automatically reversing.

Before moving on, you will want to experiment with the preceding program, trying different properties, changing the duration of a key value, and so on. Although **Timeline** is a feature that you may not need often, it provides a flexible approach to certain animation tasks.

Animating 3-D Shapes

So far, we have been animating in only two dimensions, but animation of three-dimensional shapes is also possible. There are two basic ways in which you can approach 3-D animation. First, if you just want to animate a single shape, you can do so by applying the animation to the shape itself, using the same general approach as that used by the preceding 2-D examples. Second, you can animate the perspective camera. This method lets you animate a group of 3-D shapes as a unit. The following example illustrates 3-D animation by adapting the 3-D transforms program from Chapter 6 so it demonstrates both approaches to 3-D animation. It uses **RotateTransition** to rotate either the camera or the 3-D box. The program is shown here:

```
// Animate 3-D shapes.

import javafx.application.*;
import javafx.scene.*;
import javafx.stage.*;
import javafx.scene.layout.*;
import javafx.scene.control.*;
import javafx.event.*;
import javafx.geometry.*;
import javafx.scene.transform.*;
import javafx.scene.paint.*;
import javafx.scene.shape.*;
import javafx.animation.*;
import javafx.util.*;

public class Animate3DDemo extends Application {

    Translate zTrans;

    double zPos = -60;

    Button btnRotateCamera;
    Button btnRotateBox;

    Box box;
    Cylinder cylinder;
```

```java
PerspectiveCamera pCamera;

public static void main(String[] args) {

  // Start the JavaFX application by calling launch().
  launch(args);
}

// Override the start() method.
public void start(Stage myStage) {

  // Give the stage a title.
  myStage.setTitle("3-D Animation Demo");

  // Use a FlowPane for the root node. In this case,
  // vertical and horizontal gaps of 10 are used.
  FlowPane rootNode = new FlowPane(10, 10);

  // Center nodes in the scene.
  rootNode.setAlignment(Pos.CENTER);

  // Create a scene.
  Scene myScene = new Scene(rootNode, 380, 440);

  // Set the scene on the stage.
  myStage.setScene(myScene);

  // Create push buttons for animations.
  btnRotateCamera = new Button("Rotate Camera");
  btnRotateBox = new Button("Rotate Box Only");

  // Create Z translation for the camera.
  zTrans = new Translate(0, 0, zPos);

  // Create the camera.
  pCamera = new PerspectiveCamera(true);

  // Set the camera's rotation axis to Y.
  pCamera.setRotationAxis(Rotate.Y_AXIS);

  // Add transform to the camera.
  pCamera.getTransforms().addAll(zTrans);

  // Set the camera's field of view and far clip.
  pCamera.setFieldOfView(45);
  pCamera.setFarClip(120);
```

```
// Create a 3-D box and cylinder.
box = new Box(10, 20, 30);
box.setMaterial(new PhongMaterial(Color.LIGHTSTEELBLUE));

// Set the rotation axis for the box to Y.
box.setRotationAxis(Rotate.Y_AXIS);

cylinder = new Cylinder(5, 20);
cylinder.setMaterial(new PhongMaterial(Color.GREEN));

// Rotate the cylinder 90 degrees so that it is horizontal.
// Translate the cylinder 10 units down so that it is half
// out of the box.
// Note: These transforms apply to the cylinder, itself,
// and not the camera.
cylinder.getTransforms().add(new Rotate(90,0,0));
cylinder.getTransforms().add(new Translate(10, 0, 0));

// Create a group that will hold the box and cylinder.
Group shapesGroup = new Group();
shapesGroup.getChildren().addAll(box, cylinder);

// Create subscene to manage the group. Notice that a
// depth buffer is enabled.
SubScene shapesSub = new SubScene(shapesGroup, 340, 340, true,
                                  SceneAntialiasing.DISABLED);
shapesSub.setFill(Color.AZURE);

// Set the camera on the subscene.
shapesSub.setCamera(pCamera);

// Create a RotateTransition that rotates the perspective
// camera for 2 seconds.
RotateTransition rotateCam =
      new RotateTransition(new Duration(2000), pCamera);

// Cycle 2 times, auto-reverse, and rotate through 360 degrees.
rotateCam.setCycleCount(2);
rotateCam.setAutoReverse(true);
rotateCam.setByAngle(360);

// Now, create a RotateTransition that rotates only the box.
RotateTransition rotateBox =
      new RotateTransition(new Duration(2000), box);

// Cycle 2 times, auto-reverse, and rotate through 360 degrees.
rotateBox.setCycleCount(2);
rotateBox.setAutoReverse(true);
rotateBox.setByAngle(360);
```

```
// Handle Rotate Camera button by rotating the camera.
// This effectively rotates both the box and the cylinder.
btnRotateCamera.setOnAction(new EventHandler<ActionEvent>() {
  public void handle(ActionEvent ae) {
    rotateCam.play();
  }
});

// Handle Rotate Box Only button by rotating only the box.
btnRotateBox.setOnAction(new EventHandler<ActionEvent>() {
  public void handle(ActionEvent ae) {
    rotateBox.play();
  }
});

  rootNode.getChildren().addAll(shapesSub, btnRotateCamera,
                               btnRotateBox);

// Show the stage and its scene.
myStage.show();
}
}
```

Here is sample output when the camera is being rotated:

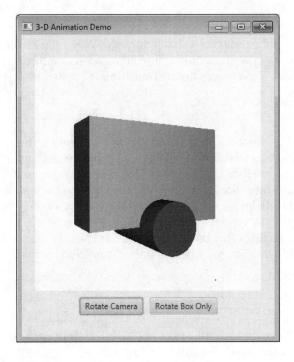

Here is sample output when only the box is being rotated:

The operation of the program is straightforward. When the Rotate Camera button is pressed, the perspective camera is animated forward and backward through a 360-degree rotation. The camera **RotateTransition** is created by this line:

```
RotateTransition rotateCam =
        new RotateTransition(new Duration(2000), pCamera);
```

At first, you might be surprised that the perspective camera can be specified for animation. However, recall from Chapter 6, that cameras, including **PerspectiveCamera**, are subclasses of **Node**. Thus, one can be used as the target node when a **RotateTransition** is created. Because it is the camera that is being rotated through the angle, it causes all shapes in the scene (in this case, both the box and the cylinder) to appear to rotate.

When the Rotate Box Only button is pressed, it causes only the box to be animated through a rotation because the **RotateTransition** for the box is created by this line:

```
RotateTransition rotateBox =
        new RotateTransition(new Duration(2000), box);
```

In this case, **box** is specified as the target node. Thus, it is the only element in the scene graph that is animated. The cylinder is unaffected.

This is another program that you will to experiment with. Try adding animations that alter the location or scale of the shapes, for example. As you will see, 3-D animation provides a dramatic effect that helps make your GUI elements stand out.

A Word About Interpolators

Before concluding this introduction to animation, it is necessary to mention *interpolators*. Interpolators are used by the transition classes and by **KeyValue**. An interpolator determines how a value changes as the animation progresses. Interpolators are instances of the **Interpolator** class. We have not needed to be concerned with interpolators in the previous examples because predefined interpolators are provided automatically for the transitions and **KeyValue**. It is possible to construct your own interpolator or to use a different predefined one. That said, in many cases, the predefined default interpolators provide appropriate action. Of course, for specialized animation needs, building your own interpolator may provide the solution you are looking for.

CHAPTER
8

Explore Menus

This chapter explores JavaFX's support for menus. Although menus have been a part of GUI programming since the beginning, they continue to form an integral, nearly indispensable part of the modern GUI. The reason for this is easy to understand: they give the user access to a program's core functionality. As a result, the proper implementation of an application's menus is a crucial part of creating a successful GUI. JavaFX provides extensive support for menus because of the key role they play in many applications. Furthermore, JavaFX's approach to menus is powerful, yet streamlined.

The JavaFX menu system supports several key elements, including

- The menu bar, which is the main menu for an application.

- The standard menu, which can contain either items to be selected or other menus (submenus).

- The context menu, which is often activated by right-clicking the mouse. Context menus are also called popup menus.

- Several different types of menu items, including the ability to create custom menu items.

- Accelerator keys, which enable menu items to be selected without having to activate the menu.

- Mnemonics, which allow a menu item to be selected by the keyboard once the menu options are displayed.

JavaFX also supports an interesting control called **MenuButton**, which lets you create a button that activates a menu. In addition to menus, JavaFX supports the *toolbar*, which provides rapid access to program functionality, often paralleling menu items. Each of these features is introduced in this chapter.

Menu Basics

The JavaFX menu system is supported by a group of related classes packaged in **javafx.scene.control**. They are shown in Table 8-1. Although JavaFX allows a high degree of customization if desired, often you will use the menu classes as-is because their default look and feel is generally what you will want.

Here is a brief overview of how the classes fit together. To provide a main menu for an application, you need an instance of **MenuBar**. This class is, loosely speaking, a container for menus. The **MenuBar** contains instances of **Menu**. Each **Menu** object defines a menu. That is, each **Menu** object contains one or more selectable items. The items displayed by a **Menu** are objects of type **MenuItem**. Thus, a **MenuItem** defines a selection that can be chosen by the user.

Class	Description
CheckMenuItem	A check menu item.
ContextMenu	A popup menu that is typically activated by right-clicking the mouse.
CustomMenuItem	A menu item that can contain any type of **Node**.
Menu	A standard menu. A menu consists of one or more **MenuItem**s.
MenuBar	An object that holds the top-level menu for the application.
MenuButton	A control that actives a drop-down menu when pressed.
MenuItem	An object that populates menus.
RadioMenuItem	A radio menu item.
SeparatorMenuItem	Provides a visual separator between menu items.
SplitMenuButton	A variation of **MenuButton** that provides both a button and a drop-down menu activator in one control.

TABLE 8-1.   *The Core JavaFX Menu Classes*

In addition to "standard" menu items, you can also include check and radio menu items in a menu. Their operation parallels check box and radio button controls. A check menu item is created by **CheckMenuItem**. A radio menu item is created by **RadioMenuItem**. Both of these classes extend **MenuItem**.

SeparatorMenuItem is a convenience class that creates a separator line in a menu. It inherits **CustomMenuItem**, which is a class that facilitates embedding other types of controls in a menu item. **CustomMenuItem** extends **MenuItem**.

One key point about JavaFX menus is that **MenuItem** does *not* inherit **Node**. Thus, instances of **MenuItem** can be used only in a menu. They cannot be otherwise incorporated into a scene graph. However, **MenuBar** does inherit **Node**, which allows the menu bar to be added to the scene graph.

Another key point is that **MenuItem** is a superclass of **Menu**. This enables the creation of submenus, which are, essentially, menus within menus. To create a submenu, you first create and populate a **Menu** object with **MenuItem**s and then add it to another **Menu** object. You will see this process in action in the examples that follow.

When a menu item is selected, an action event is generated. The text associated with the selection will be the name of the selection. Thus, when using one action event handler to process all menu selections, one way to determine which item was selected is to examine the name. Of course, you can also use separate anonymous inner classes or lambda expressions to handle each menu item's action events. In this case, the menu selection is already known and there is no need to examine the name to determine which item was selected.

As an alternative or adjunct to menus that descend from the menu bar, you can also create stand-alone context menus, which pop up when activated. To create a context menu, first create an object of type **ContextMenu**. Then, add **MenuItem**s to it. A context menu is often activated by clicking the right mouse button when the mouse is over a control for which a context menu has been defined. It is important to point out that **ContextMenu** is not derived from **MenuItem**. Rather, it inherits **PopupControl**.

Another way to create a stand-alone menu is to use the **MenuButton** or **SplitMenuButton** controls. **MenuButton** displays a button control that is used to activate a drop-down menu. **SplitMenuButton** displays both a button and a menu activator box, which is used to activate a drop-down menu. Both controls are quite useful when screen space is limited.

A feature related to the menu is the *toolbar*. In JavaFX, toolbars are supported by the **ToolBar** class. It creates a stand-alone component that is often used to provide fast access to functionality contained within the menus of the application. For example, a toolbar might provide fast access to the formatting commands supported by a word processor.

An Overview of MenuBar, Menu, and MenuItem

Before you can create a menu, you need to know some specifics about **MenuBar**, **Menu**, and **MenuItem**. These form the minimum set of classes needed to construct a main menu for an application. **MenuItem**s are also used by context (i.e., popup) menus and menu buttons. Thus, these classes form the foundation of the menu system.

MenuBar

MenuBar is essentially a container for menus. It is the control that supplies the main menu of an application. Like all JavaFX controls, it inherits **Node**. Thus, it can be added to a scene graph. **MenuBar** has two constructors. The first is the default constructor. Therefore, when using this constructor, initially, the menu bar will be empty and you will need to populate it with menus prior to use. The second constructor, which has been recently added, lets you specify the items in the menu. As a general rule, an application has one and only one menu bar.

MenuBar defines several methods, but often you will use only one: **getMenus( )**. It returns a list of the menus managed by the menu bar. You can add menus that you create to this list. The **getMenus( )** method is shown here:

```
final ObservableList<Menu> getMenus( )
```

A **Menu** instance is added to this list of menus by calling **add( )**. You can also use **addAll( )** to add two or more **Menu** instances in a single call. The added menus are positioned in the menu bar from left to right, in the order in which they are added. If you want to add a menu at a specific location, then use this version of **add( )**:

    void add(int *idx*, Menu *menu*)

Here, *menu* is added at the index specified by *idx*. Indexing begins at 0, with 0 being the left-most menu. Once a menu bar has been created and populated, it is added to the scene graph in the normal way.

One other point: Recall that **ObservableList** implements the **List** collections interface, which gives you access to all the methods defined by **List**. For example, to remove a menu that is no longer needed, call **remove( )**. To obtain a count of the number of items in a menu bar, call **size( )**.

Menu

Menu encapsulates a menu, which is populated with **MenuItem**s. As explained earlier, it is derived from **MenuItem**. This means that one **Menu** can be a selection in another **Menu**, enabling one menu to be a submenu of another. **Menu** defines several constructors. Perhaps the most commonly used is shown here:

    Menu(String *name*)

It creates a menu that has the name specified by *name*. You can specify an image along with text with this constructor:

    Menu(String *name*, Node *image*)

Here, *image* specifies the image that is displayed. The default constructor is also supported, and a constructor has been recently added that lets you specify the items in the menu. In all cases, the menu is empty until menu items are added to it. Furthermore, you can add or change a name and/or image after the fact by calling **setText( )** or **setGraphic( )**.

Each menu maintains a list of menu items that it contains. After a menu has been constructed, you can add an item to the menu by adding items to this list. To do so, first call **getItems( )**, shown here:

    final ObservableList<MenuItem> getItems( )

It returns the list of items currently associated with the menu. To this list, add menu items by calling either **add( )** or **addAll( )**. Among other actions, you can remove an item by calling **remove( )** and obtain the size of the list by calling **size( )**.

One other point: You can add a menu separator to the list of menu items, which is an object of type **SeparatorMenuItem**. Separators help organize long menus by allowing you to group related items together. A separator can also help set off an important item, such as the Exit selection in a menu.

MenuItem

MenuItem encapsulates an element in a menu. This element can either be a selection linked to some program action, such as Save or Close, or it can cause a submenu to be displayed. **MenuItem** defines the following three constructors:

MenuItem( )

MenuItem(String *name*)

MenuItem(String *name*, Node *image*)

The first creates an empty menu item. The second lets you specify the name of the item, and the third enables you to include an image.

A **MenuItem** generates an action event when selected. You can register an action event handler for such an event by calling **setOnAction( )**, just as you do when handling button events. You can fire an action event on a menu item by calling **fire( )**.

MenuItem defines several methods. One that is often useful is **setDisable( )**, which you can use to enable or disable a menu item. It is shown here:

final void setDisable(boolean *disable*)

If *disable* is **true**, the menu item is disabled and cannot be selected. If *disable* is **false**, the item is enabled. Using **setDisable( )**, you can turn menu items on or off, depending on program conditions.

Create a Main Menu

As a general rule, the most commonly used menu of any application is the *main menu*. This is the menu defined by the menu bar, and it is the menu that defines all (or nearly all) of the functionality of the program. As you will see, JavaFX streamlines the process of creating and managing the main menu. Here, you will learn how to construct a simple main menu. Subsequent sections will show various options.

Constructing the main menu requires several steps. Here is one approach. First, create the **MenuBar** instance that will hold the menus. Next, construct each menu that will be in the menu bar. In general, a menu is constructed by first creating a **Menu** object and then adding **MenuItem**s to it. After the menus have been created, add them to the menu bar. Then, the menu bar itself must be added to the scene graph. Finally, for each menu item, you must add an action event handler that responds to the action event fired when a menu item is selected.

NOTE
If you are using a recent version of JavaFX 8 (one that incorporates update 40), then you can also add menu items when you construct the menu and specify the menus when you construct the menu bar, although this approach may not be applicable to all situations. This book will use the traditional approach.

A good way to understand the process of creating and managing menus is to work through an example. Here is a program that creates a simple menu bar that contains three menus. The first is a standard File menu that contains Open, Close, Save, and Exit selections. The second menu is called Options, and it contains two submenus called Input Devices and Clock Style, and a Reset entry. The third menu is called Help, and it has one item: About. When a menu item is selected, the name of the selection is displayed in a label.

```java
// Demonstrate Menus

import javafx.application.*;
import javafx.scene.*;
import javafx.stage.*;
import javafx.scene.layout.*;
import javafx.scene.control.*;
import javafx.event.*;
import javafx.geometry.*;

public class MenuDemo extends Application {

  Label response;

  public static void main(String[] args) {

    // Start the JavaFX application by calling launch().
    launch(args);
  }

  // Override the start() method.
  public void start(Stage myStage) {

    // Give the stage a title.
    myStage.setTitle("Demonstrate Menus");

    // Use a BorderPane for the root node.
    BorderPane rootNode = new BorderPane();

     // Create a scene.
    Scene myScene = new Scene(rootNode, 300, 300);

    // Set the scene on the stage.
    myStage.setScene(myScene);

    // Create a label that will report the selection.
    response = new Label("Menu Demo");

    // Create the menu bar.
    MenuBar mb = new MenuBar();
```

```
// Create the File menu.
Menu fileMenu = new Menu("File");
MenuItem open = new MenuItem("Open");
MenuItem close = new MenuItem("Close");
MenuItem save = new MenuItem("Save");
MenuItem exit = new MenuItem("Exit");
fileMenu.getItems().addAll(open, close, save,
                           new SeparatorMenuItem(), exit);

// Add File menu to the menu bar.
mb.getMenus().add(fileMenu);

// Create the Options menu.
Menu optionsMenu = new Menu("Options");

// Create the Input Devices submenu.
Menu inDevicesMenu = new Menu("Input Devices");
MenuItem keyboard = new MenuItem("Keyboard");
MenuItem mouse = new MenuItem("Mouse");
MenuItem touchscreen = new MenuItem("Touchscreen");
inDevicesMenu.getItems().addAll(keyboard, mouse, touchscreen);
optionsMenu.getItems().add(inDevicesMenu);

// Create the Clock Style submenu.
Menu clockMenu = new Menu("Clock Style");
MenuItem analog = new MenuItem("Analog");
MenuItem digital = new MenuItem("Digital");
clockMenu.getItems().addAll(analog, digital);
optionsMenu.getItems().add(clockMenu);

// Add a separator.
optionsMenu.getItems().add(new SeparatorMenuItem());

// Create the Reset menu item.
MenuItem reset = new MenuItem("Reset");
optionsMenu.getItems().add(reset);

// Add Options menu to the menu bar.
mb.getMenus().add(optionsMenu);

// Create the Help menu.
Menu helpMenu = new Menu("Help");
MenuItem about = new MenuItem("About");
helpMenu.getItems().add(about);

// Add Help menu to the menu bar.
mb.getMenus().add(helpMenu);

// Create one event handler that will handle all menu action events.
EventHandler<ActionEvent> MEHandler =
                       new EventHandler<ActionEvent>() {
```

```
   public void handle(ActionEvent ae) {
     String name = ((MenuItem)ae.getTarget()).getText();

     // If Exit is chosen, the program is terminated.
     if(name.equals("Exit")) Platform.exit();

     response.setText( name + " selected");
   }
};

// Set action event handlers for the menu items.
open.setOnAction(MEHandler);
close.setOnAction(MEHandler);
save.setOnAction(MEHandler);
exit.setOnAction(MEHandler);
keyboard.setOnAction(MEHandler);
mouse.setOnAction(MEHandler);
touchscreen.setOnAction(MEHandler);
analog.setOnAction(MEHandler);
digital.setOnAction(MEHandler);
reset.setOnAction(MEHandler);
about.setOnAction(MEHandler);

// Add the menu bar to the top of the border pane and
// the response label to the center position.
rootNode.setTop(mb);
rootNode.setCenter(response);

// Show the stage and its scene.
myStage.show();
  }
}
```

Sample output is shown here:

Let's examine in detail how the menus in this program are created, beginning with the **MenuDemo** constructor. Note that it uses a **BorderPane** instance for the root node. As explained in Chapter 5, it defines a layout that has five areas: top, bottom, left, right, and center. Later in the program, the menu bar is positioned in the top location and a label that displays the menu selection is set to the center position. Setting the menu bar to the top position ensures that it will be shown at the top of the application and will automatically be resized to fit the horizontal width of the window. This is why **BorderPane** is used in the menu examples. Of course, other layouts, such as using a **VBox**, are also valid.

Much of the code in the program is used to construct the menu bar, its menus, and menu items, and this code warrants a close inspection. First, the menu bar is constructed and a reference to it is assigned to **mb** by this statement:

```
// Create the menu bar.
MenuBar mb = new MenuBar();
```

At this point, the menu bar is empty. It will be populated by the menus that follow.

Next, the File menu and its menu entries are created by this sequence:

```
// Create the File menu.
Menu fileMenu = new Menu("File");
MenuItem open = new MenuItem("Open");
MenuItem close = new MenuItem("Close");
MenuItem save = new MenuItem("Save");
MenuItem exit = new MenuItem("Exit");
```

The names Open, Close, Save, and Exit will be shown as selections in the menu. The menu entries are added to the File menu by this call to **addAll( )** on the list of menu items returned by **getItems( )**:

```
fileMenu.getItems().addAll(open, close, save,
                    new SeparatorMenuItem(), exit);
```

Recall that **getItems( )** returns the menu items associated with a **Menu** instance. To add menu items to a menu, you can add them to this list. Notice that a separator is used to visually separate the Exit entry from the others.

Finally, the File menu is added to the menu bar by this line:

```
// Add File menu to the menu bar.
mb.getMenus().add(fileMenu);
```

Once the preceding code sequence completes, the menu bar will contain one entry: File. The File menu will contain four selections in this order: Open, Close, Save, and Exit.

The Options menu is constructed using the same basic process as the File menu. However, the Options menu consists of two submenus, Input Devices and Clock Style, and a Reset entry. The submenus are first constructed individually and then added to the Options menu. As explained, because **Menu** inherits **MenuItem**, a **Menu** can be added as an entry into another **Menu**. This is the way submenus are created. The Reset item is added last. Then, the Options menu is added to the menu bar. The Help menu is constructed using the same process.

After all of the menus have been constructed, an **ActionEvent** handler called **MEHandler** is created that will process menu selections. For demonstration purposes, a single handler will process all selections, but in a real-world application, it is often easier to specify a separate handler for each individual selection by use of anonymous inner classes or lambda expressions. The **ActionEvent** handler for the menu items is shown here:

```
// Create one event handler that will handle all menu events.
EventHandler<ActionEvent> MEHandler = new EventHandler<ActionEvent>() {
  public void handle(ActionEvent ae) {
    String name = ((MenuItem)ae.getTarget()).getText();

    // If Exit is chosen, the program is terminated.
    if(name.equals("Exit")) Platform.exit();

    response.setText( name + " selected");
  }
};
```

Inside **handle( )**, the target of the event is obtained by calling **getTarget( )**. The returned reference is cast to **MenuItem** and its name is obtained by calling **getText( )**. This string is then assigned to **name**. If **name** contains the string "Exit", the application is terminated by calling **Platform.exit( )**. Otherwise, the name is displayed in the **response** label.

Before continuing, it must be pointed out that a JavaFX application must call **Platform.exit( )**, not **System.exit( )**. The **Platform** class is defined by JavaFX and packaged in **javafx.application**. Its **exit( )** method causes the **stop( )** life-cycle method to be called; **System.exit( )** does not.

Finally, **MEHandler** is registered as the action event handler for each menu item by the following statements:

```
// Set action event handlers for the menu items.
open.setOnAction(MEHandler);
close.setOnAction(MEHandler);
save.setOnAction(MEHandler);
exit.setOnAction(MEHandler);
keyboard.setOnAction(MEHandler);
mouse.setOnAction(MEHandler);
touchscreen.setOnAction(MEHandler);
analog.setOnAction(MEHandler);
digital.setOnAction(MEHandler);
reset.setOnAction(MEHandler);
about.setOnAction(MEHandler);
```

Notice that no listeners are added to the Input Devices or Clock Style items because they are not actually selections. They simply activate submenus.

Finally, the menu bar is added to the root node by the following line:

```
rootNode.setTop(mb);
```

This causes the menu bar to be placed at the top of the window.

At this point, you might want to experiment a bit with the **MenuDemo** program. Try adding another menu or adding more items to an existing menu. It is important that you understand the basic menu concepts before moving on because this program will evolve throughout the remainder of this chapter.

Add Mnemonics and Accelerators to Menu Items

The menu created in the preceding example is functional, but it is possible to make it better. In real applications, a menu usually includes support for keyboard shortcuts. These come in two forms: accelerators and mnemonics. An *accelerator* is a key combination that lets you select a menu item without having to first activate the menu. As it applies to menus, a *mnemonic* defines a key that lets you select an item from an active menu by typing the key. Thus, a mnemonic allows you to use the keyboard to select an item from a menu that is already being displayed.

An accelerator can be associated with a **Menu** or **MenuItem**. It is specified by calling **setAccelerator( )**, shown next:

final void setAccelerator(KeyCombination *keyComb*)

Here, *keyComb* is the key combination that is pressed to select the menu item. **KeyCombination** is a class that encapsulates a key combination, such as CTRL-S. It is packaged in **javafx.scene.input**.

KeyCombination defines two **protected** constructors, but often you will use the **keyCombination( )** factory method, shown here:

static KeyCombination keyCombination(String *keys*)

Here, *keys* is a string that specifies the key combination. It typically consists of a modifier, such as CTRL, ALT, or SHIFT, and a letter, such as s. There is a special value, called **shortcut**, which can be used to specify the control key in a Windows system and the meta key on a Mac. (It also maps to the typically used shortcut key on other types of systems.) Therefore, if you want to specify CTRL-S as the key combination for Save, then use the string "shortcut+S". This way, it will work for both Windows and Mac, and elsewhere.

The following sequence adds accelerators to the File menu created by the **MenuDemo** program in the previous section. After making this change, you can directly select a File menu option by pressing CTRL-O, CTRL-C, CTRL-S, or CTRL-E.

```
// Add keyboard accelerators for the File menu.
open.setAccelerator(KeyCombination.keyCombination("shortcut+O"));
close.setAccelerator(KeyCombination.keyCombination("shortcut+C"));
save.setAccelerator(KeyCombination.keyCombination("shortcut+S"));
exit.setAccelerator(KeyCombination.keyCombination("shortcut+E"));
```

You will also need to import **javafx.scene.input.***;.

A mnemonic can be specified for both **MenuItem** and **Menu** objects, and it is easy to do. Simply precede the letter in the name of the menu or menu item with an underscore. For example, in the preceding example, to add the mnemonic *F* to the File menu, declare **fileMenu** as shown here:

```
Menu fileMenu = new Menu("_File"); // now defines a mnemonic
```

After making this change, you can select the File menu by pressing ALT and then F. However, mnemonics will be active only if mnemonic parsing is enabled (as it is by default). You can turn mnemonic parsing on or off by using **setMnemonicParsing( )**, shown here:

final void setMnemonicParsing(boolean *enable*)

Here, if *enable* is **true**, then mnemonic parsing is turned on. Otherwise, it is turned off.

After making these changes, the File menu will now look like this:

Add Images to Menu Items

You can add images to menu items or use images instead of text. The easiest way to add an image is to specify it when the menu item is being constructed using this constructor:

MenuItem(String *name*, Node *image*)

It creates a menu item with the name specified by *name* and the image specified by *image*. For example, here the Clock Style menu items are associated with images when they are created:

```
MenuItem analog = new MenuItem("Analog", new ImageView("analog.png"));
MenuItem digital = new MenuItem("Digital", new ImageView("digital.png"));
```

You will also need to import **javafx.scene.image.***. After these additions, the images will be displayed next to the text when the Clock Style menu is displayed, as shown here:

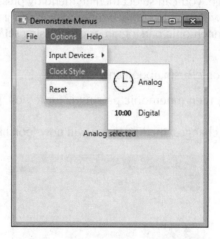

One last point: You can also add an image to a menu item after the item has been created by calling **setGraphic( )**. This lets you change the image during program execution.

Use RadioMenuItem and CheckMenuItem

In addition to the standard type of menu items just shown, JavaFX defines two others: check menu items and radio menu items. These elements can streamline a GUI by allowing a menu to provide functionality that would otherwise require additional stand-alone components. Also, sometimes check or radio menu items simply seem the most natural way to include a specific set of options. Whatever your reason, it is easy to use check and/or radio menu items in menus, and both are examined here.

To add a check menu item to a menu, use **CheckMenuItem**. It defines three constructors, which parallel the ones defined by **MenuItem**. The one used in this chapter is shown here:

CheckMenuItem(String *name*)

Here, *name* specifies the name of the item. The initial state of the check box is unchecked. If you want to check a check menu item under program control, call **setSelected( )**, shown here:

final void setSelected(boolean *selected*)

If *selected* is **true**, the menu item is checked. Otherwise, it is unchecked.

Like stand-alone check boxes, check menu items generate action events when their state is changed. Check menu items are especially appropriate in menus when you have options that can be selected and you want to display their selected/ deselected status.

A radio menu item can be added to a menu by creating an object of type **RadioMenuItem**. **RadioMenuItem** defines a number of constructors. The one used in this chapter is shown here:

RadioMenuItem(String *name*)

It creates a radio menu item that has the name passed in *name*. The item is not selected. As with the case of check menu items, to select a radio menu item, call **setSelected( )**, passing **true** as an argument.

RadioMenuItem works like a stand-alone radio button, generating both change and action events. Like stand-alone radio buttons, radio menu items must be put into a toggle group in order for them to exhibit mutually exclusive selection behavior.

Because both **CheckMenuItem** and **RadioMenuItem** inherit **MenuItem**, each has all of the functionality provided by **MenuItem**. Aside from having the extra capabilities of check boxes and radio buttons, they act like and are used like other menu items.

To try check and radio menu items, first remove the code that creates the Options menu in the **MenuDemo** example program. Then substitute the following code sequence, which uses check menu items for the Input Devices submenu and radio menu items for the Clock Style submenu:

```
// Create the Options menu.
Menu optionsMenu = new Menu("Options");

// Create the Input Devices submenu.
Menu inDevicesMenu = new Menu("Input Devices");

// Use check menu items for input devices. This allows
// the user to select more than one device.
```

```
CheckMenuItem keyboard = new CheckMenuItem("Keyboard");
CheckMenuItem mouse = new CheckMenuItem("Mouse");
CheckMenuItem touchscreen = new CheckMenuItem("Touchscreen");

inDevicesMenu.getItems().addAll(keyboard, mouse, touchscreen);

optionsMenu.getItems().add(inDevicesMenu);

// Select mouse for the default selection.
mouse.setSelected(true);

// Create the Clock Style submenu.
Menu clockMenu = new Menu("Clock Style");

// Use radio menu items for the clock style.
// This lets the menu show which clock is used
// and also ensures that one and only one clock
// can be selected at any one time.
RadioMenuItem analog = new RadioMenuItem("Analog");
RadioMenuItem digital = new RadioMenuItem("Digital");

// Create a toggle group and use it for the radio menu items.
ToggleGroup tg = new ToggleGroup();
analog.setToggleGroup(tg);
digital.setToggleGroup(tg);

// Select Analog for the default selection.
analog.setSelected(true);

// Add the radio menu items to the Clock Style menu and
// add it to the Options menu.
clockMenu.getItems().addAll(analog, digital);
optionsMenu.getItems().add(clockMenu);

// Add a separator.
optionsMenu.getItems().add(new SeparatorMenuItem());

// Create the Reset menu item.
MenuItem reset = new MenuItem("Reset");
optionsMenu.getItems().add(reset);

// Add Options menu to the menu bar.
mb.getMenus().add(optionsMenu);
```

After making the substitution, the check menu items in the Input Devices submenu will look like those shown here:

Here is how the radio menu items in the Clock Style submenu now look:

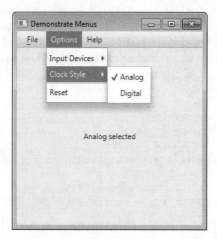

Although the two types of menu items look similar, they behave differently. With radio menu items, you can select only one at a time. With check menu items, you can select zero or more items.

Create a Context Menu

A popular alternative or supplement to the menu bar is the popup menu, which in JavaFX is referred to as a *context menu*. Typically, a context menu is activated by clicking the right mouse button when over a control. Popup menus are supported in JavaFX by the **ContextMenu** class. The direct superclass of **ContextMenu** is

PopupControl. An indirect superclass of **ContextMenu** is **javafx.stage.PopupWindow**, which supplies much of its basic functionality.

ContextMenu has two constructors. The one used in this chapter is shown here:

ContextMenu(MenuItems ... *menuItems*)

Here, *menuItems* specify the menu items that will constitute the context menu. The second **ContextMenu** constructor creates an empty menu to which items must be added.

In general, context menus are constructed like regular menus. Menu items are created and added to the menu. Menu item selections are also handled in the same way: by handling action events. The main difference between a context menu and regular menu is the activation process.

To associate a context menu with a control is amazingly easy. Simply call **setContextMenu( )** on the control, passing in a reference to the menu that you want to pop up. When you right-click on that control, the associated context menu will be shown. The **setContextMenu( )** method is shown here:

final void setContextMenu(ContextMenu *menu*)

Here, *menu* specifies the context menu associated with the invoking control.

To demonstrate a context menu, we will add one to the **MenuDemo** program. The context menu will present a standard "Edit" menu that includes the Cut, Copy, and Paste entries. It will be set on a text field control. When the mouse is right-clicked while in the text field, the context menu will pop up. To begin, create the context menu as shown here:

```
// Create the context menu items
MenuItem cut = new MenuItem("Cut");
MenuItem copy = new MenuItem("Copy");
MenuItem paste = new MenuItem("Paste");

// Create a context (i.e., popup) menu that shows edit options.
final ContextMenu editMenu = new ContextMenu(cut, copy, paste);
```

This sequence begins by constructing the **MenuItem**s that will form the menu. It then creates an instance of **ContextMenu** called **editMenu** that contains the items.

Next, add the action event handler to these menu items, as shown here:

```
cut.setOnAction(MEHandler);
copy.setOnAction(MEHandler);
paste.setOnAction(MEHandler);
```

This finishes the construction of the context menu, but the menu has not yet been associated with a control.

Now, add the following sequence that creates the text field:

```
// Create a text field and set its column width to 20.
TextField tf = new TextField();
tf.setPrefColumnCount(20);
```

Next, set the context menu on the text field:

```
// Add the context menu to the text field.
tf.setContextMenu(editMenu);
```

Now, when the mouse is right-clicked over the text field, the context menu will pop up.

To add the text field to the program, you must create a flow pane that will hold both the text field and the response label. This pane will then be added to the center of the **BorderPane**. This step is necessary because only one node can be added to any single location within a **BorderPane**. First, remove this line of code:

```
rootNode.setCenter(response);
```

Replace it with the following code:

```
// Create a flow pane that will hold both the response
// label and the text field.
FlowPane fpRoot = new FlowPane(10, 10);

// Center the controls in the scene.
fpRoot.setAlignment(Pos.CENTER);

// Add both the label and the text field to the flow pane.
fpRoot.getChildren().addAll(response, tf);

// Add the flow pane to the center of the border layout.
rootNode.setCenter(fpRoot);
```

Of course, the menu bar is still added to the top position of the border pane. After making these changes, when you right-click over the text field, the context menu will pop up, as shown here:

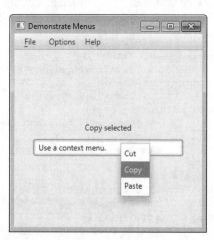

Create a Toolbar

A toolbar is a component that can serve both as an alternative and as an adjunct to a menu. Typically, a toolbar contains a list of buttons that give the user immediate access to various program options. For example, a toolbar might contain buttons that select various font options, such as bold, italics, highlighted, or underlined. These options can be selected without the need to drop through a menu. As a general rule, toolbar buttons show images rather than text, although either or both are allowed. Furthermore, often tooltips are associated with image-based toolbar buttons.

In JavaFX, toolbars are instances of the **ToolBar** class. It defines the two constructors. Here is the one we will use:

ToolBar(Node ... *nodes*)

This constructor creates a horizontal toolbar that contains the specified nodes, which are usually some form of button. If you want to create a vertical toolbar, call **setOrientation( )** on the toolbar, passing in **Orientation.VERTICAL**.

Buttons (or other controls) can be added to a toolbar in much the same way that they are added to a menu bar: by calling **add( )** on the reference returned by the **getItems( )** method. Often, however, it is easier to specify the items in the **ToolBar** constructor, and that is the approach used in this chapter. Once you have created a toolbar, add it to the scene graph. For example, when using a border layout, it could be added to the bottom location. Of course, other approaches are commonly used. For example, it could be added to a location directly under the menu bar or on the side of the window (if using a vertical toolbar).

To illustrate a toolbar, we will add one to the **MenuDemo** program. The toolbar will present four color options: Red, Green, Blue, and Black. Selecting a color causes the text displayed in the **response** label to be set to that color. We will also add tooltips to these items. Recall from Chapter 3, a *tooltip* is a small message that describes an item. It is automatically displayed if the mouse remains over the item for a moment. Tooltips are especially useful when applied to image-based toolbar controls because sometimes it's hard to design images that are intuitive to all users.

First, add the following code, which creates the colors toolbar:

```
// Define a toolbar. First, create toolbar items.
Button btnRed = new Button("Red",
                          new ImageView("red.png"));
Button btnGreen = new Button("Green",
                          new ImageView("green.png"));
Button btnBlue = new Button("Blue",
                          new ImageView("blue.png"));
Button btnBlack = new Button("Black",
                          new ImageView("black.png"));

// Now, turn off text in the buttons.
btnRed.setContentDisplay(ContentDisplay.GRAPHIC_ONLY);
btnGreen.setContentDisplay(ContentDisplay.GRAPHIC_ONLY);
btnBlue.setContentDisplay(ContentDisplay.GRAPHIC_ONLY);
btnBlack.setContentDisplay(ContentDisplay.GRAPHIC_ONLY);
```

```
// Set tooltips.
btnRed.setTooltip(new Tooltip("Select red label text."));
btnGreen.setTooltip(new Tooltip("Select green label text."));
btnBlue.setTooltip(new Tooltip("Select blue label text."));
btnBlack.setTooltip(new Tooltip("Select black label text."));

// Create the toolbar.
ToolBar tbTextColor = new ToolBar(btnRed, btnGreen, btnBlue, btnBlack);
```

Let's look at this code closely. First, four buttons are created that correspond to the text colors. Notice that each has an image associated with it. The images display the letters *ABC* in the indicated color. Next, each button deactivates the text display by calling **setContentDisplay( )**. As a point of interest, it would have been possible to leave the text displayed, but for the sake of illustration, the text is not used here. (The text for each button is still needed, however, because it will be used by the action event handler for the buttons.) Tooltips are then set for each button. Finally, the toolbar is created, with the buttons specified as the contents.

Next, add the following sequence, which defines an action event handler for the toolbar buttons:

```
// Create a handler for the toolbar buttons.
EventHandler<ActionEvent> btnHandler = new EventHandler<ActionEvent>() {
  public void handle(ActionEvent ae) {
    String color = ((Button)ae.getTarget()).getText();
    response.setText("Label text set to " + color);
    switch(color) {
      case "Red": response.setTextFill(Color.RED);
        break;
      case "Green": response.setTextFill(Color.GREEN);
        break;
      case "Blue": response.setTextFill(Color.BLUE);
        break;
      case "Black": response.setTextFill(Color.BLACK);
    }
  }
};

// Set the toolbar button action event handlers.
btnRed.setOnAction(btnHandler);
btnGreen.setOnAction(btnHandler);
btnBlue.setOnAction(btnHandler);
btnBlack.setOnAction(btnHandler);
```

Notice that the text color of the **response** label is set by a call to **setTextFill( )**. This method is provided by the **Labeled** class. Thus, it can be used with any labeled control. Each time a color is selected, the color of the text in **response** is changed. Because **Color** is in **javafx.scene.paint**, you will need to import this package.

Finally, add the toolbar to the bottom of the border layout by use of this statement:

```
rootNode.setBottom(tbTextColor);
```

After making these additions, each time the user presses a toolbar button, an action event is fired and it is handled by displaying the button's text in the **response** label. The following output shows the toolbar in action:

Use MenuButton

Both context menus and toolbars expand the ways in which a menu can be integrated into your design. JavaFX offers one more option: the menu button. Menu buttons are supported by the **MenuButton** class. It provides a mechanism that links a push button with a drop-down menu. Normally, only the button is shown, but when it is pressed, a menu drops down. Therefore, the menu button offers a compact way to add a menu to a layout because it will show only when needed. This makes **MenuButton** especially useful when screen space is limited.

MenuButton defines several constructors. The one we will use is shown here:

MenuButton(String *str*)

Here, *str* is the text shown in the button.

You can add menu items to a **MenuButton** just as you do when using **Menu**. For example, you can add them to the list of items returned by **getItems( )**, shown here:

final ObservableList<MenuItem> getItems( )

Because **MenuButton** holds **MenuItem**s, the same mechanism used to handle menu selections in a **Menu** also applies to menu selections in a **MenuButton** menu.

You can try **MenuButton** by adding these lines to the **MenuDemo** program. It creates a menu that lets you choose a network connection.

```
// Create a menu button.
MenuButton mBtnConnect = new MenuButton("Connection");
MenuItem wireless = new MenuItem("Wireless");
```

```
MenuItem wifi = new MenuItem("Wi-Fi");
MenuItem satellite = new MenuItem("Satellite");

// Add the menu items to the menu button.
mBtnConnect.getItems().addAll(wireless, wifi, satellite);
```

As is the case with any other **MenuItem**, each time one of the menu items is selected from a button menu, an action event is generated. For example, here is a lambda expression that handles the **wifi** item:

```
wifi.setOnAction( (ae) -> response.setText("Wi-Fi Selected."));
```

You might want to try adding handlers for the other buttons on your own. Of course, you don't have to use a lambda expression. You can use any appropriate method to implement the action event handler. For example, in the **MenuDemo** program, you can simply let **MEHandler** handle the events, as it does for the other menu items.

You will also need to add **mBtnConnect** to **fpRoot** (which was added by the context menu example), as shown here:

```
fpRoot.getChildren().addAll(response, tf, mBtnConnect);
```

Here is sample output after these changes have been made:

There is a subclass of **MenuButton** called **SplitMenuButton**. It provides a sometimes useful variation of **MenuButton** that contains two parts. The first is a button, which works like any other button. The second is a drop-down menu activator. When pressed, it causes the menu to drop down. You might find it interesting to experiment with **SplitMenuButton** on your own.

Create a CustomMenuItem

Although not needed in many situations, one of JavaFX's most exciting menu options is **CustomMenuItem** because it enables you to include a control (or any other **Node**) in a menu. For example, you might include a button to activate some function, a slider to set some program parameter, or a list view to select an option. Although a custom menu item won't often be needed, when it is needed, it can be quite effective.

Custom menu items are supported by the **CustomMenuItem** class. It inherits **MenuItem**, so it can be an entry in any type of menu. **CustomMenuItem** offers three constructors. The one we will use is shown here:

CustomMenuItem(Node *item*)

Here, *item* specifies the node to be added, which will often be some form of control. For example, the following creates a Stop button in a menu item:

```
Button btnStop = new Button("Stop!");
CustomMenuItem stop = new CustomMenuItem(btnStop);
```

Because the custom menu item is a button, you can respond to events on that button using the same basic approach as you would with any other button. For example, here is an action event handler that can be used with the **MenuDemo** program:

```
btnStop.setOnAction(new EventHandler<ActionEvent>() {
  public void handle(ActionEvent ae) {
    response.setText("Transfer stopped!");
  }
});
```

To see the effect of the Stop menu button, add it to the end of the menu button **mBtnConnect** from the previous example. After doing so, the menu will look like the one shown here:

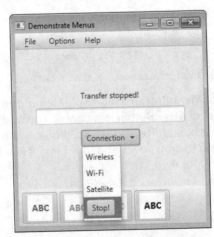

In some cases, such as if you embed a slider as a menu item, you may not want the menu to disappear when you adjust the setting. To prevent the menu from disappearing, set the **hideOnClick** property to **false**. One way to do this is to use this constructor:

CustomMenuItem(Node *item*, boolean *hide*)

If *hide* is **true**, the menu is hidden after a click. If it is **false**, the menu stays displayed. Understand, however, that this setting won't affect the button in the preceding example. In this case, whether **hideOnClick** is **true** or **false**, once you click the button, the menu will disappear because the button action is complete.

One more point: although you can include just about any control (or other **Node**) in a menu via a **CustomMenuItem**, don't be surprised if some of them seem awkward and inappropriate. The effective use of custom menu items is often more a matter of art than science.

Put the Entire MenuDemo Program Together

Throughout the course of this discussion, many changes and additions have been made to the **MenuDemo** program shown at the start of the chapter. Before concluding, it will be helpful to assemble all the pieces. Doing so not only eliminates any ambiguity about the way the pieces fit together, but it also gives you a complete menu demonstration program with which you can experiment.

The following version of **MenuDemo** includes all of the additions and enhancements described in this chapter. For clarity, the program has been reorganized, with separate methods being used to construct the various menus and toolbar. Notice that several of the menu-related variables, such as **mb** and **tbTextColor**, have been made into instance variables so they can be directly accessed by any part of the class.

```
// Demonstrate Menus -- Final Version

import javafx.application.*;
import javafx.scene.*;
import javafx.stage.*;
import javafx.scene.layout.*;
import javafx.scene.control.*;
import javafx.event.*;
import javafx.geometry.*;
import javafx.scene.input.*;
import javafx.scene.image.*;
import javafx.beans.value.*;
import javafx.scene.paint.*;
```

```java
public class MenuDemoFinal extends Application {

  MenuBar mb;
  EventHandler<ActionEvent> MEHandler;
  ContextMenu editMenu;
  ToolBar tbTextColor;
  MenuButton mBtnConnect;

  Label response;

  public static void main(String[] args) {

    // Start the JavaFX application by calling launch().
    launch(args);
  }

  // Override the start() method.
  public void start(Stage myStage) {

    // Give the stage a title.
    myStage.setTitle("Demonstrate Menus -- Final Version");

    // Use a BorderPane for the root node.
    final BorderPane rootNode = new BorderPane();

     // Create a scene.
    Scene myScene = new Scene(rootNode, 300, 300);

    // Set the scene on the stage.
    myStage.setScene(myScene);

    // Create a label that will report the selection.
    response = new Label();

    // Create one event handler for all menu action events.
    MEHandler = new EventHandler<ActionEvent>() {
      public void handle(ActionEvent ae) {
        String name = ((MenuItem)ae.getTarget()).getText();

        if(name.equals("Exit")) Platform.exit();

        response.setText( name + " selected");
      }
    };

    // Create the menu bar.
    mb = new MenuBar();

    // Create the File menu.
    makeFileMenu();
```

```
    // Create the Options menu.
    makeOptionsMenu();

    // Create the Help menu.
    makeHelpMenu();

    // Create the context menu.
    makeContextMenu();

    // Create a text field and set its column width to 20.
    TextField tf = new TextField();
    tf.setPrefColumnCount(20);

    // Add the context menu to the text field.
    tf.setContextMenu(editMenu);

    // Create the toolbar.
    makeToolBar();

    // Create the menu button.
    makeMenuButton();

    // Add the menu bar to the top of the border pane.
    rootNode.setTop(mb);

    // Create a flow pane that will hold both the response
    // label and the text field.
    FlowPane fpRoot = new FlowPane(10, 10);

    // Center the controls in the scene.
    fpRoot.setAlignment(Pos.CENTER);

    // Use a separator to better organize the layout.
    Separator separator = new Separator();
    separator.setPrefWidth(260);

    // Add the label, separator, text, and menu button
    // field to the flow pane.
    fpRoot.getChildren().addAll(response, separator,  tf, mBtnConnect);

    // Add the toolbar to the bottom of the border pane.
    rootNode.setBottom(tbTextColor);

    // Add the flow pane to the center of the border layout.
    rootNode.setCenter(fpRoot);

    // Show the stage and its scene.
    myStage.show();
}
```

```
// Create the File menu.
void makeFileMenu() {
  // Create the File menu, including a mnemonic.
  Menu fileMenu = new Menu("_File");

  // Create the File menu items.
  MenuItem open = new MenuItem("Open");
  MenuItem close = new MenuItem("Close");
  MenuItem save = new MenuItem("Save");
  MenuItem exit = new MenuItem("Exit");

  // Add items to File menu.
  fileMenu.getItems().addAll(open, close, save,
                             new SeparatorMenuItem(), exit);

  // Add keyboard accelerators for the File menu.
  open.setAccelerator(KeyCombination.keyCombination("shortcut+O"));
  close.setAccelerator(KeyCombination.keyCombination("shortcut+C"));
  save.setAccelerator(KeyCombination.keyCombination("shortcut+S"));
  exit.setAccelerator(KeyCombination.keyCombination("shortcut+E"));

  // Set action event handlers.
  open.setOnAction(MEHandler);
  close.setOnAction(MEHandler);
  save.setOnAction(MEHandler);
  exit.setOnAction(MEHandler);

  // Add File menu to the menu bar.
  mb.getMenus().add(fileMenu);
}

// Create the Options menu.
void makeOptionsMenu() {
  Menu optionsMenu = new Menu("Options");

  // Create the Input Devices submenu.
  Menu inDevicesMenu = new Menu("Input Devices");

  // Use check menu items for input devices. This allows
  // the user to select more than one device.
  CheckMenuItem keyboard = new CheckMenuItem("Keyboard");
  CheckMenuItem mouse = new CheckMenuItem("Mouse");
  CheckMenuItem touchscreen = new CheckMenuItem("Touchscreen");

  // Add the check menu items to the Input Devices menu and
  // then add this menu to the Options menu.
  inDevicesMenu.getItems().addAll(keyboard, mouse, touchscreen);
  optionsMenu.getItems().add(inDevicesMenu);
```

```
// Select mouse for the default selection.
mouse.setSelected(true);

// Create the Clock Style submenu.
Menu clockMenu = new Menu("Clock Style");

// Use radio menu items for the clock style.
// This lets the menu show which clock is used
// and also ensures that one and only one clock
// can be selected at any one time.
RadioMenuItem analog =
  new RadioMenuItem("Analog", new ImageView("analog.png"));
RadioMenuItem digital =
  new RadioMenuItem("Digital", new ImageView("digital.png"));

// Create a toggle group and use it for the radio menu items.
ToggleGroup tg = new ToggleGroup();
analog.setToggleGroup(tg);
digital.setToggleGroup(tg);

// Select Analog for the default selection.
analog.setSelected(true);

// Add the radio menu items to the Clock Style menu and
// then add the menu to the Options menu.
clockMenu.getItems().addAll(analog, digital);
optionsMenu.getItems().add(clockMenu);

// Add a separator.
optionsMenu.getItems().add(new SeparatorMenuItem());

// Create the Reset menu item and add it to the Options menu.
MenuItem reset = new MenuItem("Reset");
optionsMenu.getItems().add(reset);

// Set action event handlers.
keyboard.setOnAction(MEHandler);
mouse.setOnAction(MEHandler);
touchscreen.setOnAction(MEHandler);
analog.setOnAction(MEHandler);
digital.setOnAction(MEHandler);
reset.setOnAction(MEHandler);

// Use a change listener to respond to changes in the radio
// menu item setting.
tg.selectedToggleProperty().addListener(new ChangeListener<Toggle>() {
  public void changed(ObservableValue<? extends Toggle> changed,
                      Toggle oldVal, Toggle newVal) {
    if(newVal==null) return;
```

```
      // Cast newVal to RadioMenuItem.
      RadioMenuItem rmi = (RadioMenuItem) newVal;

      // Display the selection.
      response.setText("Clock Style selected is " + rmi.getText());
    }
  });

  // Add Options menu to the menu bar.
  mb.getMenus().add(optionsMenu);
}

// Create the Help menu.
void makeHelpMenu() {

  // Create the Help menu.
  Menu helpMenu = new Menu("Help");

  // Create the About menu item and add it to the Help menu.
  MenuItem about = new MenuItem("About");
  helpMenu.getItems().add(about);

  // Set action event handler.
  about.setOnAction(MEHandler);

  // Add Help menu to the menu bar.
  mb.getMenus().add(helpMenu);
}

// Create the context menu items.
void makeContextMenu() {

  // Create the edit context menu items.
  MenuItem cut = new MenuItem("Cut");
  MenuItem copy = new MenuItem("Copy");
  MenuItem paste = new MenuItem("Paste");

  // Create a context (i.e., popup) menu that shows edit options.
  editMenu = new ContextMenu(cut, copy, paste);

  // Set the action event handlers.
  cut.setOnAction(MEHandler);
  copy.setOnAction(MEHandler);
  paste.setOnAction(MEHandler);
}

// Create the toolbar.
void makeToolBar() {
  // Create toolbar items.
  Button btnRed = new Button("Red",
                             new ImageView("red.png"));
```

```
   Button btnGreen = new Button("Green",
                                new ImageView("green.png"));
   Button btnBlue = new Button("Blue",
                                 new ImageView("blue.png"));
   Button btnBlack = new Button("Black",
                                 new ImageView("black.png"));

   // Turn off text in the buttons.
   btnRed.setContentDisplay(ContentDisplay.GRAPHIC_ONLY);
   btnGreen.setContentDisplay(ContentDisplay.GRAPHIC_ONLY);
   btnBlue.setContentDisplay(ContentDisplay.GRAPHIC_ONLY);
   btnBlack.setContentDisplay(ContentDisplay.GRAPHIC_ONLY);

   // Set tooltips.
   btnRed.setTooltip(new Tooltip("Select red label text."));
   btnGreen.setTooltip(new Tooltip("Select green label text."));
   btnBlue.setTooltip(new Tooltip("Select blue label text."));
   btnBlack.setTooltip(new Tooltip("Select black label text."));

   // Create the toolbar.
   tbTextColor = new ToolBar(btnRed, btnGreen, btnBlue, btnBlack);

   // Create a handler for the toolbar buttons.
   EventHandler<ActionEvent> btnHandler = new EventHandler<ActionEvent>() {
     public void handle(ActionEvent ae) {
       String color = ((Button)ae.getTarget()).getText();
       response.setText("Label text set to " + color);
       switch(color) {
         case "Red": response.setTextFill(Color.RED);
           break;
         case "Green": response.setTextFill(Color.GREEN);
           break;
         case "Blue": response.setTextFill(Color.BLUE);
           break;
         case "Black": response.setTextFill(Color.BLACK);
       }
     }
   };

   // Set the toolbar button action event handlers.
   btnRed.setOnAction(btnHandler);
   btnGreen.setOnAction(btnHandler);
   btnBlue.setOnAction(btnHandler);
   btnBlack.setOnAction(btnHandler);
}

// Create a menu button.
void makeMenuButton() {
  mBtnConnect = new MenuButton("Connection");
```

```
MenuItem wireless = new MenuItem("Wireless");
MenuItem wifi = new MenuItem("Wi-Fi");
MenuItem satellite = new MenuItem("Satellite");

wireless.setOnAction(MEHandler);
wifi.setOnAction(MEHandler);
satellite.setOnAction(MEHandler);

Button btnStop = new Button("Stop!");
CustomMenuItem stop = new CustomMenuItem(btnStop);
// Assign a handler for the button.
btnStop.setOnAction(new EventHandler<ActionEvent>() {
  public void handle(ActionEvent ae) {
    response.setText("Transfer stopped!");
  }
});

// Add the menu items to the menu button.
mBtnConnect.getItems().addAll(wireless, wifi, satellite, stop);
  }
}
```

CHAPTER
9

Charts, WebView,
and Canvas

To conclude this introduction to JavaFX programming, we will look at three more user interface elements. The first is the chart. JavaFX supports several different types of chart classes, including **BarChart**, **LineChart**, and **PieChart**. The second is **WebView**, which is an extraordinarily powerful node that gives your program access to Web content. The third element is **Canvas**, which provides a surface upon which output can be directly drawn through the use of a graphics context. All three elements offer capabilities that streamline the use of JavaFX for a wide range of tasks.

Charts

JavaFX contains rich support for the graphical representation of data in a chart. You are no doubt familiar with charts because they are the means by which data is commonly depicted in its visual form. For example, stock prices, average rainfall, and sales figures are often displayed as a time series in a chart. There are several different types of charts, including bar, scatter, line, and pie. As a result, JavaFX supports several different chart classes. Although significant customization is possible, you will often find that the default configuration and features of these classes are just what you want. This makes JavaFX's approach to charts powerful, yet easy to use.

JavaFX supports eight types of charts, which are encapsulated by the following classes:

AreaChart	BarChart	BubbleChart
LineChart	PieChart	ScatterChart
StackedAreaChart	StackedBarChart	

Of these, all but **PieChart** work in the same general way. Thus, once you know how to use one, you can easily use others. In fact, as you will see, in many cases you can change the chart used in a program by simply substituting one chart class for another. No other changes are needed. This makes it easy to experiment with different chart types to see which best fits your application.

All charts in JavaFX are subclasses of the abstract **Chart** class. A superclass of **Chart** is **Node**. Thus, all chart classes are nodes that can be added to a scene graph. There are two subclasses of **Chart**, called **XYChart** and **PieChart**. **XYChart** is a superclass for all charts based on an X,Y graph. This includes all chart classes except **PieChart**. **PieChart** works a bit differently than those based on **XYChart**, but **PieChart** still inherits all of the functionality found in **Chart**. All chart classes are packaged in **javafx.scene.chart**.

Before looking at any specific chart classes, it is helpful to discuss a few commonly used methods defined by **Chart** because they are supported by all charts and are used by one or more of the examples that follow. The first is **setTitle( )**. It sets the name of the chart and is shown here:

    final void setTitle(String *name*)

Here, *name* specifies the title of the chart. By default, the title of a chart is on the top, but you can change this by calling **setTitleSide( )**, shown next:

    final void setTitleSide(Side *side*)

Here, *side* must be one of the values defined by the **Side** enumeration, which are **TOP**, **LEFT**, **RIGHT**, and **BOTTOM**. **Side** is packaged in **javafx.geometry**.

In general, a chart will have a legend that describes the information in the chart. Although it is possible to specify this legend explicitly, it is usually best to let it be defined automatically by the chart class (and that is what the following examples will do). However, you might want to specify which side of the chart the legend is on. By default, the legend is shown on the bottom. You can change this by calling **setLegendSide( )**, shown here:

    final void setLegendSide(Side *side*)

The side is passed in *side*. If you don't want a legend displayed, you can call **setLegendVisible( )**, passing in **false**.

Creating XYChart-Based Charts

As mentioned, all JavaFX charts except for **PieChart** are subclasses of **XYChart**. Charts derived from **XYChart** display their data in a two-dimensional X,Y coordinate plane. Often, one axis represents time and the other represents a value. For example, a year's worth of stock prices are commonly represented with time (in days) being on the horizontal (X) axis and the prices being on the vertical (Y) axis. Of course, the meaning of the axes is under your control, and you are not restricted in this regard. For example, you might use a line chart to show the graph of the equation $x = 2y + 12$. In general, if your data can be represented in an X,Y coordinate plane, then it is likely that one or more subclasses of **XYChart** is appropriate to display it.

XYChart is an abstract generic class declared like this:

    abstract class XYChart<X, Y>

Here, **X** and **Y** specify the type of data depicted by the X and Y axes. Thus, all subclasses of **XYChart** are also generic.

Key to using any of the **XYChart**-based classes is creating the data that will be displayed. For all **XYChart**s, data is represented in a *series*. A series defines a sequence of data for a specific item. For example, the series might contain the high temperature for a week, stock price over a year, or lines of code produced by a programmer over a month. All **XYChart**s can display one or more series. For example, you might have a bar chart that shows the relative productivity of three different programmers from month to month. Each series would define the data for a single programmer. All three series would then be displayed in the chart, side by side.

A series is an object of type **XYChart.Series**. **Series** is a generic class declared like this:

static final class XYChart.Series<X, Y>

Here, **X** and **Y** specify the type of data depicted by the X and Y axes. **Series** defines three constructors. We will use the default constructor. Other constructors let you specify a list of the data and give the series a name. However, using those constructors may result in an "unchecked generic array creation" warning. Therefore, we will set the name and the data with method calls after a **Series** instance has been created.

You can set the name of the series by calling **setName( )**, shown next:

final void setName(String *name*)

Here, *name* specifies the name of the series. This name will be shown on the chart to identify the data.

You can set the data for the series by adding it to the list of data obtained by calling **getData( )** on the **Series** instance. It is shown here:

final ObservableList<XYChart.Data<X,Y>> getData( )

This method returns a reference to the list of data in the series. You can add to the list by calling **add( )**, for example. Notice that the data type of the objects in the list is **XYChart.Data**. This is a generic class declared as shown here:

static final class XYChart.Data<X, Y>

Again, **X** and **Y** also specify the type of data depicted by the X and Y axes. **Data** defines three constructors. The one we will use is shown here:

Data(X *valX*, Y *valY*)

Here, *valX* and *valY* specify the data for the indicated axis.

Once you have created a series of data, you can add it to an **XYChart** by calling **add( )** on the list returned by the **XYChart's getData( )** method. This method is shown here:

final ObservableList<XYChart.Series<X,Y>> getData( )

A reference to the current series list is returned.

As a general rule, once you have constructed a chart and set its data, you can display it. JavaFX automatically creates the chart, providing a default layout that will often be just what you want. Of course, a number of customizations are supported, if needed. Frankly, the default layout will be appropriate for a large number of applications.

When you create any of the concrete **XYChart** classes you will need to specify two **Axis** objects, which define the axes. **Axis** is an abstract class from which two concrete classes are derived. The first is **CategoryAxis**, which encapsulates descriptive names in string form. The second is **NumberAxis**, which encapsulates values in numeric form. These classes are used to tell the concrete chart classes what type of data each axis represents. In both cases, you can specify the values or let them be computed automatically by the concrete chart class. Here, we will use the latter approach. You can label an axis by calling **setLabel( )**, passing in the label as a string. Various other aspects of the axis can also be controlled, such as how tick marks are represented. However, for our purposes only the label will be set.

A BarChart Example

Now it is time to put the preceding discussion into action by creating an example that uses **BarChart**. Because all of the concrete **XYChart** subclasses work in a similar fashion, the same general techniques used here with **BarChart** will apply to the other **XYChart** subclasses. The bar chart used in the example displays the quarterly productivity of three programmers, named John, Mary, and Terry, on a monthly basis. The horizontal axis shows the months (January through March). The vertical axis shows the number of lines of code produced. Notice that aside from setting the title, the series names, the programmer names, and the data, the chart itself is constructed and organized automatically by JavaFX.

```
// Demonstrate a BarChart

import javafx.application.*;
import javafx.scene.*;
import javafx.stage.*;
import javafx.scene.layout.*;
import javafx.scene.control.*;
import javafx.event.*;
import javafx.geometry.*;
import javafx.scene.chart.*;

public class BarChartDemo extends Application {

  public static void main(String[] args) {

    // Start the JavaFX application by calling launch().
    launch(args);
  }

  // Override the start() method.
  public void start(Stage myStage) {

    // Give the stage a title.
    myStage.setTitle("BarChart Demo");
```

```
// Use a FlowPane for the root node.
FlowPane rootNode = new FlowPane();

// Center the controls in the scene.
rootNode.setAlignment(Pos.CENTER);

// Create a scene.
Scene myScene = new Scene(rootNode, 600, 600);

// Set the scene on the stage.
myStage.setScene(myScene);

// Create the two axes.
CategoryAxis hAxis = new CategoryAxis();
hAxis.setLabel("Programmers");

NumberAxis vAxis = new NumberAxis();
vAxis.setLabel("Lines of Code");

// Create a bar chart that shows the first quarter
// productivity in terms of lines of code produced per
// month for John, Mary, and Terry.
BarChart<String, Number> bcProgProd = new BarChart<>(hAxis, vAxis);
bcProgProd.setTitle("1st Qtr Productivity");

// Create the series for the chart.
XYChart.Series<String, Number> january = new XYChart.Series<>();
XYChart.Series<String, Number> february = new XYChart.Series<>();
XYChart.Series<String, Number> march = new XYChart.Series<>();

// Populate each series with data.
january.setName("January");
january.getData().add(new XYChart.Data<String, Number>("John", 300));
january.getData().add(new XYChart.Data<String, Number>("Mary", 325));
january.getData().add(new XYChart.Data<String, Number>("Terry", 247));

february.setName("February");
february.getData().add(new XYChart.Data<String, Number>("John", 242));
february.getData().add(new XYChart.Data<String, Number>("Mary", 183));
february.getData().add(new XYChart.Data<String, Number>("Terry", 354));

march.setName("March");
march.getData().add(new XYChart.Data<String, Number>("John", 195));
march.getData().add(new XYChart.Data<String, Number>("Mary", 224));
march.getData().add(new XYChart.Data<String, Number>("Terry", 288));

// Add the series to the chart.
bcProgProd.getData().add(january);
bcProgProd.getData().add(february);
bcProgProd.getData().add(march);
```

```
      // Add the chart to the scene.
      rootNode.getChildren().add(bcProgProd);

      // Show the stage and its scene.
      myStage.show();
    }
}
```

The output is shown here:

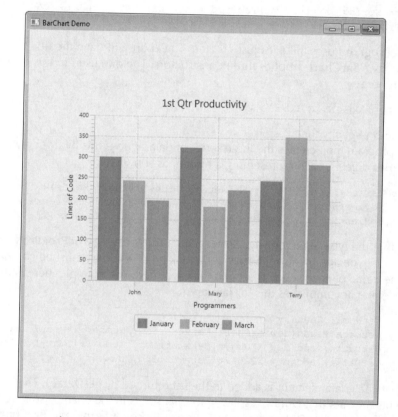

As you can see, the chart includes the title at the top, a legend (which was automatically created by **BarChart**) at the bottom, and labels on the axes. Also, note that the chart is appropriately scaled. As a result, **BarChart** is amazingly easy to use. Let's now look closely at key parts of this program.

Notice first how the **Axis** instances are created:

```
CategoryAxis hAxis = new CategoryAxis();
hAxis.setLabel("Programmers");

NumberAxis vAxis = new NumberAxis();
vAxis.setLabel("Lines of Code");
```

As the output shows, the program displays programmer productivity over a period of three months, with the programmer names shown on the horizontal axis and the lines of code produced shown on the vertical axis. As a result, the horizontal axis uses **CategoryAxis( )** and the vertical axis uses **NumberAxis( )**. Each is given a label that states its meaning.

Next, a **BarChart** called **bcProgProd** is created and its title is set by these statements:

```
BarChart<String, Number> bcProgProd = new BarChart<>(hAxis, vAxis);
bcProgProd.setTitle("1st Qtr Productivity");
```

Here, **bcProgProd** uses the axes just created. The chart will have the title "1st Qtr Productivity." **BarChart** supplies three constructors. The one used in this example is shown here:

BarChart(Axis<X> x, Axis<Y> y)

Here, x and y specify the axes.

The program then creates the three series of data. It does this by first constructing three **Series** objects, each representing a month, as shown here:

```
XYChart.Series<String, Number> january = new XYChart.Series<>();
XYChart.Series<String, Number> february = new XYChart.Series<>();
XYChart.Series<String, Number> march = new XYChart.Series<>();
```

Notice that the type arguments for **Series** match those used by **bcProgProd**. In general, the type arguments for **Series** and any kind of **XYChart** must be compatible. Next, the name of each series is set and data is added. For example, here is the sequence that accomplishes this for **january**:

```
january.setName("January");
january.getData().add(new XYChart.Data<String, Number>("John", 300));
january.getData().add(new XYChart.Data<String, Number>("Mary", 325));
january.getData().add(new XYChart.Data<String, Number>("Terry", 247));
```

Note that each data element is added to the list returned by **getData( )**. This list represents the data that will be displayed for that series in the chart. Also note that the type arguments for **Data** are also the same as those for **Series** and **BarChart**. Again, type compatibility is required between the data and the series of which it is part. The other series are constructed using the same general approach.

Finally, the series are added to the chart by these statements:

```
bcProgProd.getData().add(january);
bcProgProd.getData().add(february);
bcProgProd.getData().add(march);
```

In each case, the series is added to the list returned by calling **getData( )** on **bcProgProd**. At this point, the bar chart is complete and can be displayed by adding it to the scene graph.

Some Things to Try with the BarChart Example

Before moving on, there are several things that you might want to experiment with. Perhaps the most important is to try substituting another **XYChart** subclass for **BarChart**. Except for **BubbleChart**, any of the other **XYChart** subclasses can be used. For example, try using **StackedBarChart**. Because all **XYChart**s work in the same general way, all you need to do is change this line:

```
BarChart<String, Number> bcProgProd = new BarChart<>(hAxis, vAxis);
```

to

```
StackedBarChart<String, Number> bcProgProd =
                          new StackedBarChart<>(hAxis, vAxis);
```

After making this change, the chart will look like this:

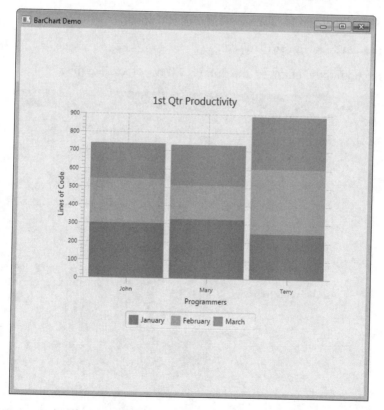

With this approach, the lines of code produced by each programmer are shown in an additive fashion. This type of chart makes it easy to gauge the total first quarter output for each programmer. You might also want to try the other two-dimensional charts. Although the way they represent the data may not be particularly appropriate for this application, they will let you see how each looks.

NOTE

*If you want to experiment with **BubbleChart**, a bit more work is required because you will need to create an example that uses **NumberAxis** for both axes.*

Another thing you might want to try is changing the location of the legend or title. For example, you can set the title to the left side in the **BarChartDemo** program by including this line:

```
bcProgProd.setTitleSide(Side.LEFT);
```

You can move the legend to the top, with this statement:

```
bcProgProd.setLegendSide(Side.TOP);
```

If you make both these changes, the output will now look like this:

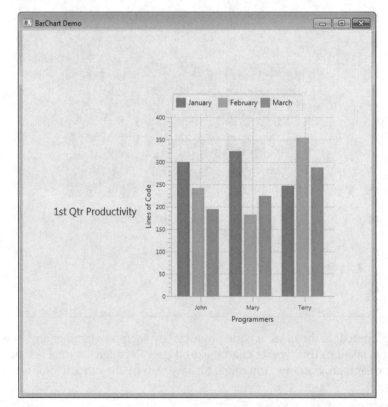

As you might expect, you can also customize the look of various aspects of a chart. For example, with **BarChart**, you can set the space between bars in the same series and the space between each series. This is done by using **setBarGap( )** and **setCategoryGap( )**, respectively. If you don't want any gap between bars, for example, simply pass 0.

One particularly pleasing aspect of charts is that any change to the data in the chart can be animated. The **Chart** class defines a property called **animated**. When this property is **true**, a change to the data in the chart will be animated. For example, in **BarChartDemo**, if you change the number of lines of code for John in January from 300 to 99 during the execution of the program, then the bar will visually descend, rather than just jump to the new value. You can determine if the **animated** property is **true** by calling **getAnimated( )**. You can set **animated** by calling **setAnimated( )**. To see the effect of this animation, add the following sequence to the program.

```
if(!bcProgProd.getAnimated()) bcProgProd.setAnimated(true);

Button btnChange = new Button("Change Data");

// Change the January data for John, Mary, and Terry.
btnChange.setOnAction(new EventHandler<ActionEvent>() {
  public void handle(ActionEvent ae) {
    january.getData().get(0).setYValue(99);
    january.getData().get(1).setYValue(400);
    january.getData().get(2).setYValue(150);
  }
});
```

This adds a button called Change Data and the action event handler that changes the data. It also ensures that the **animated** property is set to **true** (as it should be by default). You will also need to add **btnChange** to the scene graph. After making these changes, when you press the Change Data button, the January data for each programmer will be changed, and each bar will animate to its new position.

One last point about **XYChart**s: they are powerful, flexible GUI elements that can be tailored to fit nearly any need. You will want to explore them fully. They can add a truly impressive element to your GUIs.

Creating a PieChart

In addition to charts based on **XYChart**, JavaFX offers one other chart type: the pie chart. Pie charts are instances of the **PieChart** class. **PieChart** is a subclass of **Chart**, so it supports all of the features common to all charts. However, **PieChart** is not based on an X,Y coordinate plane. Instead, it represents its data as slices of a circle.

You are no doubt familiar with pie charts because they are quite commonly used to show the relative magnitude of a group of related values. For example, you might use a pie chart to display the revenue produced by a set of products. Whatever the use, **PieChart** provides an easy, but effective, way to create a pie chart.

PieChart defines two constructors. The first is the default constructor. The second lets you specify a list of the data that will make up the pie. This is the one we will use. It is shown here:

PieChart(ObservableList<PieChart.Data> *list>*

Here, *list* specifies the data that will be displayed in pie form. Notice the data type of the elements in the list is **PieChart.Data**. Therefore, to create a **PieChart**, you need first to create **PieChart.Data** elements.

PieChart.Data has one constructor, shown here:

Data(String *sliceName*, double *sliceValue*)

Here, *sliceName* specifies the name of the slice that is shown, and *sliceValue* specifies its value.

The following program demonstrates **PieChart**. It creates a pie that depicts the number of programmer hours used to create various subsystems in an application. As the program shows, **PieChart**s are surprisingly easy to construct because all you need to do is create the data, instantiate a **PieChart** object, and include that object in the scene graph.

```
// Demonstrate a PieChart

import javafx.application.*;
import javafx.scene.*;
import javafx.stage.*;
import javafx.scene.layout.*;
import javafx.scene.control.*;
import javafx.event.*;
import javafx.geometry.*;
import javafx.scene.chart.*;
import javafx.collections.*;

public class PieChartDemo extends Application {

  public static void main(String[] args) {
```

```
    // Start the JavaFX application by calling launch().
    launch(args);
  }

  // Override the start() method.
  public void start(Stage myStage) {

    // Give the stage a title.
    myStage.setTitle("PieChart Demo");

    // Use a FlowPane for the root node.
    FlowPane rootNode = new FlowPane();

    // Center the Chart in the scene.
    rootNode.setAlignment(Pos.CENTER);

    // Create a scene.
    Scene myScene = new Scene(rootNode, 600, 600);

    // Set the scene on the stage.
    myStage.setScene(myScene);

    // Create the list of hours used for each subsystem.
    ObservableList<PieChart.Data> pieData =
      FXCollections.observableArrayList (
        new PieChart.Data("Printing", 1200),
        new PieChart.Data("Network Support", 800),
        new PieChart.Data("Data Analysis", 1450),
        new PieChart.Data("Storage", 450),
        new PieChart.Data("Security", 745),
        new PieChart.Data("Formatting", 190)
      );

    // Create a pie chart that shows the hours consumed by
    // various parts of a software project.
    PieChart pieHours = new PieChart(pieData);
    pieHours.setTitle("Programmer Hours by Subsystem");

    // Add the chart to the scene.
    rootNode.getChildren().add(pieHours);

    // Show the stage and its scene.
    myStage.show();
  }
}
```

Output from the program is shown here:

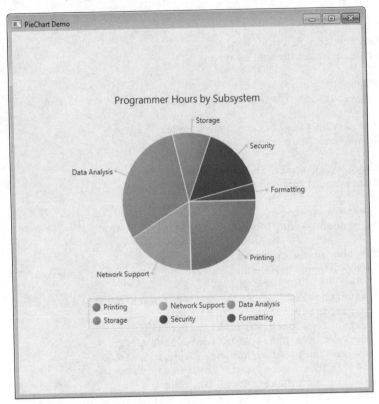

As you can see, **PieChart** automatically constructs the pie from the given values, includes labels for the slices, and supplies a legend. The title, which is set in the program, is located on top. Furthermore, all of this is accomplished by only a few lines of code. This makes it difficult to justify *not* using **PieChart** when a pie chart is needed. **PieChart** is just too convenient to ignore.

Although the default pie chart produced by **PieChart** will fit many situations, several customizations are possible. You can specify the direction of rotation in which the data will be added to the pie by calling **setClockwise( )**. By default, the direction is clockwise. If you pass **false** to **setClockwise( )**, the rotation will be counterclockwise. You can specify the start angle for adding the data. By default, this angle is 0. You can set it by calling **setStartAngle( )**, passing in the new angle. For example, passing 90.0 causes the pie to be rotated by 90 degrees. You can hide the slice labels by calling **setLabelsVisible(false)**. Of course, you can also change several features that **PieChart** inherits from **Chart**, such as the ability to hide the legend and change the side of the legend or title.

Display Web Content with WebView

If you want to embed Web-based content in your application, JavaFX provides a convenient, yet powerful, solution with the **WebView** class. You can think of **WebView** as a type of high-level control that displays content from a website. The content is provided by an instance of **WebEngine**, which is associated with a **WebView**. **WebEngine** handles the actual loading, processing, and styling of a web page. Thus, you will use **WebEngine** to load and otherwise manage access to the Web. You will use **WebView** to display the information.

WebView offers an easy way to display a wide variety of Web-based content. Uses for **WebView** are easy to imagine. Here are two examples. You might have an application for which the instructions are provided online, through a **WebView** window. You might use **WebView** to support a "mini-browser" that allows access to only certain sites. Whatever your use, integrating **WebView** into your applications is a straightforward process.

WebView

In some ways, **WebView** is a bit like **ImageView** described in Chapter 5 because its primary role is to display content. However, because the content can contain active elements, such as a hyperlink, **WebView** implicitly supports user interaction. For example, if a **WebView** is displaying a web page and that page contains a link, the user can click that link to display the linked page. Thus, the user can interact with a page displayed by **WebView** in the same way as he or she does with a page displayed in a browser window. (In fact, as the following example shows, it is possible—indeed easy—to use **WebView** to create a browser-like application.) The key point is that even though **WebView** is essentially a passive window, what it displays supports user interaction.

WebView is a subclass of **Node**, which means that **WebView** can be part of a scene graph. **WebView** defines only the default constructor. You can set the preferred size of a **WebView** as you do with any other **Node**, by use of methods such as **setPrefWidth( )**, **setPrefHeight( )**, and **setPrefSize( )**. **WebView** also defines methods that let you scale the font size or scale the entire image. To scale the font, call **setFontScale( )**, passing in the scale factor. The default is 1.0, so if you want text displayed twice as big, pass 2.0. As useful as scaling the font can be in some cases, it won't change the size of other items on the page, such as images. If you want to change the scale of the entire page, use **setZoom( )**, passing in the zoom factor.

Perhaps the most important method that **WebView** provides is **getEngine( )** because it returns a reference to the **WebEngine** that powers the **WebView**. It is the **WebEngine** that lets you load a page or gain access to the user's history list. The **getEngine( )** method is shown here:

```
final WebEngine getEngine( )
```

The **WebEngine** associated with the **WebView** is returned. In essence, after you have created a **WebView**, you will obtain and use its **WebEngine** to perform Web-based actions.

WebEngine

WebEngine provides access to the Web. In addition to loading pages and managing content, it maintains a history list, reports errors, and offers a way to print a page, among other capabilities. Because **WebEngine** uses a worker thread to handle page loading, an application that uses **WebEngine** will not stall when a page load takes place. Frankly, **WebEngine** is a truly powerful, impressive part of JavaFX.

Although **WebEngine** has two constructors, when using **WebView** you won't be using either. The reason is that when a **WebView** is created, a **WebEngine** is automatically created for it. Instead, to obtain a reference to this engine, call **getEngine( )** on the **WebView** instance, as explained in the previous section.

Once you have a reference to the engine, you can use it to perform various Web-based actions, the most fundamental of which is loading a page. To load a page, call **load( )**, shown here:

    void load(String *urlOfPage*)

Here, *urlOfPage* specifies the URL of the page to be loaded. As mentioned, the page is actually loaded by a worker thread, which means that **load( )** will return immediately. As a point of interest, **WebEngine** also supplies a method called **loadContent( )**, which lets you pass a string containing HTML.

Notice that **load( )** does not return anything, such as a status code. To obtain information about the page load, you will register a change listener on the **state** property associated with the worker thread. Each time the state changes, the listener will be called. To add a change listener for the **state** property, you will first call **getLoadWorker( )** on the **WebEngine**. It is shown here:

    final Worker<Void> getLoadWorker( )

Worker is an interface defined in **javafx.concurrent**. Its purpose is to carry out some action in a background thread. It defines several methods, but the only one that we need here is **stateProperty( )**. It returns a reference to the **state** property, to which you will add the change listener.

The **stateProperty( )** method returns a reference to the current state of the worker thread. It can be one of the following values defined by the **Worker.State** enumeration. The names describe the state.

CANCELLED	FAILED	READY
RUNNING	SCHEDULED	SUCCEEDED

When **WebEngine** loads a page, the **Worker**'s state will change to **SUCCEEDED** if the page is successfully loaded. It will change to **FAILED** if an error occurs. If an error occurs, you can obtain the exception by calling **getException( )** on the **Worker** object.

Another useful method defined by **WebEngine** is **getLocation( )**. It returns the page currently loaded and is shown here:

final String getLocation( )

This method is particularly useful when the user has followed a link to a new page. This method lets you get its URL.

One of the most useful features of **WebEngine** is its support for a Web history list. This list keeps track of visited web pages. You could use this list to implement forward and back navigation buttons, for example, thus allowing users to move forward and backward through the list. To obtain the history, call **getHistory( )**, shown here:

WebHistory getHistory( )

It returns a **WebHistory** object that you can use to obtain the list and to load pages from the list.

WebHistory

Using the **WebHistory** reference returned by **getHistory( )**, you can retrieve the history list by calling **getEntries( )**. It is shown here:

ObservableList<WebHistory.Entry> getEntries( )

It returns a read-only list of the entries. Recall that **ObservableList** implements the **List** interface, so you have access to all list-management methods. For example, you can call **size( )** to obtain the length of the list. **WebHistory.Entry** encapsulates the page entry, giving you access to various pieces of page-related information. For example, you can call **getUrl( )** to obtain the URL.

Perhaps the most important method defined by **WebHistory** is **go( )**. It loads a page from the history list. It is shown here:

void go(int *offset*) throws IndexOutOfBoundsException

Here, *offset* specifies an offset from the current page in the history list. To load the preceding page, pass –1. To load the next page, pass 1. Of course, you can pass a value greater than 1 (or less than –1). For example, passing 2, loads the page two places forward in the list. An attempt to overrun or underrun the list results in an exception. The **go( )** method makes it easy to navigate through the history list.

Another very useful method provided by **WebHistory** is **getCurrentIndex( )**, shown next:

int getCurrentIndex( )

As its name suggests, **getCurrentIndex( )** returns the index of the current page. Using this index you can determine if the current page is at the beginning or the end of the list, for example.

A WebView Demonstration: Mini-Browser

The following program demonstrates **WebView**, **WebEngine**, and **WebHistory** by implementing a mini-browser. The mini-browser has limited functionality because it includes only the **WebView**, Back and Forward buttons, and a text field that lets you enter a URL. However, despite its limitations, it will display all Web content that is compatible with **WebView**. It also lets you move forward and backward through the history list and enter a URL to display. You can also click a link in the **WebView** window and that link will be followed.

```java
// Demonstrate WebView by building a mini-browser.

import javafx.application.*;
import javafx.scene.*;
import javafx.stage.*;
import javafx.scene.layout.*;
import javafx.scene.control.*;
import javafx.event.*;
import javafx.geometry.*;
import javafx.scene.web.*;
import javafx.concurrent.*;
import javafx.beans.value.*;

public class WebViewDemo extends Application {

  public static void main(String[] args) {

    // Start the JavaFX application by calling launch().
    launch(args);
  }

  // Override the start() method.
  public void start(Stage myStage) {
    String homepage = "http://www.HerbSchildt.com";

    // Give the stage a title.
    myStage.setTitle("WebView-Based Mini-Browser");

    // Use a FlowPane for the root node. In this case,
    // vertical and horizontal gaps of 10.
    FlowPane rootNode = new FlowPane(10, 10);

    // Center the controls in the scene.
    rootNode.setAlignment(Pos.CENTER);

    // Create a scene.
    Scene myScene = new Scene(rootNode, 500, 500);
```

```java
// Set the scene on the stage.
myStage.setScene(myScene);

// Create navigation push buttons.
Button btnBack = new Button("Back");
Button btnForward = new Button("Forward");

// Initially disable the buttons.
btnBack.setDisable(true);
btnForward.setDisable(true);

// Create a text field for user-specified URLs.
TextField tfUrl = new TextField(homepage);
tfUrl.setPrefColumnCount(25);

// Use an HBox to hold the navigation controls.
HBox navBox = new HBox(10);
navBox.getChildren().addAll(btnBack, btnForward, tfUrl);

// Create the WebView.
WebView myWV = new WebView();
myWV.setPrefSize(450, 450); // change this size as needed

// Obtain the web engine.
WebEngine myWE = myWV.getEngine();

// Initially load a home page.
myWE.load(homepage);

// Handle the action events for the Back button.
btnBack.setOnAction(new EventHandler<ActionEvent>() {
  public void handle(ActionEvent ae) {
    try {
      // Load the previous page.
      myWE.getHistory().go(-1);
    } catch(IndexOutOfBoundsException exc) { }
  }
});

// Handle the action events for the Forward button.
btnForward.setOnAction(new EventHandler<ActionEvent>() {
  public void handle(ActionEvent ae) {
    try {
      // Load the next page.
      myWE.getHistory().go(1);
    } catch(IndexOutOfBoundsException exc) { }
  }
});
```

```
// Handle the action events for the text field.
tfUrl.setOnAction(new EventHandler<ActionEvent>() {
  public void handle(ActionEvent ae) {
    // Load the specified page.
    myWE.load(tfUrl.getText());
  }
});

// Monitor the status of the page load by watching changes to
// the worker thread's state
myWE.getLoadWorker().stateProperty().addListener(
                      new ChangeListener<Worker.State>() {
  public void changed(ObservableValue<? extends Worker.State> changed,
                    Worker.State oldVal, Worker.State newVal) {

    // If the load was successful, update the navigation controls.
    if(newVal == Worker.State.SUCCEEDED) {
      WebHistory myWH = myWE.getHistory();

      // Set the new location in the text field.
      tfUrl.setText(myWE.getLocation());

      // If not the first entry, enable the Back button.
      if(myWE.getHistory().getCurrentIndex() > 0)
        btnBack.setDisable(false);
      else // Otherwise, disable the Back button.
        btnBack.setDisable(true);

      // If at end of the entries list, then disable the
      // Forward button.
      if(myWH.getCurrentIndex() == myWH.getEntries().size()-1)
        btnForward.setDisable(true);
      else // Otherwise, enable Forward button.
        btnForward.setDisable(false);
    }
    else // Otherwise, report the error.
      if(newVal == Worker.State.FAILED) {
        // Report a load error in the text field.
        tfUrl.setText("Error " +
                myWE.getLoadWorker().getException().getMessage());
      }
  }
});

// Add the HBox and WebView to the scene graph.
rootNode.getChildren().addAll(navBox, myWV);
```

```
    // Show the stage and its scene.
    myStage.show();
  }
}
```

Sample output is shown here:

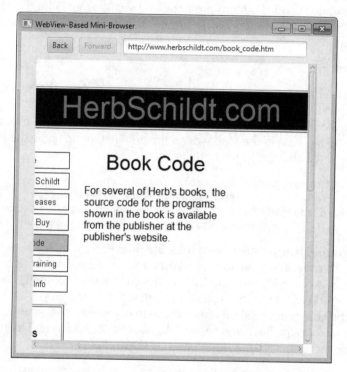

Most of the program is easy to understand, but a few key sections merit a close look. First, notice how the **WebView** is created and the first page is loaded:

```
// Create the WebView.
WebView myWV = new WebView();
myWV.setPrefSize(450, 450); // change this size as needed

// Obtain the web engine.
WebEngine myWE = myWV.getEngine();

// Initially load a home page.
myWE.load(homepage);
```

Here, a **WebView** called **myWV** is created and given a preferred size of 450 by 450. This creates a small window that automatically provides scroll bars as needed. (This size was chosen for demonstration purposes. You might want to try making it larger as an experiment.) Next, a reference to the **WebEngine** associated with the **WebView** is obtained and stored in **myWE**. Using this engine, the first page is loaded by calling **load( )**. The URL of this page is stored in **homepage**, which in the program is set to **http://www.HerbSchildt.com**, but you can change this to another page of your own choosing.

The Back and Forward buttons are handled by calling **go( )** on the history list, moving in the desired direction. For example, here is the call to **go( )** for the Forward button:

```
myWE.getHistory().go(1);
```

When you enter a URL in the text field, that URL is loaded by passing it to **load( )**, called on **myWE** directly.

Perhaps the most interesting part of the program is found in the event handler for changes to the state of the load worker thread. First, notice how the handler is registered and the **changed( )** method declared:

```
myWE.getLoadWorker().stateProperty().addListener(
                    new ChangeListener<Worker.State>() {
   public void changed(ObservableValue<? extends Worker.State> changed,
                    Worker.State oldVal, Worker.State newVal) {
```

This registers the change listener with the **state** property associated with the **Worker** used to load a page. The state is of type **Worker.State**. Now, any changes to the state will cause an event to be generated. Next, the **changed( )** method is declared, specifying **Worker.State** as the type of value that has changed.

Then, the **changed( )** method tests if the load completed successfully. If it did, **changed( )** updates the Back and Forward buttons (if necessary) and then updates the text field so it reflects the current page, as shown here:

```
// If the load was successful, update the navigation controls.
if(newVal == Worker.State.SUCCEEDED) {
  WebHistory myWH = myWE.getHistory();

  // Set the new location in the text field.
  tfUrl.setText(myWE.getLocation());

  // If not the first entry, enable the Back button.
  if(myWE.getHistory().getCurrentIndex() > 0)
    btnBack.setDisable(false);
  else // Otherwise, disable the Back button.
    btnBack.setDisable(true);

  // If at end of the entries list, then disable the
  // Forward button.
  if(myWH.getCurrentIndex() == myWH.getEntries().size()-1)
```

```
   btnForward.setDisable(true);
else // Otherwise, enable Forward button.
   btnForward.setDisable(false);
}
```

Notice how the current index of the history list determines how the Back and Forward buttons are set. Essentially, if the current index is greater than zero, the current page is not the first page to be displayed. If the current index is equal to the last entry in the list, then there is at least one previous page, but no next page.

Finally, if an error occurs in the load process, then the state will be **FAILED** and the error is reported by these lines:

```
else // Otherwise, report the error.
  if(newVal == Worker.State.FAILED) {
    // Report a load error in the text field.
    tfUrl.setText("Error " +
          myWE.getLoadWorker().getException().getMessage());
  }
```

Notice the error is displayed in the navigation text field. For example, if you enter an invalid URL, you will see the message "Error Malformed URL".

Before moving on, you might find it interesting to experiment with the **setZoom( )** method. For example, try calling **setZoom( )** with the value 0.5. Doing so will reduce the display size of the content by 50 percent. You might also try implementing the zoom feature by adding a control, such as a **Slider**. Each time the control is moved, the size of the content can be adjusted.

Drawing Directly on a Canvas

As you saw in Chapter 6, **javafx.scene.shape** defines several classes that can be used to draw various types of graphical shapes, such as circles, arcs, and lines. These are represented by nodes and can, therefore, be part of the scene graph. However, it is also possible to draw various graphics objects directly on the surface of a window through the use of graphics methods found in the **GraphicsContext** class. This class is packaged in **javafx.scene.canvas**. Its methods can be used to draw directly on the surface of a *canvas*, which is encapsulated by the **Canvas** class in **javafx.scene.canvas**. When you draw something on a canvas, such as a line or a circle, JavaFX automatically renders it whenever it needs to be redisplayed. This makes it easy to manage sophisticated graphics applications. This section provides an introduction to **Canvas** and **GraphicsContext** and to the techniques required to use them.

Before you can draw on a canvas, you must perform two steps. First, you must create a **Canvas** instance. Second, you must obtain a **GraphicsContext** object that refers to that canvas. You can then use the methods defined by **GraphicsContext** to draw output on the canvas.

The **Canvas** class is derived from **Node**, so it can be used as a node in a scene graph. **Canvas** defines two constructors. One is the default constructor; the other is the one shown here:

Canvas(double *width*, double *height*)

Here, *width* and *height* specify the dimensions of the canvas.

To obtain a **GraphicsContext** that refers to a canvas, call **getGraphicsContext2D( )**. Here is its general form:

GraphicsContext getGraphicsContext2D( )

The graphics context for the canvas is returned. **GraphicsContext** defines a large number of methods that draw shapes, text, and images and supports effects and transforms. Here, we will use only a few of these methods, but they will give you a sense of the power available to your applications.

You can draw a line by use of **strokeLine( )**, shown here:

void strokeLine(double *startX*, double *startY*, double *endX*, double *endY*)

It draws a line from *startX,startY* to *endX,endY*, using the current stroke, which can be a solid color or some more complex style.

To draw a rectangle, use either **strokeRect( )** or **fillRect( )**, shown here:

void strokeRect(double *topX*, double *topY*, double *width*, double *height*)

void fillRect(double *topX*, double *topY*, double *width*, double *height*)

The upper-left corner of the rectangle is at *topX,topY*. The *width* and *height* parameters specify its width and height. The **strokeRect( )** method draws the outline of a rectangle using the current stroke, and **fillRect( )** fills the rectangle with the current fill. The current fill can be as simple as a solid color or something more complex.

To draw an ellipse, use either **strokeOval( )** or **fillOval( )**, shown next:

void strokeOval(double *topX*, double *topY*, double *width*, double *height*)

void fillOval(double *topX*, double *topY*, double *width*, double *height*)

The upper-left corner of the rectangle that bounds the ellipse is at *topX,topY*. The *width* and *height* parameters specify its width and height. The **strokeOval( )** method draws the outline of an ellipse using the current stroke, and **fillOval( )** fills the oval with the current fill. To draw a circle, pass the same value for both *width* and *height*.

You can draw text on a canvas by use of the **strokeText( )** and **fillText( )** methods. We will use this version of **fillText( )**:

void fillText(String *str*, double *topX*, double *topY*)

It displays *str* starting at the location specified by *topX,topY*, filling the text with the current fill. You can set the font and font size of the text being displayed by using **setFont( )**. You can obtain the font used by the canvas by calling **getFont( )**. By default, the system font is used. You can create a new font by constructing a **Font** object, as described in Chapter 5.

You can specify the fill and stroke by use of these two methods defined by **Canvas**:

void setFill(Paint *newFill*)

void setStroke(Paint *newStroke*)

Notice that the parameter of both methods is of type **Paint**. As mentioned earlier in this book, **Paint** is an abstract class packaged in **javafx.scene.paint**. Its subclasses define fills and strokes. The one we will use is **Color**, which simply describes a solid color. **Color** defines several static fields that specify a wide array of colors, such as **Color.BLUE**, **Color.RED**, **Color.GREEN**, and so on.

GraphicsContext also supports a number of transforms, including scaling, translation, and rotation. These are set by using the **scale( )**, **translate( )**, and **rotate( )** methods. A generalized transform is supported by **transform( )**. To give you a sense of the power that these transforms offer, we will use **scale( )** in the following example program. It is shown here:

void scale(double *hScale*, double *vScale*)

Here, *hScale* specifies the horizontal (X) scale factor and *vScale* specifies the vertical (Y) scale factor.

If you want to clear (i.e., erase) all or a portion of a canvas, you can use **clearRect( )**, shown here:

void clearRect(int *upperX*, int *upperY*, int *width*, int *height*)

The upper-left corner of the region to be cleared is specified by *upperX* and *upperY*. The width and height of the region are passed to *width* and *height*. Clearing a canvas is especially useful when you want to replace what was previously drawn with new output.

The following program uses the aforementioned methods to demonstrate drawing on a canvas. It first displays a few graphic shapes on the canvas. Then, each time the Change Color button is pressed, the color of three of the objects changes. If you run the program, you will see that the shapes whose color is not changed are unaffected by the change in color of the other objects. Pressing the Change Scale button toggles between a half-scale and a full-scale image. Notice that even though the scale changes, the relative location of the items remains the same. One other thing: if you try covering and then uncovering the window, you will see that the canvas is automatically repainted, without any other actions on the part of your program. That is, it is not necessary for you to redraw the graphical elements. JavaFX does this for you.

```
// Demonstrate drawing on a canvas.

import javafx.application.*;
import javafx.scene.*;
import javafx.stage.*;
```

```
import javafx.scene.layout.*;
import javafx.scene.control.*;
import javafx.event.*;
import javafx.geometry.*;
import javafx.scene.shape.*;
import javafx.scene.canvas.*;
import javafx.scene.paint.*;
import javafx.scene.text.*;

public class DirectDrawDemo extends Application {
  Color[] colors = { Color.RED, Color.BLUE, Color.GREEN, Color.BLACK };
  int colorIdx = 0;
  boolean isSmall = false;

  public static void main(String[] args) {

    // Start the JavaFX application by calling launch().
    launch(args);
  }

  // Override the start() method.
  public void start(Stage myStage) {

    // Give the stage a title.
    myStage.setTitle("Draw Directly to a Canvas.");

    // Use a FlowPane for the root node.
    FlowPane rootNode = new FlowPane(10, 10);

    // Center the nodes in the scene.
    rootNode.setAlignment(Pos.CENTER);

    // Create a scene.
    Scene myScene = new Scene(rootNode, 450, 480);

    // Set the scene on the stage.
    myStage.setScene(myScene);

    // Create a canvas.
    Canvas myCanvas = new Canvas(400, 400);

    // Get the graphics context for the canvas.
    GraphicsContext gc = myCanvas.getGraphicsContext2D();

    // Create buttons that change color and scale.
    Button btnChangeColor = new Button("Change Color");
    Button btnChangeScale = new Button("Change Scale");

    // Handle the action events for the Change Color button.
    btnChangeColor.setOnAction(new EventHandler<ActionEvent>() {
      public void handle(ActionEvent ae) {
```

```
      // Set the stroke and fill color.
      gc.setStroke(colors[colorIdx]);
      gc.setFill(colors[colorIdx]);

      // Redraw the line, text, and filled rectangle in the
      // new color. This leaves the color of the other items
      // unchanged.
      gc.strokeLine(0, 0, 200, 200);
      gc.fillText("This is drawn on the canvas.", 60, 50);
      gc.fillRect(100, 320, 300, 40);

      // Change the color.
      colorIdx++;
      if(colorIdx == colors.length) colorIdx= 0;
    }
  });

  // Handle the action events for the Change Scale button.
  btnChangeScale.setOnAction(new EventHandler<ActionEvent>() {
    public void handle(ActionEvent ae) {
      // Clear the canvas and reset the colors to black and
      // and the color index to 0.
      gc.clearRect(0, 0, 400, 400);
      colorIdx = 0;
      gc.setStroke(Color.BLACK);
      gc.setFill(Color.BLACK);

      // Switch between small and large scale.
      if(!isSmall) {
        // Scale to one half size.
        gc.scale(0.5, 0.5);
      } else {
        // Scale to full size
        gc.scale(2.0, 2.0);
      }
      isSmall = !isSmall;

      // Redisplay the graphics and text.
      gc.strokeLine(0, 0, 200, 200);
      gc.strokeOval(100, 100, 200, 200);
      gc.strokeRect(0, 200, 50, 200);
      gc.fillOval(0, 0, 20, 20);
      gc.fillRect(100, 320, 300, 40);
      gc.setFont(new Font(20));
      gc.fillText("This is drawn on the canvas.", 60, 50);
    }
  });

  // Draw initial output on the canvas.
  gc.strokeLine(0, 0, 200, 200);
  gc.strokeOval(100, 100, 200, 200);
  gc.strokeRect(0, 200, 50, 200);
```

```
      gc.fillOval(0, 0, 20, 20);
      gc.fillRect(100, 320, 300, 40);

      // Set the font size to 20 and draw text.
      gc.setFont(new Font(20));
      gc.fillText("This is drawn on the canvas.", 60, 50);

      // Add the canvas and button to the scene graph.
      rootNode.getChildren().addAll(myCanvas, btnChangeColor, btnChangeScale);

      // Show the stage and its scene.
      myStage.show();
    }
}
```

Output from the program is shown here:

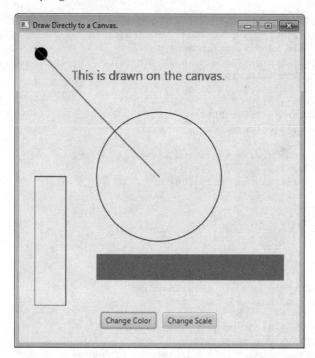

Most of the program should be easy to understand, but let's look closely at a couple of key parts. First, notice the declaration of the instance variables **colors**, **colorIdx**, and **isSmall**:

```
Color[] colors = { Color.RED, Color.BLUE, Color.GREEN, Color.BLACK };
int colorIdx = 0;
boolean isSmall = false;
```

The **colors** array contains a list of the colors that will be cycled through each time the Change Color button is pressed. The index of the current color is contained in **colorIdx**. The **isSmall** variable is used by the handler for the Change Scale button. It indicates the current scale of the image. If it is **true**, the image is small. Otherwise, it is full size.

Now, notice how the canvas is created and the graphics context is obtained by this sequence:

```
// Create a canvas.
Canvas myCanvas = new Canvas(400, 400);

// Get the graphics context for the canvas.
GraphicsContext gc = myCanvas.getGraphicsContext2D();
```

This creates a **Canvas** called **myCanvas** that is 400 units square. The graphics context, **gc**, is obtained by calling **getGraphicsContext2D( )** on **myCanvas**.

Next, notice each button handler. Each time a button is pressed, the indicated action takes place. In the case of Change Color, the color of the line, text, and filled rectangle are redisplayed in the new color. The other items remain unchanged. In the case of Change Scale, the entire canvas is cleared by a call to **clearRect( )**. Next, the **isSmall** variable is tested to determine which scale to use. If **isSmall** is **false**, then the scale of the canvas is reduced by 50 percent. Otherwise, it is increased by a factor of 2. In either case, the value of **isSmall** is reversed. Thus, each time the Change Scale button is pressed, the image will switch between small and large.

It is important to emphasize that **GraphicsContext** supports many more features than discussed and demonstrated here. Despite its power, its features are easy to master and use. The best way to learn is to experiment with them. If sophisticated graphics programming is in your future, then **GraphicsContext** is a class about which you will need to be knowledgeable. Drawing directly to a **Canvas** offers a flexible solution to many graphics-intensive tasks.

What Next?

JavaFX is a rich and powerful framework that supports the modern GUI environment. This book has introduced several of its key aspects, but it has only scratched the surface. As you progress in your study of JavaFX, here are two important places to start. As mentioned in Chapter 1, JavaFX supports the use of Cascading Style Sheets (CSS), and this support is something you will want to explore. JavaFX also supports FXML, which can be used to separate the design of the interface from other aspects of your program. For many applications, designing a GUI with FXML will be easier than doing so with Java language statements. Also, Oracle's visual design tool Scene Builder generates FXML code. If you want to use that tool, you will need at least a general familiarity with FXML.

Several packages were used in this book, and all of those packages support additional features you will want to explore. In addition to these packages, here are a few others of particular interest. If you want to use JavaFX with a Swing application, then you will want to study the **javafx.embed.swing** package. JavaFX supports printing in **javafx.print**. The key class there is **PrintJob**. To use audio or video in your application, you will want to use features in **javafx.scene.media**.

One final comment: JavaFX has set a new standard in Java GUIs. Not only does it offer a powerful, modern approach, it also makes the process of creating a GUI easier. It represents a major step forward and is worthy of all the effort needed to master it. JavaFX is truly that important.

Index

T

Join the Largest Tech Community in the World

 Download the latest software, tools, and developer templates

 Get exclusive access to hands-on trainings and workshops

 Grow your professional network through the Oracle ACE Program

 Publish your technical articles – and get paid to share your expertise

**Join the Oracle Technology Network
Membership is free. Visit oracle.com/technetwork**

@OracleOTN   facebook.com/OracleTechnologyNetwork

Reach More than 700,000 Oracle Customers with Oracle Publishing Group

Connect with the Audience that Matters Most to Your Business

Oracle Magazine
The Largest IT Publication in the World
Circulation: 550,000
Audience: IT Managers, DBAs, Programmers, and Developers

Profit
Business Insight for Enterprise-Class Business Leaders to Help Them Build a Better Business Using Oracle Technology
Circulation: 100,000
Audience: Top Executives and Line of Business Managers

Java Magazine
The Essential Source on Java Technology, the Java Programming Language, and Java-Based Applications
Circulation: 125,000 and Growing Steady
Audience: Corporate and Independent Java Developers, Programmers, and Architects

For more information or to sign up for a FREE subscription:
Scan the QR code to visit Oracle Publishing online.